A SURVEY BETWEEN THE TESTAMENTS

By W. W. SLOAN

About the Author

Dr. Sloan is a graduate of the College of Wooster, McCormick Theological Seminary, and Northwestern University, at which latter seat of learning he received his Ph.D. degree.

After teaching at the American Mission College in Alexandria, Egypt, he returned to the United States where he served churches on the west coast. Later, he was both teacher and dean in midwest colleges, and in 1947 he joined the faculty of Elon College, North Carolina, as professor of Bible.

He has travelled extensively, making addresses in approximately fifty nations. In Palestine, he became well acquainted with research in the Dead Sea Scrolls.

Dr. Sloan is the author of numerous articles for magazines and the World Book Encyclopedia. His *A Survey of the Old Testament,* adopted by more than a hundred colleges, has appeared in four editions in the United States and England.

About the Book

What took place between the last event of the Old Testament, the building of a wall around Jerusalem in 444 B.C., and the beginning of Christianity? This book deals with the history and literature of this intertestamental period. Written for laymen and college undergraduates by the professor of Bible at Elon College, it surveys the religious development as revealed in the Dead Sea Scrolls, the Apocrypha, the Pseudepigrapha, and other writings of the period. Thought-provoking questions and suggestions for additiona' ____ _____ ____ __ the forty chapters.

A SURVEY BETWEEN THE TESTAMENTS

by

W. W. SLOAN

1964

LITTLEFIELD, ADAMS & CO.

PATERSON, NEW JERSEY

PREFACE

Discovery of the Qumran Dead Sea Scrolls and the publication of the Revised Standard Version of the Apocrypha have stimulated interest in the history and literature of the Jewish people in the period between the Old Testament and the New Testament. The Old Testament is a record of the development of Jewish thought and religion. The New Testament indicates considerable advance over the Old Testament. Most people know very little about how this advance took place.

In the Apocrypha, the Pseudepigrapha, the Dead Sea Scrolls, and the writings of such Jewish authorities of about the time of Jesus as Philo and Josephus, we are able to outline this progress between the Testaments. The student of the Jewish and Christian religions should become acquainted with this period of history. That is why this book has been written.

My *A Survey of the Old Testament,* published by Abingdon Press in 1957, put the findings of Biblical scholars into simple terms. This brought requests from all parts of the world for a similar book about the New Testament. Philosophical Library in 1961 and Littlefield, Adams and Company in 1962 published my *A Survey of the New Testament.* Then came inquiries, What lay between the two Testaments? There are many books dealing with various phases of this, especially with the Dead Sea Scrolls, but nothing that brings together in terms the layman can easily understand the numerous factors of the history and development between the return of the Jews from the Babylonian captivity and the organization of Christianity. This book fills that need.

As with my other books, this text has been worked out with my undergraduate students at Elon College. As I taught a course on the intertestamental period, I developed chapters and then went over them with my students. In one class session, as I was noting down a suggestion made by the class, I overheard one student remark, "Gee! We are helping write a book!" This has now been done several times. Other students and also teachers have helped write this book. Most credit should be given to my wife, Bessie Pickett Sloan, assistant professor of Romance languages at Elon College. Four visits to the lands of the Bible, including research in the Qumran caves and the ruins of the Essene community center, have helped.

Quotations from the books of the Pseudepigrapha have, in general, followed the translation of R. H. Charles; those from the Qumran Scrolls are largely patterned from the translation of T. H. Gaster. Quotations from the Bible and the Apocrypha are from the Revised Standard Version. It is well to read the books of the Apocrypha in connection with chapters 8 and 24-28, and the Qumran Scrolls with chapters 18-22. Gaster's *The Dead Sea Scriptures* is available as a paperback edition. Most of the Pseudepigrapha have not been printed in English since 1913, but are soon to be re-published.

W. W. SLOAN

Contents

Contents

vii

Chapter 1

The Old Testament Background

Nehemiah built a wall around Jerusalem. Ezra conducted the dedication exercises. This occurred in 444 B.C. These are the last two men told about in the Old Testament. What took place between this occasion and the ministry of Jesus? Is this really a "period of silence"? What are the significant events? What thinking and literature developed? This book attempts to answer these questions in accord with the instructions given to the prophet Habakkuk:

> Make it plain upon tablets,
> so he may run who reads it (Hab. 2:2).

To understand this we must have some background, know what led up to Nehemiah. The Hebrew people were taught to say, "A wandering Aramean was my father" (Deut. 26:5). This was Jacob, whose grandfather is said to have been Abraham. Abraham left the region of the Tigris and Euphrates Rivers about 1900 B.C. and settled in what we today call Palestine. Tradition says that Jacob reared a family north of Palestine and that one of his sons, Joseph, was sold into Egypt as a slave. We are told that Joseph eventually became prime minister and brought his relatives into the northeastern part of Egypt. As they grew in numbers, they came to be feared by the Egyptians, who put them to forced labor.

From this group there arose an able leader, Moses, who about 1300 B.C. led them out of Egyptian captivity. After some time in the Sinai desert, they penetrated Palestine, the land of the Canaanites. Other small groups joined these Israelites. The largest single invasion took place under the leadership of Joshua about 1250 B.C. The agricultural Canaanites occupied the valleys, but the invading Israelites with their cattle, sheep, and goats settled on the mountainsides. From there they gradually captured Canaanite villages and towns.

A little previous to 1,000 B.C., the vigorous Israelites became powerful enough to set up their own government. Saul, their first king, led them to the conquest of Canaanite and neighboring strongholds. He was largely a farmer-soldier. His successor, David, conquered the central Canaanite city, Jerusalem, and made it his capital. Here he built a palace and secured the respect of neighboring nations. His son and successor, Solomon, was able to dedicate his energies to a building program—palaces, temples, roads, water supply. He enhanced his standing through the Middle East by numerous marriages to foreign princesses.

Solomon's building enterprises proved so expensive that many people criticized him. Upon his death the northern part of his kingdom, considerably more than half the population, rebelled against his son. The date generally given for this event is 922 B.C. The new northern nation continued the name, the Kingdom of Israel. The southern nation became known as the Kingdom of Judah. The little southern country was able to keep Jerusalem with its great religious and government buildings. Each of its kings, until its destruction three centuries later, was a descendant of King David, the glamorous hero of all the Hebrew people.

These two tiny nations soon became the prey of their strong neighbors. The northern kingdom suffered numerous civil wars with resulting changes in dynasty. Finally, in 722 B.C., it was conquered by the powerful nation to the east, Assyria. Most of its people were resettled in Mesopotamia, where they came to be absorbed by the Assyrians. Crippled, sick, blind, and elderly people, and some who were able to hide, were left. Migrants were sent from Assyria. In time these groups intermarried and became known as Samaritans, from the chief city of the region, Samaria.

The southern kingdom, Judah, was more successful, but in 586 B.C. was destroyed by Assyria's successor, Babylonia. The majority of the people were deported to Babylonia, where they were well treated. They maintained their religion and their separateness. The prophets Ezekiel and Second Isaiah helped them maintain a dream of eventual release. In 538 B.C. Babylonia was taken over by Cyrus of Persia. Cyrus allowed captured people to return to their homelands. Many of those who considered Judah home did return, although a large number, possibly more than half, remained in the much more fertile region along the Tigris and Euphrates Rivers. Probably a few people whose ancestors had come from Israel also returned, but two hundred years had almost destroyed loyalty to Israel, and to its god, Yahweh.

Since those who returned to Palestine were nearly all people whose parents or grandparents had lived in Judah, the group became known as Jews. They soon cleared the debris from the site of the temple and built an altar for the worship of Yahweh. They expected to build a new temple, but other matters took their energy. Eventually a new leader, Zerubbabel, brought other Jews from the east. He was determined to build a temple. Two prophets, Haggai and Zechariah, in 520 B.C., aroused support for the building enterprise. As a result, the temple was completed four years later.

The Jews continued to be dissatisfied. They were having trouble with the Samaritans and other neighbors, who feared being dominated. Jews in Jerusalem were uneasy, for the city wall still lay in ruins.

At this time Nehemiah, a Jew who had risen to a high position in the Persian government, asked for a leave of absence to go to Jerusalem and supervise the erection of a city wall. The Persian ruler not only granted permission, but made Nehemiah governor of the province of Judah. Nehemiah proved to be a good administrator. Before long he had the wall built. Ezra, the priest and scribe, apparently had brought a group of Jews from Persia a few years earlier. He was determined to tie the Jews' enthusiasm for their new wall into a loyalty to their religion. He organized a great dedication celebration lasting eight days. This included singing, instrumental music, marching, and sacrifices. A portion of the Torah, the first five books of our Bible, was read and explained each day. The people made solemn pledges to obey the rules set forth in the Torah.

Nehemiah visited Jerusalem again a few years later and was discouraged by his discovery that many Jews had fallen away from loyalty to their religion. No further events in the history of the Hebrew people are recorded in the Old Testament. The story of Ruth was written to refute some of Ezra's teaching; the story of Esther was composed much later. The prophecies of Joel and Jonah and parts of the poetic books were written at a later time and reflect later thinking. The Apocalypse of Daniel was written about 165 B.C. as a contribution to the solution of a problem of that time. However, no definite history of the Hebrew people is recorded in our Old Testament after the accounts of Nehemiah and Ezra. Therefore, we consider their time as the beginning of the intertestamental period.

But there is much more to Hebrew history than migrations, the rise and fall of leaders, the building of cities, walls, palaces, and temples. Much more important is the rise of ideas.

The Hebrews were a religious people, basically loyal to their god, Yahweh. It took them a long time to understand Yahweh. We know almost nothing about their religious thinking previous to Moses. The accounts of earlier events were written several hundred years after the time of Moses and, therefore, reflect ideas that not even Moses held. We have no way of knowing how accurate even reports about Moses are. Doubtless his ancestors had been animists, as were nearly all primitive people, trying to please spirits which they felt lived in stones, trees, mountains, clouds.

Abraham seems to have had a higher concept of deity, but Moses gives us the first picture of God. Moses combined ideas from Egypt, Midian, and his own ancestors. He evidently felt that there were many gods, but was convinced that he and his Israelites should be completely loyal to one god, Yahweh—"You shall have no other gods before me" (Ex. 20:30). The idea of many gods is called polytheism. The idea held by Moses, or at least his early successors, that Yahweh is much greater than other gods is known as henotheism. This is the thought through much of the Old Testament:

O give thanks to the God of Gods (Ps. 136:2).

The first definite expression of monotheism, that there is but one god, was made in Babylonian captivity about 540 B.C. by the second Isaiah:

I am the LORD, and there is no other,
besides me there is no God (Isa. 45:5).

Along with the question as to how many gods exist, the Hebrews asked, What is our god like? In a harsh, cruel world deity was thought of as cruel, notionate, vengeful, killing Er and Onan (Gen. 38:7-10), trying to kill Moses as he was carrying out Yahweh's will (Ex. 4:24), and killing numerous men "because they looked into the ark of the LORD" (1 Sam. 6:19). Moses attempted to teach his followers that Yahweh could be depended upon, although at least once Moses thought that he persuaded God to change his mind (Ex. 32:14). However, Moses said nothing about the love of God. Eventually, the Hebrews came to think that God loved them as a people when they did his will. But, when they disobeyed God, they believed that God turned his back on them (Judges 2:20-21).

It was not until about 745 B.C. that the Israelites began to feel that God loved their nation even when it sinned. The prophet Hosea found his wife unfaithful to him, becoming a prostitute. Still, since he loved his wife when she was a rascal, God must love Israel and Judah when they sinned as well as when they obeyed him. Hosea did not teach that God loved other nations or individual people. Jeremiah, around 600 B.C., was the first to attribute these qualities to God. Both Hosea and Jeremiah used the word "father" in referring to deity. By intertestamental times this was a common term for God.

In a similar way, the Old Testament records the evolution of the idea of the proper relation of men to men. Genesis pictures Lamech proclaiming:

> If Cain is avenged sevenfold,
>   truly Lamech seventy-sevenfold (4:24).

Such multiple vengeance did not bring happiness. Moses, in turn, taught, "You shall give life for life, eye for eye, tooth for tooth, hand for hand, foot for foot, burn for burn, wound for wound, stripe for stripe" (Ex. 21:24-25). This one-for-one vengeance came to be questioned in the case of accidentally injuring another. After settling in Canaan, the Israelites established six cities of refuge, "that the manslayer who kills any person without intent may flee there" (Joshua 20:3).

Hosea spoke of the forgiveness of God and asked the question, Should not we too forgive? This led to discussion as to how often one should forgive a person who has harmed him. The general conclusion reached was, Forgive once, twice, three times, but if one injures you four times, hit him hard. It is after the intertestamental period that we find Peter suggesting a sevenfold forgiveness, and Jesus insisting upon forgiving "seventy times seven" (Mt. 18: 21-22).

Men's relation to God also evolved through the Old Testament. In the time of Moses, people were afraid of God. They told Moses, "You speak to us, and we will hear; but let not God speak to us, lest we die" (Ex. 20:19). God was too great to deal with common people. God would listen only to priests or outstanding individuals. Even these got the ear of Yahweh by first offering him a sacrifice. As men enjoyed food and were often brought into good humor by being given a good meal, so God might be humored by being given the smell or essence of food. Sacrifice did not mean giving up something. When the Ark of the Covenant, which had been captured by the Philistines, was returned, the Israelites sacrificed cattle which did not belong to them but to the Philistines (1 Sam. 6:14). When David was being chased by King Saul, he told Saul, "if it is the LORD who has stirred you up against me, may he accept an offering" (1 Sam. 26:19). However, toward the end of his life, David came to feel that genuine sacrifice meant giving up something. When he was offered sacrificial material as a gift, he declined: "I will not offer burnt offerings to the LORD my God which cost me nothing" (2 Sam. 24:24).

The idea that there are other things more important than sacrifice evolved through Hebrew scripture. Samuel told Saul, "To obey is better than sacrifice" (1 Sam. 15:22). The prophet Amos insisted that God preferred justice to sacrifice. His successor, Hosea, maintained that kindness or love is of even greater importance. Some of the writing prophets would have been glad to do away with sacrifices; but, during Babylonian captivity, Ezekiel looked forward to the re-establishment of sacrifices. About 460 B.C. Malachi put a new emphasis upon the value of sincere sacrifices.

Here and there in the Old Testament we find the practice of prayer apart from sacrifices. The taboo against common people praying may have been first broken by Hannah, who prayed that she might have a son (1 Sam. 1:9-18). In his letter from Jerusalem to the captives in Babylonia, the prophet Jeremiah urged them to pray (Jer. 29:7). As we come to the end of the Old Testament history, we find Nehemiah, not a priest or prophet, not a scribe or rabbi, praying from time to time. In the Apocalypse of Daniel, another layman, Daniel himself, is pictured as having regular daily prayer habits. Development of prayer in the intertestamental period will be discussed in Chapter 36.

Other concepts developed through the Old Testament. War was considered the will of God, to be actively participated in on frequent occasions—"In the spring of the year, the time when kings go forth to battle" (2 Sam. 11:1). However, David, before his death, believed that God told him, "You have shed much blood and have waged great wars; you shall not build a house in my name" (2 Chron. 22:8). The prophets Isaiah and Micah were both convinced that in time men would abolish war (Isa. 2:4 and Mic. 4:3-4).

The picture of life beyond the grave also changed through the Old Testament. That there is some such existence seems to have been taken for granted. It was not considered a question of religion. Therefore, there is no definite reference to a future life earlier than the story of Saul's wanting to confer with Samuel, who was dead (1 Sam. 23:3-19). The dead were called shades, having a very hazy existence. Their state was called Sheol. Even as late a writer as that of Ecclesiastes stated, "There is no work or thought or knowledge or wisdom in Sheol, to which you are going" (9:10).

However, as the Hebrews came to think of God as just, they came to think of reward and punishment in the next life. Certainly some people do not receive justice in this life. The Persian Zoroastrian religion, contacted in Babylonian captivity, probably influenced the ideas of a future life. In Palestine the Hebrews were eager to live in a walled city, safe from their enemies. The prophet Micah criticized people for rushing to the cities. Jerusalem was their major city. Therefore, it was natural that they dreamed of the desirable future life as a new, much more beautiful, Jerusalem. South of the city in the valley of Hinnom (Gehenna) was a garbage dump where bodies of criminals and beggars were sometimes put. The third Isaiah doubtless reflected a common feeling when he suggested that those who rebelled against God deserved a similar fate, being where "their worm shall not die, their fire shall not be quenched" (Isa. 66:24).

In writings of the intertestamental period, changing ideas of all these questions are expressed. There is a definite gap between concepts given in the Old Testament and those in the New Testament. How this gap was bridged is the theme of this book. The time from Ezra to Jesus was definitely not a silent or inactive period. To many people they are forgotten or hidden years. This need not be.

ASSIGNMENT

1. Trace the history of the Hebrew people from Abraham through Ezra. Give approximate dates for the chief characters and events.
2. Trace the step-by-step development of the concept of God found in the Old Testament.
3. Trace the Old Testament development of man's concept of his relation to God. Include sacrifice and prayer.
4. Trace the step-by-step development of the concept of man's proper relation to his fellow man as found in the Old Testament.

SUPPLEMENTARY READING

A bibliography for all supplementary reading suggestions is given on pages 216-7.

Fosdick

Sloan: *Old Testament*—Chapters 1 and 42

Chapter 2

Hebrew Captivity— Jewish Return

The evolution of religious and social thought of the Hebrew people was slow, but during the period of captivity in Babylonia, it made a tremendous leap forward. They were taken into captivity as conservative Hebrews. They returned as progressive Jews. To understand the intertestamental period it is necessary to know what took place during this time of exile.

The religion of our forefathers was eclectic—that is, it borrowed ideas from other religions. We have mentioned the influence of Egypt and Midian upon Moses. Recent discoveries in the Middle East indicate that a number of ideas we had thought original among the Hebrews were Canaanite, adopted by the Hebrews after they entered Canaan. We do not know what ideas Abraham brought from the valleys of the Tigris and Euphrates Rivers, but we find that this region had stories of creation, the flood, and other legends recorded before Abraham was born. These are very similar to those reported in Genesis. Genesis and the other books of the Torah were edited during Babylonian captivity, but doubtless most of what they contained was a part of the Hebrew lore before 586 B.C. Many new ideas were adopted during the Babylonian captivity.

Jeremiah was the leading prophet in Jerusalem when people of Judah were captured by the Babylonians. He was never in Babylonia, but he greatly influenced the captives. Read his letter to these captives as given in the twenty-ninth chapter of his prophecy. He feared that the people of Judah would be swallowed up in captivity and disappear as their northern cousins had. During the Deuteronomic Reform, Jeremiah had preached that Yahweh must be worshiped only in Jerusalem. Such a practice would have destroyed the religion of the captives. Therefore, Jeremiah reversed himself and insisted that the captives worship Yahweh in Babylonia—"Seek the welfare of the city where I have sent you into exile, and pray to the LORD on its behalf" (29:7). He instructed, "Build houses . . . plant gardens . . . take wives . . . and multiply there" (29:5-6).

This letter probably would have been of little value had it not been for Ezekiel. Ezekiel was a priest who was among those taken to Babylonia eleven years before the destruction of Jerusalem. He could no longer function as a priest, but was still very much concerned about his people and their religion. Therefore, he became a prophet, despite the fact that prophets and priests disliked each other. In general, priests were conservative, wanting to keep things "the good old way"; prophets were seeking for better ways. Ezekiel set about implementing Jeremiah's letter. People still felt that they could not worship Yahweh apart from the temple. Ezekiel felt otherwise. Evidently he invited a group of Jews to his home. There they prayed, read from what scriptures they had, and discussed the will of God in the light of what they had read. This proved so valuable that groups began to meet in other homes each Sabbath. These gatherings came to be called synagogues. They soon became social and educational institutions as well as worship centers. When many of the Jews returned to Judah and rebuilt their temple there, they took the synagogue with them. During the intertestamental period, Jews scattered throughout the known world. In every town where they settled they established a synagogue.

One of the Hebrew "Ten Commandments" was "Remember the sabbath day, to keep it holy" (Ex. 20:8). To the early Hebrews, keeping the Sabbath holy was primarily resting from labor. Ezekiel added the element of group worship to Sabbath observance. This became one of the distinguishing marks of the Jews during the intertestamental period.

When Israel had been destroyed by the Assyrians in 722 B.C., and when Judah met a similar fate at the hands of the Babylonians in 586 B.C., the prophets did not come to distrust Yahweh or think him weaker than the gods or kings of their enemies. They recognized that the people had sinned, had failed to obey the will of Yahweh. Therefore, Yahweh was punishing them. Jeremiah wrote the captives that " 'I know the plans I have for you,' says the LORD, 'plans for welfare and not for evil, to give you a future and a hope. Then you will call upon me and come

and pray to me, and I will hear you. . . . I will bring you back
to the place from which I sent you into exile' " (29:11-14).
Ezekiel, and later the second Isaiah, kept reminding the exiles
of this promise. They remained united and were ready for the
opportunity when it came. This is why Ezekiel is considered
the father of Judaism. The Jewish people list him as one of the
four greatest heroes of Hebrew history, along with Abraham,
Moses, and David.

The second Isaiah, author of Isa. 40-55, was a product of the
Babylonian captivity. He is responsible for much of the finest
literature of the Hebrew scriptures. Writing about 540 B.C.,
he not only comforted the exiles, but challenged them. As far as
our records show, he was the first Hebrew to proclaim that there
is but one God, "the LORD who made all things" (44:24).
He felt that the Jews had a great task, that of telling the world
about Yahweh. He, therefore, insisted that Judah was the suffering servant of Yahweh.

Since Israel and Judah had become separated about 922 B.C.,
the Hebrews had looked forward to a great leader, the Anointed
One or Messiah. Kings and high priests were anointed. Some
day God would raise up one who would be not just *an* anointed,
but *the* Anointed. The second Isaiah believed he had found
this person. His nominee was the Persian king Cyrus (45:1).

In 559 B.C. Cyrus inherited a tiny kingdom which was tribu-
tary to the Median Empire east of Babylonia. A decade later
he revolted against his emperor. The emperor sent two armies
against Cyrus. Because their overlord had been so cruel, both
armies deserted to Cyrus. Cyrus was a generous conqueror and
allowed many government officials to keep their positions.
Cyrus then marched north and conquered Lydia, which we today call Turkey. He took over the Greek cities on the eastern
shore of the Aegean Sea. Primitive people as far east as the
edge of China soon recognized him as the "Great King."

Cyrus then turned toward Babylonia, where he was welcomed
in what was almost a bloodless conquest. The Babylonian king,
Nabonidus, was chiefly interested in archaeology and spent much
time exploring in Arabia. He left his nation in charge of his
son, Belshazzar, who was not interested in the dead past, but in
wine, women, and song! Neither Nabonidus nor his son was
popular. Graft and mismanagement had brought about suffering. Therefore, the Babylonians considered Cyrus as a deliverer
when he took over Babylon in October 538 B.C., diverting the

Euphrates River and entering the city through the water channel. Cyrus had established the first world empire, Persia.

Nabonidus had hoped to secure protection by bringing to his capital the statues of many foreign gods. This was opposed by the local priests. Cyrus immediately cooperated with the Babylonian priests by participating in the ritual of their new year festival and returning the idols to their original places. He found that Assyrians and their successors had moved about many people whom they had conquered. In his own account of his dealings with the people in Babylonia, Cyrus writes: "I gathered all their [former] inhabitants and returned [to them] their habitations."

Ezra (2:64-65) and Nehemiah doubtless exaggerate in reporting that as many as 50,000 Jews took advantage of this opportunity and returned to the province of Judah. Other groups followed later. Cyrus was happy to have them do this. The one important part of the world he had not conquered was Egypt. If the Jews could be contentedly settled, they would form a buffer state. Cyrus' son Cambyses later conquered Egypt for the empire. Persia lasted for two hundred years after the fall of Babylonia, or until it was conquered by Alexander the Great as a part of his Greek empire.

Although certain Babylonian religious ideas influenced the Jews, greater contributions were made by the Persian religion, Zoroastrianism. This was much superior to the Marduk worship of Babylonia and had begun to influence the Babylonians and the Jews before the coming of Cyrus.

Perhaps the chief Zoroastrian contribution to Jewish thinking was that of Angra Mainyu, or Satan, later referred to as the devil. The Hebrews had originally thought of Yahweh as the great power, without much concern as to whether he was good or evil. Many cruel deeds were attributed to him, such as demanding that Abraham sacrifice to him his son Isaac (Gen. 22:2). Hannah, in her song of gratitude for the birth of Samuel, sang:

> The LORD kills and brings to life;
> he brings down to Sheol and raises up.
> The LORD makes poor and makes rich;
> he brings low, he also exalts (1 Sam. 2:6-7).

But, as the Hebrews grew in their belief in the justice, even the love and kindness of God, the idea that God is the source of evil bothered them. A solution was presented by the Zoroastrian concept of Ahura Mazda, the power of light and right, and of Angra Mainyu, the power of darkness and evil. Therefore, the idea of Satan was adopted into the Jewish religion.

This is well illustrated by the story of King David's census. In 2 Sam. 24:1 we read "The anger of the LORD was kindled against Israel, and he incited David against them, saying, 'Go, number Israel and Judah.' " The author later says that God punished David for taking the census. This account was written shortly before, or early in, the Babylonian captivity. The Jewish people began to ask, Would God punish a man for obeying him? After the return from captivity, a group of priests rewrote much of the material found in the books of Samuel and Kings. This revised record we call Chronicles. In it this problem is solved. In 1 Chron. 21:1 we read, relative to the same census, "Satan stood up against Israel, and incited David to number Israel."

The Zoroastrians contributed not only Satan but also angels and demons. They felt that between God and man there were various degrees of helpers, messengers of good and light; that between man and Satan there were also various degrees of messengers of evil and darkness. The term angel originally meant messenger. The Hebrews had used it earlier for human beings. Lot's visitors, reported in Gen. 19, are referred to as men and as angels. In Gen. 28:12 we read that Jacob dreamed of angels ascending and descending a ladder—they had not yet sprouted wings! It was not too difficult for Jews to adopt the idea of non-human angels. If good angels, why not evil ones as well? Development of the idea of non-human beings during the intertestamental period will be discussed in Chapter 39.

A constant struggle between the powers of light and those of darkness, in which light and good would eventually win, is another Zoroastrian idea that appealed to the Jews. It has already been mentioned that Jewish pictures of the future life indicate an influence from the religion of the Persians. The intertestamental development of this concept will be dealt with in Chapter 38.

Their return from Babylonian captivity started an entirely new life for the Jewish people. Their religion had greatly changed during the exile. They soon came to recognize this and began to think of everything previous to it as their childhood and adolescence. God had brought them to maturity. He spoke to them through prophets. Now the prophets were practically a thing of the past. The Jews had become people of a book, but the book should be completed. Historical writings were edited; collections were made of sayings and poems attributed to pre-exile people; but the idea that their scriptures should be a continually growing thing was rejected.

Official action as to what books were to be included in their Bible was not taken until after the close of the intertestamental period. In A.D. 90 a list of accepted books was drawn up. This practically repudiated anything that seemed to originate after the time of Ezra. Naturally, when books were compiled and edited, some post-Ezra ideas crept in. However, the Bible, as most of us recognize it, leaves us ignorant of the events and thinking between Ezra and the development of Christianity. The history and literature of this intertestamental period are rich. To understand Christianity we must become acquainted with the events and developing concepts of the centuries immediately preceding the birth of the Christian religion.

ASSIGNMENT

1. Trace the story of the captivity of Israel.
2. Trace the story of the captivity of Judah.
3. What theological concept did the prophets express when the Hebrew nations were destroyed?
4. Outline the advice Jeremiah sent to the captives of Judah.
5. Who was Ezekiel? What contributions did he make to the religion of his people?
6. Who was II Isaiah? What were his major contributions?
7. Tell briefly the rise and success of Cyrus. How did II Isaiah consider him?
8. Identify Zoroastrianism. What did it contribute to the religion of the Hebrews? What is religious eclecticism?
9. Why is this chapter not entitled "Hebrew Captivity and Return"?
10. Identify Ezra, Nehemiah. When was Nehemiah's wall built?

SUPPLEMENTARY READING

Enslin—Chapter I
Lamb: *Cyrus*
Pfeiffer, R. H.: *History*—Pages 5-8
Sloan: *Old Testament*—Chapter 5
Snaith—Chapters I and II

Chapter 3

The Coming of the Greeks

Cyrus and his successor Cambyses were conquerors. Cambyses'
son, Darius I, was an organizer. He established a postal system
by which riders on fast horses carried news from one part of the
empire to another. He conquered territory north of Greece and
invaded Greece itself, but was defeated at Marathon. Ten years
later his successor, Xerxes I, with soldiers of forty-six nations
and a fleet reported to have consisted of 1207 fighting vessels
and 3000 transport ships, conquered much of Greece. He defeated the Spartans at Thermopylae and burned the city of
Athens, but soon lost his fleet and most of his army. In 465
B.C. Xerxes was poisoned. Several later kings and generals were
poisoned. This weakened the empire; a number of sections
secured independence.

In time, much of Greece was conquered by Philip of Macedonia to the North. Philip was murdered in 336 B.C. He was
succeeded by his nineteen-year-old son, Alexander, who had
already been a general for three years. He soon completed the
conquest of Greece and marched eastward to conquer Persia.
Greek culture had already penetrated much of the Middle East.
Alexander successfully counted upon this to find allies in destroying the increasingly degenerate Persian Empire.

Alexander quickly defeated a Persian army three times as
large as his own and took what we now call Turkey. He easily
captured Damascus, but it required seven months to secure the
submission of the island stronghold of Tyre. The fall of Tyre
permanently destroyed the commercial prominence of the Phoe-
nicians, the able seafaring nation along the Mediterranean,
northwest of Palestine. Despite a heroic but short-lived re-
sistance upon the part of the ancient Philistine city of Gaza,
Alexander conquered Palestine in 332 B.C. He went on to
Egypt, where he was greeted as a deliverer from Persian control.
He spent the winter along the Mediterranean coast and founded

the city that bears his name. This was the first of a dozen Alexandrias, the only one that lasted any great length of time. It soon replaced Tyre as the commercial center of the eastern Mediterranean. From a cultural standpoint, it became the Athens of the East. Jewish and Greek colonists were encouraged to settle there and develop the city. During the intertestamental period, we have more references to Alexandria than to any other city.

The next spring Alexander went on to Mesopotamia, where he defeated the main Persian army east of the Tigris River and north of Nineveh. About a year later the Persians murdered their king and the Empire belonged to Alexander. After taking some of what is now southern Russia, and marrying Roxana, a princess of that region, he pushed on into India. His soldiers, worn out and far from home, threatened to rebel. Alexander was persuaded to return to Babylon, where he died in 323 B.C., before reaching the age of thirty-three.

Alexander's conquest had a much more lasting effect than did that of the Persians, for he spread Greek ideas and Greek culture. This had its influence on the Jewish religion and had a very definite impact upon Christianity. Rome took over Greek culture and even the Greek language and built its civilization upon that of Greece. This is the background of much of our western life.

Much credit for this goes to the Greek philosopher Aristotle, who became Alexander's tutor when the prince was thirteen years old, and kept up a correspondence with him throughout his campaigns. Alexander had already learned to love Greek poetry, especially that attributed to Homer. On all his marches he carried copies of the Iliad and the Odyssey with him. As a boy, he had come to think of himself as a son of the Greek gods. Aristotle developed in him a great reverence for all things Greek —art, literature, language, and style of government. He was determined to plant Greek culture wherever he went. As he marched farther and farther from home, many of his soldiers, because of age or wounds, were unable to continue the campaign. Alexander discharged them in groups and settled them in communities to marry native women and raise families as Greeks. He married a Persian princess and some eighty of his officers took Persian wives. Thus many centers of Greek life were established through the Middle East. After every conquest Alexander was followed by Greek-speaking merchants, tourists, scholars, and settlers. They, too, commonly married local women. They brought Greek ideas of architecture, government, and philosophy. The many cities built by Alexander or his successors were definitely Greek, with theaters, baths, gymnasiums, and forums. Northeast of Palestine a group of Greek cities developed. Known as the Decapolis (Ten Cities), they greatly influenced the environment into which Christianity was born. The Greeks from the west changed Jewish life much more than did the oriental Persians.

Before his death, Alexander lost many of his Greek ways. He adopted Persian dress, insisted upon being treated as a god, and became a harsh oriental potentate. However, Greek culture outlived him. Although his empire soon broke up, every piece remained Greek. The intertestamental period was in reality a Greek period. The three centuries after Alexander's time are often called the Hellenistic age.

Alexander left no legitimate heirs. Who should succeed him? He had a half-witted half-brother. Alexander's wife, Roxana, was "expecting." The brother was undesirable. Roxana's child might be a girl! Alexander's generals finally decided to take over the empire themselves, in the name of the descendants of Philip and Alexander. This immediately resulted in fighting among the generals. A dozen of them had ambitions. Most of them took over sections of the empire for themselves and plotted to undermine neighboring generals or satraps. Alexander's mother, his half-brother, his wife, and posthumous son were murdered. By 312 B.C. the ruling generals had been reduced to four. The author of the book of Daniel describes Alexander's empire as being "broken and divided toward the four winds of heaven" (11:4). Daniel uses even more figurative language in describing this in 8:8.

Ptolemy Lagi, a boyhood companion of Alexander, one of his stalwarts from the time he entered Asia, decided to take Egypt for his own. It would be the easiest territory to defend. The woman he loved was an Egyptian and kept urging him to return to Egypt. He stole the body of Alexander and hurried off to Alexandria, where he established a dynasty that ran through fourteen members, ending with the infamous Cleopatra and the Roman conquest of 30 B.C. With Egypt, Ptolemy took southern Syria or Palestine. He moved a large number of Jews, possibly 100,000, into northern Egypt. Many were already living in Alexandria. Ptolemy collected tribute from the Jews in Palestine, but, in general, allowed them to govern themselves under the supervision of their high priests.

Near the end of Alexander's life, a young man named Seleucus became one of his favorite generals. However, in the division of territory among the generals, he did not receive a satrapy. He entered the contest and by 311 B.C. had made himself master of Babylon. Before long he had secured northern Syria and determined to take Palestine from Ptolemy. By 281 B.C. Seleucus possessed all of Alexander's Asian territory, except Palestine. He was murdered as he was about to take control of Macedonia, the birthplace of both Alexander and himself. Another leader secured Macedonia. This division of Alexander's kingdom into Asian, African, and European territories lasted until the rise of Rome. Seleucus built himself a capital on the Orontes River, north of Palestine. He named it Antioch in honor of his father, one of Philip's right-hand men. Of the sixty Greek cities he built from the Hellespont to the Indus, sixteen were called Antioch. His nation took over the ancient name Syria.

The descendants of Seleucus were still determined to take Palestine from the descendants of Ptolemy. Numerous attempts were made, some temporarily successful. Finally, in 198 B.C. the great-great-grandson of Seleucus wrested Palestine from the great-great-grandson of the first Ptolemy. Dan. 11:10-17 tells how "the king of the north" defeated "the king of the south" and took his stand "in the glorious land" (Palestine).

Under the Ptolemies the Jews prospered, although they were required to pay heavy taxes. Probably Chronicles, Ezra, Nehemiah, the book of Proverbs, and some of the Psalms were written at this time. A translation of the Hebrew scriptures into Greek, the Septuagint, was begun in Alexandria. Some attempts were made to persuade the Jews to adopt Greek ways, but little pressure was brought to bear. However, under the Seleucids the situation was much different.

Antiochus III, the Great, who took Palestine from the Ptolemies, increased the heavy taxes, but otherwise treated the Jews kindly. The younger of his two sons, Antiochus IV, was born in Greece and served as chief magistrate of Athens. He also spent twelve years as a hostage in Rome. He saw the world dividing between a coarse Roman civilization and Greek culture. He determined to bring culture to his territory, which meant making Palestine Greek.

In Palestine Antiochus built theaters and amphitheaters, stadiums and baths. In Jerusalem he had a gymnasium constructed. There, in accord with the Greek custom, young men exercised in the nude. The word gymnasium is derived from the Greek word for naked. This practice antagonized pious Jews. On the other hand, some Jews welcomed the Greek influence as a means of their becoming part of a great world civilization; they were glad to be called "citizens of Antioch"—many even migrated to Syria.

The high priest of the Jews, Onias III, was required to pay tribute to the Seleucids. His brother Jason offered to pay a larger tribute and persuaded Antiochus to appoint him in the place of Onias. Antiochus thought of the high priesthood as a political office and saw nothing wrong in selling it to the highest bidder. The Hasideans, or "pious" Jews, feeling that this was a sin against God, opposed the Seleucids.

A third contender for the high priesthood, Menelaus, who did not even belong to the priestly family, offered to pay still higher tribute and was given the position. Naturally, this increased Jewish antagonism. It even led to civil war among the Jews.

Antiochus came to think of orthodox Jews as his enemies. After invading Egypt, he had been forced to withdraw by threats from Rome. To appease his anger, Antiochus sent an army to occupy Jerusalem. He attacked the city on a Sabbath, knowing that the orthodox would not fight on that day. A fortress was built in Jerusalem and a program of forcing Greek culture onto the Jews was instituted. Orders were given that Greek gods be worshiped. Jews were forbidden to observe the Sabbath or their religious feasts. The practice of circumcision was not allowed. Copies of the Hebrew scriptures were ordered destroyed.

In December, 168 B.C., licentious heathen rites were performd in the temple courts, and—worst of all from a Jewish viewpoint—a pig was sacrificed on the altar. Dan. 11:31 calls this "the abomination that makes desolate."

An elderly scribe was flogged to death for refusing to eat pork. Two mothers were thrown headlong over the city wall because they had circumcised their new-born sons. Menelaus, the high priest, submitted and offered worship to Zeus in place of Yahweh. This led to the Maccabean Revolt, which will be discussed in Chapter 8.

It is not surprising to find Daniel referring to Antiochus as "a contemptible person" (11:21), a little horn, "with eyes like the eyes of a man, and a mouth speaking great things" (7:8). He took for himself the title Epiphanes, the brilliant. Behind his back the Jews called him Epimanes, the fool.

ASSIGNMENT

1. Identify Philip of Macedon.
2. Give in some detail the story of Alexander the Great.
3. Identify Ptolemy, Seleucus, Antiochus III, Antiochus IV.
4. What was "the abomination that makes desolate"?

SUPPLEMENTARY READING

Dentan—Pages 23-28
Pfeiffer, R. H.: *History*—Pages 8-9
Lamb: *Alexander*
Snaith—Chapters III and IV
Toombs—Pages 24-7

Chapter 4

Greek Thought
and Influence

While Daniel is the only book in our Old Testament that discusses the taking over of Palestine by the Syrian Greeks, the influence of the Greeks is not lacking elsewhere. Joel 3:6 refers to people of Judah and Jerusalem being sold to the Greeks and removed "far from their own border." This was written shortly before the coming of Alexander. In the appendix to the book of Zechariah, a group of writings brought together between 300 and 250 B.C., there is reference to the coming of Greeks. Optimistically the writer proclaims, "I will brandish your sons, O Zion, over your sons, O Greece" (9:12).

Much of the third section of the Old Testament, the Holy Writings, was composed after the time of Alexander and reflects Greek thought. The pessimistic book of Ecclesiastes has a Greek outlook. Evidently the writer of Job had a knowledge of Greek drama and philosophy. A few Psalms and numerous portions of the book of Proverbs express Greek thought. Like Ecclesiastes, the Song of Solomon contains a number of Greek words put into Hebrew.

What were the major differences between Jews and Greeks? Jewish life centered around religion; Greek, around philosophy. Although the two tend to overlap in our minds today, religion was not originally a concern of Greek philosophy. Jewish life was God-centered; Greek, self-centered.

The Jews thought of their god, Yahweh, as directing their lives. He was concerned with their progress. He had set up laws. Those who obeyed these laws found life good. A leading Greek philosopher said, "If you wish good, get it yourself." But the Greeks could not stay away from the idea of deity. The ordinary Greek thought there were many gods. Socrates said there is but one God, but Socrates was put to death for this in 399 B.C. on the charge of corrupting the morals of youth. However, the Greek gods had very little to do with morals. They were thought of as quite immoral, quarreling among themselves, stealing each other's wives. To the Jew, Yahweh was above all wrong. The earlier Jews attributed to God certain deeds we today would not consider moral. On the other hand, all Jews would have agreed with the thought accredited to Abraham, "Shall not the Judge of all the earth do right?" (Gen. 18:25). To the Jew, God was above all matters of sex. The idea of God's having parents, wife, or children was unthinkable, although by intertestamental times the term Father was considered an appropriate title for God. Yahweh was all powerful, the creator of the universe. The Greeks thought their gods weak; many men were stronger.

The Greek was cosmopolitan, tolerant of other people's ideas and religions. The Jew was sure he had the only truth, that the Jewish people were the chosen of God. They had a covenant, an agreement, with him.

As we look back over history now, we see a definite evolution of the Jewish religion, but the Jew did not understand this. He believed that everything had been revealed by Yahweh to Moses on Mount Sinai. God knew how to have a perfect world. This could be brought about by obeying God's laws. If Israel would keep all the law for a single day, the golden age would dawn. Their religion had been revealed to them by God. It was recorded in their basic scriptures, the Torah (Genesis, Exodus, Leviticus, Numbers, and Deuteronomy). By intertestamental times it was realized that there were many questions of worship and ethics not answered in the Torah. Therefore the Jews, especially those who called themselves the Pharisees, developed what became known as the oral Torah. This consisted of a great number of detailed rules. However, they denied that they made up these rules. They asserted that God had given them to Moses, but Moses or his successors had failed to record them, and they had been handed down by word of mouth. When this was challenged, the answer was that the rules were right: God could see ahead to any circumstances and, therefore, must have made such laws. He would not have omitted anything in giving his directions to Moses.

Sin was considered defiance of the laws of God. Ethics was a part of the will of God. To many Greeks, however, virtue was an important means to real pleasure; but pleasure was the end, virtue only a means.

To the Greek, not deity, but the mind of man was supreme. It was the permanent and controlling principle of the natural order. Some Greeks went on from this to the idea of one supreme intelligence. On the other hand, the Jews started from their concept of the supreme creator who made man somewhat in his own image. The Jew was not expected to think, but to obey. God's will had become his will.

Although they made their temple a thing of beauty, the Hebrews borrowed its design from others. They failed to develop an architecture of their own. They thought of "the beauty of holiness," but had almost no concern for art. Life on their bare hills was harsh. They had little interest in esthetics. They considered attempts at beauty as vanity, pride, trying to improve on what God had done. Very early in their religion they had been told "you shall not make yourself a graven image, or any likeness of anything that is in heaven above, or that is in the earth beneath, or that is in the water under the earth" (Ex. 20:4). This practically prohibited all visual arts.

In contrast, the Greeks loved beauty and art. They sought expression in painting and sculpture, in poetry and music. They developed a system of musical notes. Philosophical discussion was to them an art. So were the theater and athletic contests. The prohibition of Deut. 22:5 was considered by the Jews as forbidding masquerading and, therefore, stage presentations. Among Greeks, races of various kinds, discus and javelin throwing, were enjoyed. To the Jew, this was very impractical. Why run unless to get some place in a hurry? Why throw a javelin unless to hit an enemy or an animal? Games were make-believe, for children. Gymnasiums and baths were social centers for the Greeks, who wanted a sane mind in a healthy body. Luxurious living was sought. Greek culture was based upon a slave society. This gave a limited group much leisure for philosophizing and recreation.

Practically all Jewish writing was religious. Not a great deal other than their scriptures and explanations of them was produced in Palestine. Schools were connected with the synagogues. They existed for the purpose of enabling boys to read the scriptures. The Greeks, on the other hand, were literary people. Their language, developed as early as 1,000 B.C., became one of the world's most expressive. Their vocabulary was richer and much more extensive than that of the Hebrews. Writings attributed to Homer, produced by 800 B.C., are still some of the world's greatest literature. Much of the later "classical" literature is read in all parts of the world today.

With so many little city-states in the Greek peninsula, it was natural that there were various dialects. Alexander, by bringing together soldiers from all parts of Greece, was responsible for the development of Koiné Greek, which became the language of the Mediterranean world and even to the borders of India, and the language in which the New Testament was written.

Interest in literary expression brought about the development of great libraries. The library at Alexandria, destroyed by the Romans in 47 B.C., is reported to have contained 700,000 scrolls. This was re-established, but destroyed again by Moslems in A.D. 640. Greek homes of means and culture had their own libraries, although all books were expensive, being copied by hand.

Great universities were developed at Athens, Alexandria, and Tarsus, and lesser ones at Antioch, Rhodes, and Marseilles. Instruction was given in oratory, law, mathematics and astronomy, medicine, geography, and botany. In each of these fields the Greeks made definite progress.

Language and dress of the Greeks were foreign to the Jews, but were adopted more readily than the elements of Greek culture and religion. During the intertestamental period, however, we find a fusing of things Jewish and Greek. This prepared the way for Christianity, which one might say had two parents, Jewish theology and Greek philosophy.

ASSIGNMENT

1. Which Old Testament books refer to the coming of the Greeks? Which other Old Testament books indicate Greek influence?
2. In what chief ways did the Greek outlook differ from the Jewish?
3. What was the Greek picture of deity?
4. What influence did the Greeks have on the life and customs of the Jews in Palestine?
5. What influence did the Greeks begin to have on Jewish religion?

6. What was the intellectual influence of the Greeks?
7. What is meant by Koiné Greek?

SUPPLEMENTARY READING

Dana—Chapter IX
Enslin—Chapter VI
Russell—Chapter I

Chapter 5

Jews in Egypt

The Jews were a prolific people; they found Palestine too small for them. Many migrated to the north, and a smaller number to Egypt. Those living outside Palestine were called Jews of the Dispersion. Often the Greek term Diaspora was used. Those who came definitely under Greek influence were known as Hellenists. We hear more of the Jews in Egypt than of those in Syria. At the time of Jesus, there seem to have been about 700,000 Jews in Palestine and a million in Egypt.

Our first Biblical record of a flight of Jews to Egypt is in the latter part of the book of Jeremiah, especially in the 43rd chapter. After Nebuchadnezzar had destroyed Jerusalem and taken a second group of Jews to Babylonia as captives, he made a Jewish leader, Gedaliah, governor with headquarters at Mizpah. Some of his fellow Jews considered Gedaliah a traitor, a quisling. About 581 B.C. they murdered him. The Jews then feared that Nebuchadnezzar would return and destroy them all. They decided to flee to Egypt. The prophet Jeremiah, who had been allowed to remain in Judah because he had advised against fighting Babylonia, opposed this flight. His advice was not taken. He was kidnapped and carried off to Egypt. The Jews settled down in Goshen, where Joseph is reported to have located their ancestors more than a thousand years before.

We learn that there were already many Jews in Egypt with colonies as far south as Elephantine Island in the Nile River near the present Aswan Dam. This was the Ethiopian border. Ezek. 29:10 and 30:6, Isa. 49:12, as well as the Greek historian Strabo, refer to the region opposite the island as Syene. This term has survived in the modern name Aswan

When the Persians secured control of Egypt in 525 B.C., the Jews had already been allowed to build a temple on Elephantine. Jews elsewhere, loyal to Jerusalem, considered this heretical and would not recognize it as a true temple. A papyrus discovered on Elephantine reports that Cambyses, the Persian conqueror, found the temple to Yahweh and did not harm it, although he destroyed the Egyptian temples.

Two early non-Biblical accounts tell of Jewish soldiers being employed by an Egyptian pharaoh to help fight Ethiopians about 580 B.C. Deut. 17:16 forbids sending people (evidently soldiers) to Egypt in exchange for horses. After the war, Jewish soldiers were probably settled at Elephantine on the Ethiopian border. Because they expressed loyalty to the Persian invaders, they were looked upon with suspicion by the Egyptians, who destroyed their temple in 410 B.C., according to papyri found in 1906. The temple evidently was rebuilt, but nothing more is heard later of this Elephantine group; they were probably killed by the Egyptians—perhaps this was the beginning of anti-Semitism. These Jews seem to have paid no attention to the Deuteronomy Reform of 621 B.C. They offered sacrifices to other gods in addition to Yahweh. Probably they absorbed migrants from northern Palestine.

A few years ago, near Cairo, jars were found which contained correspondence between Jews living in northern Egypt and those in the Elephantine region. Greetings were sent, not in the name of Yahweh, but in that of the Egyptian queen of heaven, Astarte or Ishtar. These letters were written about the time Jeremiah was urging Jews in Egypt to return to the service of Yahweh.

Jeremiah found many of the Jews throughout Egypt unfaithful to Yahweh. We hear him reprimanding them for burning incense and pouring out libations to the queen of heaven, who was also considered a goddess of fertility and as such served by many Jewish women. In their homeland they had been friendly to the Canaanite god of fertility, Baal.

Jews doubtless continued to filter into Egypt after the time of Jeremiah. The next big influx was in connection with the developing of the city of Alexandria. Not many real Egyptians lived in the region where Alexander decided to erect a commercial city. Therefore, he invited both Greeks and Jews to take part in the city's development. Eventually, two of the five sections of the city were called Jewish, although Jews lived and had synagogues in all parts of it. One synagogue is reported to have been so large that to let the congregation know the proper time for the "Amens" it was necessary to wave flags. Jews were not confined to a ghetto and had definite civil rights. However, only those who worshiped the gods of the city-state were considered full citizens.

In his letter to Philocrates, Aristeas says that Ptolemy I "transported more than a hundred thousand persons from the country of the Jews to Egypt. Of these he armed some thirty thousand chosen men and settled them in garrisons in the country . . . the remaining bulk, those too old or too young and also the women, he reduced to bondage" (12-14). He also mentions that "previously many had come into the country along with the Persians." These Jewish slaves, he says, were given their freedom by Ptolemy II, Philadelphus.

The accusation reportedly made against Jews in Persia applied in Alexandria, and wherever Jews were found during the inter-testamental period: "There is a certain people scattered abroad and dispersed among the peoples in all the provinces of your kingdom; their laws are different from those of every other people, and they do not keep the king's laws" (Esther 3:8). They enjoyed considerable autonomy, but were not especially liked by their neighbors. However, until the coming of the Romans, the controversies between Jews and Gentiles remained oral or literary. When the Romans took control in 30 B.C., the Jews proclaimed loyalty to the new rulers. The Greeks despised this. The Romans managed to prevent violence between the two groups until about A.D. 35, when the Greeks hit upon the scheme of putting statues of the Roman emperor in the synagogues. The emperor was demanding divine worship for himself. The Jews refused to offer this, and thus came to be persecuted by both Greeks and Romans. Jews were then forced to live in a ghetto.

When Claudius became Roman emperor in A.D. 41, he condemned to death two of the leaders in earlier anti-Jewish riots. He confirmed privileges and rights Jews had had in Alexandria. He insisted that they should be allowed to enjoy the prosperity of the city "not their own," but forbade them to invite other Jews to Alexandria. Peace ruled until the Palestinian Jews rebelled against Rome in A.D. 66, when anti-Semitism naturally broke forth again in northern Egypt.

Not only did the first Ptolemy bring a large number of Jews to Egypt. Throughout the Ptolemy dynasty, others settled in various parts of Egypt, setting up synagogues in many towns. About 160 B.C., a high priest escaped from Jerusalem when Syrians had plotted against him. In the southern part of the

Egyptian delta, he was permitted by Ptolemy VI to build a small replica of the Jerusalem temple. Here, contrary to Jewish law, he offered sacrifices. Many Jewish farmers lived in villages. Other Jews served as merchants and tax collectors.

In Egypt, especially in Alexandria, Jews became acquainted with Greeks on about an equal footing. Greeks in Palestine were despised as intruders. Jews in Greece were looked upon in much the same way. In Egypt both groups, being foreigners, came to have respect for one another.

These Jews began to feel that they should share their knowledge of God. In Babylonian captivity, Second Isaiah had insisted that those who knew God should tell others about him, even if this made them the suffering servant of Yahweh. About 300 B.C., an unknown Jew, probably in Alexandria, produced a book to emphasize this belief. It was the story of Jonah. First Isaiah and Jeremiah had indicated that their people should share their religious understanding. They had not done so, and God had allowed them to be swallowed in captivity. Jeremiah had said, "Nebuchadnezzar . . . has swallowed me like a monster" (51:34).

God had given the Jews a second chance, which they should utilize. To point up this idea, the writer retold an ancient story of a man being swallowed by a sea-monster, Jonah and the great fish (referred to in the New Testament as a whale). Jonah had been commanded to go to Nineveh in Assyria to tell about God. He went in the opposite direction, met the whale, and three days later was spit out. He then went to Nineveh and proclaimed that the city would be destroyed within forty days. When his prediction was not fulfilled, he was angry with God, who pointed out to Jonah that his great concern was with the people of Nineveh. This would not have been accepted by the orthodox Jews of Palestine, who were still nationalistic, insisting that God had chosen them and them alone. One non-Biblical writing represents the Palestine Jews as saying that to God the Gentiles were so unimportant that they were but a drop in a bucket.

We do not know how effective the book of Jonah was. A few years later a definite attempt was made to help Greek-reading people to understand Yahweh. Jews had built synagogues in Alexandria. They made much of their basic scripture, the Torah. When book-loving Greeks asked about it, they were doubtless told to go ahead and read it, but to the Greeks the

Hebrew letters looked like chicken-tracks. They could not read Hebrew. Neither could many of the Jewish young people. Probably many Jewish adults were in the same situation. To make the Torah available to these groups, Jewish scholars proceeded to translate it into Greek. This was started about 250 B.C. However, rabbis in Jerusalem disapproved. They felt that Hebrew was the language of heaven, spoken by the angels, God's native tongue.

Our earliest story of this translation into Greek says that the second Ptolemy had it translated to add it to the Alexandrian library. This story says that the high priest sent him seventy-two scholars from Jerusalem. When they arrived in Alexandria, Ptolemy gave them a great banquet. He asked them numerous philosophical questions and was greatly impressed by the wisdom revealed by their answers. Seventy-two days later a Greek translation of the Torah had been completed. This was highly praised by both the Jewish community and the king. It came to be called the Septuagint, from the Latin word for seventy, septuaginta, commonly referred to by Biblical scholars by the symbol LXX.

The Greek Torah was divided into five scrolls. A Greek name was given to each scroll. In English translation they are known as Genesis (meaning beginning), Exodus (the way out), Leviticus (rules for priests and Levites), Numbers (beginning with statistics) and Deuteronomy (second law). The term Pentateuch, meaning five books, was often used for the scrolls of the Torah.

Eventually, all the Hebrew scriptures were translated. There was no official list of the books constituting the third section of the Hebrew Bible, the Holy Writings. Jewish scholars in Egypt included all the Jewish religious writings which they had found especially helpful. Some of these were originally written in Greek or Aramaic rather than Hebrew. The term Septuagint came to be applied to the entire Greek-language Old Testament. It turnd out to be a larger Bible than the Hebrew canon. The additional books were eventually classed as the Apocrypha. Thus, the Septuagint had four sections, the Torah, the Prophets (both Former Prophets or history, and Latter Prophets or sermons), the Holy Writings, and the Apocrypha. Other translations of parts of the Hebrew scriptures into Greek were made, but the Septuagint became the accepted version. It was used by early Christians as they spread their religion, and with it the

Old Testament, over the Mediterranean world.

However, the Septuagint at certain points differs extensively from the Hebrew on which our English translations are based, known as the Masoretic text. Because of this, English translations of the Septuagint have been made. The New Testament writers used the Septuagint. Therefore, many quotations from the Old Testament in our Bible differ from the corresponding Old Testament verses. Until recently it has been taken for granted that the Septuagint translators condensed some parts they thought too drawn out, and expanded some parts they thought needed to be explained. They also seemed to change figures of speech here and there. But the finding of the Dead Sea Scrolls suggests that this is not always true. The oldest Hebrew copy we had of the Old Testament was made about A.D. 900. Now we have copies of at least parts of every Old Testament book (with the possible exception of Esther) nine hundred to a thousand years older. In many places the reading in the scrolls is more in agreement with the Septuagint than it is with the Hebrew we have been using. Can it be that the Septuagint is closer the original, and it is the Hebrew that was changed? This is discussed in Chapter 20.

The attempt to have the Greeks understand the Jewish religion and their God resulted in an effort to fuse the two cultures on a philosophical and religious level. The outstanding leader of this movement was Philo, sometimes called Philo Judaeus. He was an Alexandrian Jew born about 20 B.C. He secured a thorough Greek philosophical education, but also became well acquainted with the Septuagint. He felt that every word in it had been inspired by God. In many, many parts of the scriptures he found what he was convinced were allegorical meanings. Other philosophers had done this with Greek history. To Philo, Abraham's journey to Palestine was the story of a Stoic philosopher leaving sensual understanding and stopping for a time (at Haran) with the senses. Abraham's marriage to Sarah was allegorized as the marriage of the philosopher to abstract wisdom.

Philo was loyal to Moses. He wrote a "Life of Moses." He found in all the teachings of Moses Greek philosophical precepts. He believed that Greek philosophers had borrowed much from Mosaic law. He considered Moses the greatest thinker of all time. Philo's concept of God was the advanced Greek idea of spirit or principle. All Biblical references that appeared to attribute human qualities to Yahweh were allegorized. In them he found some hidden meaning. Many of Philo's ideas could not be considered Christian, yet it has been well said that "Philo was the bridge between Judaism and Hellenism over which Christian theology advanced."

The interest in Greek people and culture that developed among Egyptian Jews exerted an influence on Christianity. Nothing is told about Alexandria in the New Testament, but an interesting character in Acts, "Apollos a native of Alexandria" (8:24), seems to have carried the Philo spirit into Christianity. It is quite possible that Apollos is the author of "The Letter to the Hebrews." Alexandria soon became a Christian center, the home of several of the "church fathers."

ASSIGNMENT

1. Identify the terms Diaspora, Hellenist.
2. Read Jeremiah 40-43. What does it tell about Jewish migration to Egypt? Where in Egypt did the Jews settle?
3. What eventually became the chief Jewish center in Egypt? How did this come about?
4. How many Jews lived in Egypt by the time of Jesus? Why had so many migrated there?
5. What Old Testament book was probably written in Egypt? How does its thinking contrast to orthodox Palestinian thinking? How did this come about?
6. What other major contribution to our Old Testament did Jews in Egypt make?
7. Identify (a) Septuagint, (b) Pentateuch, (c) Apocrypha, (d) Philo, (e) Apollos. In what way is each connected with Egypt?
8. Discuss the difference between the Septuagint and the Masoretic text.

SUPPLEMENTARY READING

Pfeiffer, C. F.—Pages 54-8, 71-5
Pfeiffer, R. H.: *History*—Pages 169-78
Sloan: *Old Testament*—Chapter 38
Wright and Freidman—Chapter 11

find all s part of the Septuagint included in the Apocrypha. Some

Chapter 6

The Apocrypha
and Pseudepigrapha

To understand the intertestamental period, the background of
Christianity, it is necessary to examine the books that are included in the Septuagint but are not a part of the Hebrew scriptures. These writings are known as the Apocrypha. The word
apocrypha is the plural of a Greek word meaning hidden or
secret. In Hebrew they were described by a term meaning "outside books." That term probably comes from a story in 2
Esdras. In it Ezra is told to rewrite all the sacred books of
Israel which had been destroyed. He is to make available the
canonical books, but hide the "outside books." These latter
were probably meant for the eyes of only the wise.

In modern English the term apocryphal is often used to mean
false or unauthentic. This doubtless is derived from the idea
that attempts were made to represent the books of the Apocrypha as canonical.

The term Apocrypha usually refers to the books appearing in
the Septuagint, or in the official Latin translation, the Vulgate,
but not in the Bible most Protestants read. There is still another
group of Jewish writings, chiefly intertestamental, which we
shall examine. These are generally called the Pseudepigrapha,
that is, books written under an assumed name. However, Roman
Catholics have this first set of extra books in their Old Testament.
Therefore, they use the term Apocrypha to refer to what Protestants call the Pseudepigrapha.

The Revised Standard Version of the Apocrypha lists its
contents as follows: The First Book of Esdras; The Second Book
of Esdras; Tobit; Judith; The Additions to the Book of Esther;
The Wisdom of Solomon; Ecclesiasticus or the Wisdom of Jesus
the Son of Sirach; Baruch; The Letter of Jeremiah; The Prayer

of Azariah and the Song of the Three Young Men; Susanna; Bel
and the Dragon; The Prayer of Manasseh; The First Book of
the Maccabees; The Second Book of the Maccabees. In other
editions of the Apocrypha, the Letter of Jeremiah is considered
the sixth chapter of Baruch. Second Esdras does not appear in
the Septuagint as we know it, but is in the Vulgate. Doubtless
not all copies of the Septuagint included the same books. Some
collections seem to have had books that were later lost. Roman
Catholics omit First and Second Esdras and the Prayer of
Manasseh from their English translations.

The collection called the Apocrypha is three-fourths as long
as our New Testament. Some books may have incorporated
earlier writings; but, in general, they were written during the two
centuries before the birth of Jesus, except for 2 Esdras, which
was composed about A.D. 90. They include history, fiction,
poetry; 2 Esdras is an apocalyptic writing.

Few Protestants use the Apocrypha. We may well ask what
has become of these books. At the time of Jesus, there were
two Jewish Bibles, the shorter Hebrew Bible used in Palestine,
and the longer Greek Bible used throughout the Dispersion.
Most New Testament quotations from the Old Testament are
directly from the Septuagint. There was much discussion among
Jews as to which Bible should be used. Conferences about this
were held from time to time. The most important of these meet-
ings took place at Jamnia, west of Jerusalem, in A.D. 90. Some
Christian Jews were wanting to include Christian writings in
their Bible. Some final decision must be reached. There was
a popular feeling among orthodox Jews that about the time of
Ezra, certainly no later than Alexander, prophetic revelation
ceased. Doubtless the better educated scribes and rabbis knew
that some of the books used in Palestine had been composed
later, but they were convinced that it was time to close, "seal"
—we might say "freeze"—the scriptures.

There seems to have been no question about the Torah and
the books classed as the Prophets. Some of the Holy Writings
were discussed at the Council of Jamnia. However, the problem centered chiefly around the Apocrypha. These were known
to the rabbis only in Greek. Hebrew was the sacred language.
The more orthodox felt that the Apocrypha added nothing to the
knowledge of God and his will. Possibly the argument also arose
that three was a sacred number; three sections was the proper
number for the Bible. If the Apocrypha were included, some

people would soon want to include the Pseudepigrapha, and probably in time a sixth and a seventh section, with no end. In India the Hindu people failed to limit their scriptures, with the result that today they are so extensive that very few people have read them all. At Jamnia the Jewish authorities vetoed the inclusion of the Apocrypha. Ever since, the Jewish people have accepted this decision.

However, Christians would take no dictation from Jews as to what should be considered scripture. Christians continued to include the Apocrypha in their Bible, but made little use of them. When Latin supplanted Greek, the church directed Jerome to make an official Latin translation of the Bible. He realized that no translation is free from error. To translate the Septuagint would double the number of errors. He, therefore, went to Palestine and, working there with Jewish scholars, translated the Old Testament directly from Hebrew. He completed this in 407. He found that the Jews did not have the books of the Apocrypha. Since they were in the Septuagint, he translated some of them from the Greek or used older Latin translations. In time, they came to be included in the Latin Vulgate. Jerome called attention to the fact that they were not a part of the Hebrew Bible. It is he who named these books the Apocrypha.

Until the time of Martin Luther in the sixteenth century, all Christian Bibles contained the Apocrypha as part of the Old Testament. The earliest English translations were made from Latin and included the Apocrypha. However, Luther translated the Old Testament into German from Hebrew. The Hebrew Bible did not have the Apocrypha, so Luther translated them from the Greek. He placed them between the Old and New Testaments. This became the general style for nearly three hundred years, although the Puritans insisted upon having Bibles without the Apocrypha. The Puritans felt that these writings were sensational and on a low moral and religious level. In 1827 the British and Foreign Bible Society printed Bibles without the Apocrypha, arguing that they were seldom read and made Bibles heavier and more expensive than necessary. Since then this practice has been commonly followed. The Church of England and the American Protestant Episcopal Church consider the Apocrypha a part of the Bible, but other Protestants pay little attention to these writings. Roman Catholic translations of the Bible follow the Septuagint order of having the books of the Apocrypha which are used by the Roman church scattered through the Old Testament. Roman Catholic scholars refer to these books as "deuterocanonical," meaning that they are of less authority than other books of the Bible.

We occasionally come across the expression New Testament Apocrypha. These are early Christian writings not included when, about A.D. 400, the church came to general agreement as to which books should constitute the Christian scriptures. Among these are: the Shepherd of Hermas and the Epistle of Barnabas, which appear in the very earliest copies we have of the entire Bible; First Clement and the Apocalypse of Peter, which some early Christians wanted in their Bibles; and other books. Not all lists of these early Christian writings agree.

Considered by both Jews and Christians as of even less value than the Apocrypha are the books classed as Pseudepigrapha. Anonymous and pseudepigraphic writing was not unusual. Various writers felt that their messages might have better reception if they were in some vague way associated with famous people of the past. The Song of Solomon in the Old Testament was written long after the life of King Solomon. The late Old Testament book of Ecclesiastes hints that it was written by the same famous king. The Jews liked to feel that their Torah had been written by Moses. David's name was associated with many Psalms composed long after his time. The Wisdom of Solomon, Baruch, the Letter of Jeremiah, and the two "Prayers" in the Apocrypha are pseudepigraphic. Later the names of Peter and Paul were similarly used in both the New Testament and the New Testament Apocrypha.

The books of the Pseudepigrapha were written between 200 B.C. and A.D. 100. Some of the earlier writings were changed considerably by later editors. The list generally given includes the following: Jubilees; Testaments of the Twelve Patriarchs; 1 Enoch; 2 Enoch; Assumption of Moses; Apocalypse of Baruch; Sibylline Oracles; Letters of Aristeas; Books of Adam and Eve; Martydom of Isaiah; Psalms of Solomon; 3 Maccabees; 4 Maccabees; Lives of the Prophets; Testament of Job. Most of the books of the Pseudepigrapha will be examined in later chapters.

At least a partial explanation of the pseudepigraphic character of these writings is the common belief that God no longer inspired writers. To give weight to their ideas the authors attributed them to authorities who lived no later than the time of Ezra.

ASSIGNMENT

1. Identify canon, Vulgate, Jerome.

2. What is the collection of writings called the Apocrypha? Where and when did these books first come into general use? Where, when, and why were they officially excluded from the Jewish canon? What does the word Apocrypha mean?

3. List the books that are generally included in the Apocrypha today. How does this differ from the Roman Catholic list?

4. What is meant by the New Testament Apocrypha? Name some of these.

5. To what does the term Pseudepigrapha refer? What is the root meaning of the word? List the chief books included under this term. What Old Testament books are pseudepigraphic. What books of the Apocrypha? Between what years were most of the Pseudepigrapha written? Why are they pseudepigraphic?

6. What do Roman Catholics call the books of the Pseudepigrapha?

SUPPLEMENTARY READING

Charles: *Religious Development*—Chapters VII and VIII
Charles: *The Apocrypha*
Denton—Chapter I
Goodspeed—Chapter I
Metzger—Introduction
Pfeiffer, R. H.: *History*—Pages 198-230
Toombs—Pages 11-6
Torrey—Pages 4-40
The Interpreter's Bible: Vol. 1—Pages 391-436

Chapter 7

Other Sources of Information

Late Old Testament writings, the Apocrypha, and the Pseude-pigrapha are not the only sources from which we learn about the intertestamental period.

The next most important source is the great rabbinic work called the Talmud, from a Hebrew word meaning "to study." This is now available in English in sixty-four large volumes. Much of it was composed orally and handed down from father to son, from rabbi to rabbi, without being completely written out. This was the oral Torah. Credit for starting it was given to Ezra, "making a hedge about the Torah."

The Talmud has two major parts. The first is the Mishna, a Hebrew word meaning "to repeat" or "to study." The present Mishna is a digest of laws reduced to writing about A.D. 200 because there had developed a difference of opinion as to what the oral laws actually were. It tended to idolize the Judaism of the intertestamental period in contrast to the New Testament tendency to note the less desirable factors of the Jewish religion of the period immediately following.

The Mishna is divided into six parts. The first, "Seeds," deals with the laws of agriculture, and has appended to it a book of prayers and blessings. The second, "Festivals," deals with the Sabbath, fasts, and feasts. The third, "Women," contains regulations about betrothal, marriage, divorce, widows, the levirate, and adultery. The fourth, "Injuries," deals with civil and criminal law. The fifth, "Holy Things," is concerned with the temple and sacrifices. The sixth, "Cleanliness," deals with numerous questions of ritual purity.

The Mishna softens and modernizes some rules of the Torah. It abhors the shedding of blood and makes the Law of the Tooth more lenient, much as Jesus does in Mt. 5:38-42. The Torah had largely a rural background. The Talmud expands its laws to cover trade, labor, and industry.

The second of the six sections of the Mishna, "Festivals," goes into detail regarding the observance of the Sabbath. It gives three hundred times as much space to this as does the Torah. Nothing heavier than a dried fig is to be carried. Rabbis are quoted on both sides of the question as to whether or not it is a sin to carry half a fig two different times on the Sabbath.

At another place we read regarding Sabbath observance, "He who has the toothache may not rinse his teeth with vinegar and spit it out again, for this would be to apply medicine; but he may wash them with the vinegar and then swallow it, as this is but taking food."

The Mishna itself quotes some 150 authorities. Naturally, these do not all agree. Rabbis in both Palestine and Babylonia proceeded to develop the Gemara, a study or completion of the Mishna. The word Gemara means "completion." This material attempts to explain contradictions in the Mishna. To help make the Mishna understood, the Gemara was written in Aramaic rather than Hebrew, in which the earlier commentary had been. Palestinian Jews continued writing Gemara until about A.D. 400; but earlier than this, Jews in and around Babylon had taken the leadership. They developed three times as much material and continued writing until nearly A.D. 500. It is this more extensive writing that Jews commonly use today.

Two types of material in the Talmud are often mentioned. One is the Midrash, a running commentary on Old Testament books, especially the books of the Torah. The Midrashes are divided into the Halakah, rules "by which one walks," dealing with the legal sections of the Bible; and the Haggada, "tales," dealing with the non-legal. The latter is a hodge-podge of vivid and sometimes humorous stories, parables, allegories, and maxims.

Expressions of wit and wisdom throughout the Talmud include such statements as: "Thy friend has a friend, and thy friend's friend has a friend; be discreet." "Two pieces of coin in a bag make more noise than a hundred." "Use thy noble vase today; tomorrow it may break." "The soldiers fight and the kings are heroes." "Commit sin twice, and it will seem a sin no longer." "The best preacher is the heart; the best teacher, time; the best book, the world; the best friend, God."

Writers in the Talmud constantly asked, Why does the Torah use this word and not that, this expression and not that? Every choice of word must have a meaning. Why does Ex. 20:12 say,

"Honor your father and your mother," while Lev. 19:3 reverses the order and says, "Every one of you shall revere his mother and his father"?

Another term often found in discussion of Jewish literature is the Targum. This means a translation. The Septuagint was a targum, but the term most often refers to Aramaic translations of portions of the Hebrew scriptures. After returning from Babylonian captivity, the Jewish people practically quit speaking Hebrew. They had learned Aramaic in captivity and continued to use it. About 500 B.C. Aramaic became the official language of the entire Persian Empire. The Jews wrote Aramaic in Hebrew letters and used many Hebrew words, but their language became basically Aramaic. When portions of the scripture were read in the synagogues it was necessary to translate them into Aramaic. This was done orally, for there was a feeling that the scriptures were too sacred to be written down in any other than their original language. Eventually this feeling disappeared and parts of the Old Testament were made available. This change of attitude made the Septuagint permissible.

Other writings help us understand the intertestamental period. We have already mentioned the Greek-educated Jew, Philo. Even better known is the historian, Flavius Josephus. He was born in Jerusalem A.D. 37 or 38 and died about 110. His father was a priest, his mother of the Jewish royal family. He experimented with the three major religious orders, Sadducees, Pharisees, and Essenes. He says that for three years he lived in the desert with a hermit. At the age of twenty-six he went to Rome to defend some Jewish priests. Here he got acquainted with Roman life and became a friend of Nero's wife. When he returned to Jerusalem the revolt against Rome had broken out. Josephus was proud of being a Jew, but he knew that Rome was unbeatable. The Jews appointed him as governor of Galilee, where he raised an army to defend it against Rome. He was forced to surrender. He told the conquering general Vespasian that he was able to see the future, that both Vespasian and his son Titus would become Roman emperors. This gained their friendship. Josephus was taken to Egypt by the general and then settled in Rome. Here he was made a Roman citizen and given a generous pension. He dedicated his life to writing. A Roman authority called him "by far the most renowned Jew of his time."

We have four of Josephus' writings. The first, the *Jewish*

War, points out that it was foolish for the Jews to think that they could defeat Rome. It is a warning to any other would-be insurgents. The emperor himself ordered it published. Josephus traces the blame for the war back to Antiochus IV of Syria.

His second book, known as *Antiquities,* tells his readers the story of the Jews from creation to the war against Rome. The first ten volumes are largely a paraphrase of the Septuagint. The latter ten volumes recount the post-Babylonian experiences of the Jews. Josephus found great prejudice against the Jews. He realized that this was based on ignorance. A Roman historian of his time, Tacitus, had written what he called a history of the Jews. In it he claimed that the Jews were descendants of Egyptian lepers and worshiped a donkey. Josephus determined to correct this misinformation. He pointed out that in the past Jews had been highly respected. In this book, published in A.D. 93, we learn something of the intertestamental period. His accounts do not always agree with those given in his earlier book.

Josephus' third book is his *Life,* written as an appendix to his *Antiquities.* It is largely a vindication of his behavior during the Jewish War.

Josephus' fourth book, *Against Apion,* is an exposition of the doctrine and practices of the Jews. He answers anti-Jewish slanders made by Apion, a lawyer of Alexandria, who had published a collection of stories unfavorable to the Jews. Josephus is quite critical of Gentile morality.

For knowledge of Persia and its expansion we go back to Herodotus, known as the father of history. A Greek born about 484 B.C. in territory already conquered by Persia, he went into great detail in giving the background of Greece's troubles with Persia. Xenophon, born about the year Nehemiah completed his wall around Jerusalem, was a Greek general who participated in a Persian civil war and led the retreat of his fellow Greeks. In his *Anabasis* he gives helpful information about the Persians.

Tacitus was a Roman historian living between A.D. 50 and 120. He was an eyewitness to the terror of the last three years of the emperor Domitian. As a senator he felt guilty for permitting the judicial murder of many of Rome's best citizens. He wrote not only a history of the Roman Empire, but also that of various parts of the known world, including a sketch of the history of Britain under the Romans. Despite an interest in ethics, his *History of the Jews* is very unfair. He was also quite superstitious, believing in astrology, omens, and portents.

Livy, a Roman historian living from 59 B.C. to A.D. 17, wrote 142 books of Roman history; we have only 35 today. These deal with the period 218 to 157 B.C. However, we also have summaries of almost all his history, compiled by someone else three hundred years after his death. Other writers give various quotations from Livy.

Strabo, a Greek geographer and to some extent a historian, was born in 63 B.C. Josephus often quotes him. Strabo probably gather his material from the Alexandrian library. He quotes Greek authorities, but seldom Roman ones. His seventeen books of geography give considerable information about Asia Minor, Persia, Babylonia, and Egypt, as well as Europe.

Another author from whom we learn something of the inter-testamental period is Plutarch, a Greek biographer and miscellaneous writer trained in philosophy in Athens. He lived A.D. 46 to 120. He was extensively acquainted with the literature of his time. His best-known work is his *Parallel Lives*. In this he tells the life of an outstanding Greek and compares it with that of an outstanding Roman; for example, Alexander and Caesar, Demosthenes and Cicero. His interest was chiefly ethical. He also published about sixty essays. Some were entitled: Should a man engage in politics when no longer young? On the education of children; How one may be conscious of progress in goodness; How a flatterer may be distinguished from a friend.

ASSIGNMENT

1. Identify Talmud, Mishna (its six parts), Gemara, Midrash, Halakah, Haggada, Targum.
2. Identify in detail each of the following and tell what contribution he made to our knowledge of the interestamental period: Philo, Josephus, Plutarch, Strabo, Tacitus, Livy, Herodotus, Xenophon.

SUPPLEMENTARY READING

Enslin—Pages 104-10
Harris
Perowe: *Later Herods*
Toombs—Pages 16-8

Chapter 8

The Maccabean Revolt

Despite political control by foreign people, the Jews had enjoyed religious freedom. Reaction to the first real attack upon their religion is reported in the book of First Maccabees in the Apocrypha. This books deals with the Maccabean Revolt. Second Maccabees makes a much different approach to the same revolt. First Maccabees starts with the ascension of Antiochus IV (Epiphanes) to the Syrian throne in 175 B.C. and ends with the death of the last of the Maccabean brothers in 134 B.C.

Written in Hebrew by a Palestinian Jew about 100 B.C., First Maccabees tells how Antiochus attacked Jerusalem: "He plundered the city, burned it with fire, tore down its houses and its surrounding walls, and they took captive the women and children, and seized the cattle" (1:31-32). "Then the king wrote to his whole people that all should be one people, and that each should give up his customs. All the Gentiles accepted the command of the king. Many even from Israel gladly adopted his religion; they sacrificed to idols and profaned the Sabbath" (1:41-43). The King ordered them "to build altars . . . to sacrifice swine . . . and to leave their sons uncircumcised" (1:47-48). On the fifteenth of Chislov, which corresponds to our December, 168 B.C. "they erected a desolating sacrilege upon the altar of burnt offering. . . . The books of the law which they found they tore to pieces and burned" (1:54-56). People were condemned to death for adhering to the book of the covenant. "But many in Israel stood firm and were resolved . . . not to eat unclean food. They chose to die . . . and they did die" (1:62-63).

A priest named Mattathias, with his family, fled northwest of Jerusalem to Modein. There an attempt was made to bribe the elderly priest to make sacrifices to heathen deities. He replied, "We will not obey the king's words by turning aside from our religion to the right hand or to the left" (2:22). Another Jew

offered to make the required sacrifice, but Mattathias killed him
and the king's representative, and with his family fled to the hills.
Other Jews went to the wilderness, where the king's officers
attacked them on the Sabbath. "They died with their wives and
children and cattle, to the number of a thousand persons"
(2:38).

Mattathias and his friends resolved to avenge this slaughter.
They were joined by a group of Jews known as Hasideans or
Asideans—that is, the pious—whose chief concern was to save
their religion. They had no political interests. "They organized
an army and struck down sinners in their anger and lawless
men in their wrath . . . and tore down the altars; they forcibly
circumcised all the uncircumcised boys" (2:44-46). Mattathias
soon died, but before his death he asked his followers to recognize his son, Judas, "a mighty warrior from his youth," as their
leader to "avenge the wrong done to your people" (2:66-67).
"He was like a lion in his deeds" (3:4).

Judas and his brothers made it difficult for the Syrians. He
soon came to be known as Maccabeus, meaning the hammerer.
A Greek general "gathered together Gentiles and a large force
from Samaria to fight against Israel. . . . Judas . . . defeated him
and killed him" (3:10-11). The Syrian commander with "a
strong army of ungodly men" attacked a much smaller number
under Judas, who insisted that "strength comes from Heaven.
. . . We will fight for our lives and laws." Eight hundred of the
Syrians fell, and "Judas and his brothers began to be feared."
After other severe defeats by Judas, the Syrians "mustered sixty
thousand picked infantrymen and five thousand cavalry" (4:28)
and attacked from the south. With ten thousand men Judas
defeated the Syrians.

Evidently the Jews were more discouraged than the author
of First Maccabees admits. Although Judas is reported to have
won all his battles, his resources were being weakened. Apparently many Jews felt that the Greek Syrians would eventually
win. The book of Daniel, which will be discussed in the next
chapter, was written to encourage the Jews. It fulfilled its purpose, made the Maccabean revolt successful. The Syrians
still held the fort in Jerusalem, but otherwise were out of the
city. The Jews were able to say, "Let us go up to cleanse the
sanctuary and dedicate it" (4:36). Not only had the altar been
profaned and much of the temple burned, but "in the courts they
saw bushes sprung up as in a thicket." They were not sure

whether the altar, defiled by its use in sacrificing pigs, should again be used for sacrifices to Yahweh. "So they tore down the altar, and stored the stones in a convenient place on the temple hill until there should come a prophet to tell them what to do with them" (4:45-46).

Three years and ten days from the "abomination that makes desolate," the temple and a new altar were dedicated. First Maccabees also contains a contradictory statement, saying that this was done in exactly three years. It was decreed that "every year at that season the days of the dedication of the altar should be observed with gladness and joy for eight days" (4:59). This is the Feast of Lights or Hanukkah (or Chanukah), referred to in John 1:22 as the "feast of Dedication." It is celebrated yet today each December.

This success in Jerusalem angered non-Jews in the regions surrounding Judah—Idumea, Ammon, Gilead, and Galilee. Judas defeated his opposition in the first three territories and sent his brother Simon to Galilee, where he "fought many battles against the Gentiles, and the Gentiles were crushed" (5:21). He then resettled the Galilean Jews in Judah. Judas even led a successful expedition against the Nabatean Arabs.

Judas' knowledge of the Palestinian hills enabled him to defeat much larger numbers of warriors trained for open fighting on the plains of Syria. A religious zeal also gave the Jewish soldiers great courage and strength. The Hasideans withdrew from the fighting when the use of the temple was regained, but many Jews were now determined to have political independence. Troubles at home forced Syrian armies to withdraw when victory might have been theirs. Antiochus Epiphanes led an army to Persia, with the hope of securing extensive plunder, and lost his life there. This led to a great internal struggle for power in Syria.

Judas determined to capture the Jerusalem fortress. The Syrians came to its defense with "a hundred thousand foot soldiers, twenty thousand horsemen, and thirty-two elephants accustomed to war" (6:30). The sixth chapter of First Maccabees gives a vivid description of how these elephants were used in battle. Judas met this force south of Jerusalem. His brother, Eleazar, noted that one elephant, larger than the others, had royal armor. He supposed that the king was on this elephant. Rushing in like a madman, he "got under the elephant, stabbed it from beneath, and killed it, but it fell to the ground upon him and there he

died" (6:46). The Jews fled and the Syrians attacked Jerusalem. Since this was the sabbatical year when Jews allowed
their fields to stand fallow, very little food was stored in the city.
Therefore, it could not be defended for long. However, the
Syrian general learned of serious trouble at home, so agreed
to let the Jews "live by their own laws," and withdrew.

Soon another army was sent against Judas. A plot to get
Judas by trickery failed. The Syrians were repulsed at Jerusalem
and defeated in a later battle. The Syrian general was killed.
Judas knew he would be unable to keep up his fighting indefinitely and turned to Rome for aid.

Too late to stop a new army from marching south, Rome
threatened Syria. The new army found Judas encamped with
only three thousand men. The Jews saw that the situation was
impossible. All but eight hundred deserted. In desperation
Judas proclaimed, "Let us die bravely for our brethren, and
leave no cause to question our honor" (9:10). "The earth was
shaken by the noise of the armies, and the battle raged from
morning till evening" (9:13). "Judas also fell, and the rest fled"
(9:18). This was in the year 161 B.C.

Judas' brother Jonathan was made his successor, although the
Syrians seemed to have complete control. Jonathan and his followers withdrew to the wilderness at the north end of the Dead
Sea where the Syrians tried to trap them. Jonathan's men killed
a large number of Syrians and then swam the Jordan River, with
the Syrians afraid to follow them. The Syrians built forts
through Judah and garrisoned them, but the high priest who had
been supporting the Syrians suddenly died. People took this as
divine intervention, the Syrian general "returned to the king, and
the land of Judah had rest for two years" (9:57). At the request of his supporters in Judah, the Syrian general came back
but was defeated by Jonathan. Disgusted with his local supporters, the Syrian killed many of them and "swore to Jonathan
that he would not try to harm him as long as he lived" (9:71).
"Thus the sword ceased from Israel" (9:73). Syria itself was
rent with civil war. Jonathan began to gain control of Judah
and put to death his local opposition. One of the Syrian leaders
decided he could use Jonathan. He encouraged him to act as
chief of his people, and "appointed" him high priest. Trying to
take sides in the Syrian internal conflicts got Jonathan into various troubles, and he was finally imprisoned by one of his Syrian
"allies."

The last, but oldest, of the sons of Mattathias, Simon, was then chosen leader of the Jews at his own request—"My brothers have perished for the sake of Israel . . . far be it from me to spare my life" (13:4-5). The Syrians made another attempt to subjugate the Jews but were stopped by a heavy snow. They killed their prisoner Jonathan and returned to Syria. "The yoke of the Gentiles was removed from Israel, and the people began to write in their documents and contracts, 'In the first year of Simon, the great high priest and leader of the Jews'" (13:41-42). Later the Jews honored Simon by setting up a bronze tablet at the temple telling of his exploits, and those of his brothers, stating that Simon (and his sons after him) had been appointed "high priest, to be commander and ethnarch of the Jews and priests, and to be protector of them all" (14:47).

A bit later a new Syrian king tried to assert his authority over Judah and collect tribute. Simon appointed his sons, Judas and John, to "take my place and my brothers', and go out and fight for our nation" (16:3). Syria was defeated. In 134 B.C. Simon and two of his sons were murdered by his son-in-law "when Simon and his sons were drunk" (16:16). An attempt was made to kill another son, John, but he got the upper hand and became high priest. He reigned as John Hyrcanus from 134 to 104 B.C.

An interesting phase of nationalism resulted from the Maccabean Revolt: First Maccabees was written in the Hebrew language. Ever since Babylonian captivity, Aramaic had largely taken the place of Hebrew, although the sacred scriptures were read in the more ancient language. As Hebrew has become the official language of twentieth century Israel, so it was to a degree restored at the time of the Maccabean Revolt. It was probably not used by the common people, but for the next three hundred years important writings were put in the highly respected Hebrew.

The first seven chapters of First Maccabees are retold in melodramatic form in the book called Second Maccabees. This book asserts that it is a condensation of a record "set forth by Jason of Cyrene in five volumes" (2:23). This was done "to please those who wish to read, to make it easy for those who are inclined to memorize" (2:25). Condensed as it may be, the book's chief contribution is the miraculous (such as the appearance of heavenly horsemen) and moral lessons found in both victories and defeats of the Jews. There is no general agreement as to the date of Jason of Cyrene, or of the compiler of the condensed story.

When an envoy of the Syrian king attempted to confiscate the temple funds, we are told "there appeared to them a magnificently caparisoned horse, with a rider of frightening mien, and it rushed furiously at Hiliodorus and struck at him with its front hoofs. Its rider was seen to have armor and weapons of gold . . . While he lay prostrate, speechless because of the divine intervention and deprived of any hope of recovery, they praised the Lord who had acted marvelously for his own place" (3:25-30).

Later, when Antiochus was about to stage a massacre, the populace of Jerusalem was warned by the appearance "for almost forty days" of "golden-clad horsemen charging through the air" (5:2).

The author of Second Maccabees was generous with large numbers. He says that in one attack by Antiochus "within the total of three days, eighty thousand were destroyed, forty thousand in hand-to-hand fighting; and as many were sold into slavery as were slain" (5:14). He "carried off eighteen hundred talents from the temple, thinking in his arrogance that he could sail on the land and walk on the sea" (5:21). The soldiers of Judas are credited with killing more than 220,000 of the enemy. Such exaggerated reports appear throughout the book.

In telling of atrocities perpetrated by the Syrians, the author moralizes: "I urge those who read this book not to be depressed by such calamities, but to recognize that these punishments were designed, not to destroy, but to discipline our people" (6:12). The most famous of the torture stories is the seventh chapter. A mother and her seven sons refused to eat pork. The king "commanded that the tongue of their spokesman be cut out and that they scalp him and cut off his hands and feet, while the rest of the brothers and the mother looked on. When he was utterly helpless, the king ordered them to take him to the fire, still breathing, and to fry him in a pan" (7:4-5). While each was similarly treated, the family encouraged one another to refuse the pork, "The Lord is watching over us" (7:6). The mother is commended: "Though she saw her seven sons perish within a single day, she bore it with good courage because of her hope in the Lord" (7:20).

With his historical inaccuracies, exaggerations, and gory

tales, the author expresses his belief that God ordains the details of the life of his people, and gives men punishment to fit their crimes. We see his picture of angels, of a future life, and of his belief in the value of prayers and sacrifices. Many Jews and later Christians were encouraged by the mother and her seven sons, and other martyrs in Second Maccabees. This book makes a definite contribution to our understanding of Jewish thinking of the intertestamental period.

ASSIGNMENT

1. Read First Maccabees in the Apocrypha, and outline the record of the revolt given there.
2. Identify Epiphanes, Mattathias, Hasideans, Judas, Hanukkah, Jonathan, Simon, John Hyrcanus, Maccabees.
3. Despite its numerous historical inaccuracies, 2 Maccabees makes what contributions to our understanding of the religious outlook of the intertestamental period?
4. Summarize the most often quoted story of 2 Maccabees, Chapter 7.
5. Contrast the account of the death of Antiochus Epiphanes as given in 1 Mac. 6 and 2 Mac. 9. What did the author of the book of Daniel expect about the death of Antiochus Epiphanes (Dan. 11:45)?
6. What were the remote and the immediate causes of the Maccabean revolt?

SUPPLEMENTARY READING

Dentan—Pages 31-2 and Chapter V
Enslin—Pages 16-27
Goodspead—Chapters XI and XII
Mathews—Chapter 5
Metzger—Chapters XIV and XV
Pfeiffer, R. H.: *History*—Pages 461-522
Schurer
Tedsche and Zeitlin: *First Maccabees*
Tedsche and Zeitlin: *Second Maccabees*
Toombs—Pages 27-30
Torrey—Pages 69-78

Chapter 9

Apocalyptic Literature

An apocalypse is something uncovered, unveiled, revealed. Apocalyptic literature was begun by the Jews some time before 200 B.C. and remained popular for four hundred years, although apocalypses have been written as late as the fourteenth century. The Jewish people got the apocalyptic idea from Zoroastrianism and handed it on to early Christians.

Apocalypses were tracts for hard times, comfort in days of trouble. They told in figurative language how God proposed to bring victory to his people. God will dramatically overcome Satan and his agents. A new age will be established. Daniel and the Revelation to John are the two extensive apocalypses in our Bible. Apocalyptic sections are found in Ezekiel, Joel, and Zechariah. There are short apocalyptic sections in the New Testament, such as Mark 13.

Apocalypses are messages of encouragement written in code, so that they could not be understood by non-Jewish government authorities. To the latter, they would seem to be harmless childish ramblings. This helped them escape the censor. They were intended to develop a feeling, an attitude, as is the purpose of oratorios today. The words of an oratorio apart from the music are repetitious, almost seem silly, but people who hear an oratorio sung are expected to be inspired, to get a very definite impression. Much the same may be said about various "modern" types of painting and sculpture. The color organ develops a feeling through both eye and ear.

Apocalyptists are sometimes confused with prophets. Both felt that they had a message from Yahweh. The word prophet means "one who speaks for another." The prophet was a preacher, giving his message orally. Later some of these sermons were written down, generally by someone who was impressed by the prophet's thundering, "Thus says the LORD."

The apocalyptist organized and wrote out his message.

Priests, people who strove to maintain the good old ways, to keep religion in its proper groove, were found in all religions. The true prophet, the pioneer who sought better ways of expressing and applying religion, seldom appeared outside Judaism previous to Christianity. The apocalyptist also was almost entirely limited to Judaism and early Christianity.

Prophets were popular among the Hebrews between the eighth and fourth centuries B.C. By the end of that period the priest had the upper hand. The priests emphasized the Law or Torah, teaching that God had told Moses all that was to be known. Legalism became absolute. The apocalyptist took the place of the prophet. To give the impression that his message was from God, he attached to it the name of some worthy who had lived before prophetic inspiration was thought to have ceased. Thus all pre-Christian apocalyptic literature was pseudepigraphic. Some Christian apocalyptists felt that revelation had begun again in Christ, and wrote under their own names. In this way they were like prophets; the writer of the Revelation to John calls himself a prophet. However, others retained the pseudepigraphic style. To fit into the idea that the apocalypse had been written by some famous person, the writer maintained a spirit of prediction, that long ago the present situation was foreseen and also its solution or outcome.

The apocalyptist did have an element of prediction on his own part, for every apocalyptist proclaimed that God would help his people out of their predicament, that they would win. The prophet was concerned with warnings and advice for immediate action. He was convinced that, regardless of the immediate outcome, there would be a remnant left who would be used by God in maintaining the Hebrew nation. Yet all prosperity and success was conditioned upon doing the will of Yahweh.

The prophet was not concerned about the future of individuals, about life beyond the grave. In Sheol, future existence would be alike for good and bad, a hazy type of vegetation. Thus the eschatology, the doctrine of last things, of the prophet and the apocalyptist differed. The apocalyptist knew that many of his people would suffer and be killed by the oppressor, but he held out a promise of a future life, a resurrection. This was a definite contribution. In the earlier apocalypses, this was a promise that the faithful would return to earth to enjoy seeing

the suffering of the unfaithful and to participate in the prosperity of the new age. Eventually, this concept of a future life
became definitely more spiritual.

Apocalyptic literature reinterpreted prophecy, pointing out
that the optimism of prophets had not been misplaced, although
perhaps misunderstood. The great anointed one, the Messiah,
who would make the Hebrews independent and powerful once
more, still would be raised up in the near future. Jeremiah had
predicted the return of captives from Babylonia at the end of
seventy years, doubtless meaning at the end of a generation.
They had returned within fifty years, but not to the utopia expected. The book of Daniel interpreted this figure to mean
seventy weeks of years or 490 years, which his readers recognized were about reached. At a later period, Enoch interpreted
it as a rule of seventy patron angels. Second Esdras interpreted
it as a time which included the rule of Rome.

The apocalyptist made extensive use of symbolism. Some of
the code has been lost. Some is known. Nations were referred
to as beasts; the Jewish people always as a domestic animal.
The beasts often had more than one head, which meant plural
dynasties. Horns were individual rulers. Stars were angels or
other superhuman beings. Today we still use symbols. Like
the apocalyptists, we use the lion to represent Great Britain; the
bear, Russia; the eagle, the United States. Numerology was also
used. This is not surprising, for neither Hebrew, Aramaic, nor
Greek had numbers as we know them. The first letter of the
alphabet was considered to have a value of one, the second two,
etc. Therefore, names and words had numerical value. Certain
numbers were considered sacred: three, four, and their combina-
tions, as seven and twelve.

Apocalyptists expected a sudden end of their unpleasant situation, probably a catastrophic end of their current world. But
they offered almost no ethical or social teaching. They felt that
their world was too wicked to contain the Kingdom of God.
They pointed out God's activity in the past; for the time being
God was relatively inactive, but they were sure of his activity
in a glorious future, the ultimate triumph of righteousness. The
prophet was much more interested in a social gospel for his own
time, an improved community which would be everlasting, but
there was no such promise for the individual.

Daniel is the apocalypse that concerns us at this point. It
was written in 165 B.C. or possibly a few months earlier. Its

purpose was to encourage the Jews in their effort to drive out the Selucid Syrians. People had raised such questions as: Does it pay to insist upon worshiping only Yahweh? Greeks worship many gods and they are on top. Why should we be strict about dietary laws? The Greeks eat pork and seem none the worse. Can we ever expect to outsmart the powerful Syrians?

There were in circulation numerous stories about a fabled hero, Daniel, reported to have lived during the Babylonian and Persian periods. We are reminded of America's Paul Bunyan. The author of the book of Daniel collected or wrote stories about Daniel and his friends in answer to questions which were bothering the Jews. Daniel's friends had refused to bow down to a great statue, had been thrown into a fiery furnace, but had come out without the smell of smoke! Daniel had worshiped Yahweh openly, despite the law that petitions must be addressed to the king only. He was thrown to the lions but survived victoriously. Daniel and his friends, as young men being prepared for government positions, had refused to eat the food provided but followed their own dietary rules. As a result, in matters of wisdom, the king found them "ten times better than all the magicians and enchanters that were in his kingdom" (1:20). Daniel was able to tell the king his dream and its interpretation when all others failed. Upon another occasion he did much the same. At a third time he interpreted handwriting upon the wall, outsmarting "all the king's wise men."

The author then turned to apocalyptic, reporting a number of dreams or visions of Daniel. In apocalyptic terminology, they told of the destruction of Babylonia by Persia, the coming of Alexander, the division of his kingdom into four parts, the oppression of the Jews by the Syrians, "the abomination that makes desolate" (desecrating the altar at Jerusalem), the rededication of the temple, and the eventual expulsion of the Syrians. Readers recognized that all these events had taken place as "predicted" except the last two, and, therefore, were assured that they would defeat the Syrians. In an early vision, it was said that the temple would be restored within three years and six months after the abomination of desolation. In a later vision, the time suggested was three years and two months. The Jews were so encouraged that they were able to have their rededication service three years and ten days (possibly exactly three years) after the sacrifice of a pig on the altar.

ASSIGNMENT

1. What is meant by "Apocalyptic literature"? What is the root meaning of the word apocalypse?

2. How does apocalypse differ from prophecy in outlook? When are most of the books of prophecy written? Most of the apocalyptic books? What caused the decline of the prophet? The rise of the apocalyptist? To what extent did the prophet exist outside the Hebrew religion? The apocalyptist outside the Judeo-Christian community?

3. What is eschatology? What differences existed between the eschatology of prophecy and that of apocalyptic?

4. What is meant by numerology?

5. Why did apocalyptic writing after 200 B.C. become pseudonymous? Why did Christian apocalyptic tend to abandon pseudonymity?

6. What apocalypses are usually included in the Pseudepigrapha? What two pseudepigraphic apocalypses are referred to in the New Testament book of Jude?

7. Why was the book of Daniel written? What was its approach to the problem? What are the six stories in Daniel? The six "visions"? What influence did the book of Daniel have in its time? Why was it included in the Old Testament canon?

8. How are Biblical apocalypses misused today?

9. What makes up the apocalypse of Esdras found in the Apocrypha? When was it written? What was the problem with which it deals? Read the fifth vision (2 Esdras 11:1-12:39) and tell in what ways it is similar to Daniel. What is the hope expressed in the sixth vision (13:1-59)?

SUPPLEMENTARY READING

Charles: *Religious Development*—Chapter I
Denton—Chapter VII
Goodspeed—Chapter XVI
Metzger—Chapter II
Pfeiffer, C. F.—Chapter 16
Pfeiffer, R. H.: *History*—Pages 81-90
Rowley
Russell—Pages 93-119
Sloan: *Old Testament*—Chapter 39
Sloan: *New Testament*—Chapter 36
Toombs—Pages 30-2
Torry—Pages 108-23
Abingdon Bible Commentary—Pages 18-190

Chapter 10

The Hasmoneans

The ruling descendants of Mattathias came to be known as Hasmoneans in honor of an ancestor of Mattathias. John Hyrcanus
may have called himself king—his son definitely did. The term
was never popular among Jews, who felt that only Yahweh
should be considered king. The high priest should be the vicar
or representative of God. When Simon and his two sons were
murdered by Ptolemy, his son-in-law, John managed to get to
Jerusalem ahead of the murderer. He was proclaimed high priest
and became ruler of the Jewish state.

Again a Syrian king attacked Jerusalem. John Hyrcanus
found his food supply scarce. He expelled the non-combatants
from the city, but they were not allowed through the enemy
lines. At the Feast of Tabernacles, Hyrcanus was forced to open
the gates and allow those who had survived to return. He found
it necessary to accede to the demands of the Syrians. The Jews
were disarmed, and openings were made in the city walls. Hyrcanus was required to pay indemnity. He also paid rent for
some non-Jewish cities he controlled. He was forced to accompany the Syrian ruler on expeditions to the east. But, when
the Syrian king died five years later, Syria, weakened by internal
rivalries and by threats from Rome, had to forego all serious
attempts to control Palestine.

Hyrcanus then employed foreign troops and proceeded to
expand his territory. He solidified his power in central Palestine,
destroying the Samaritan temple on Mount Gerazim, and, after
a year's siege, the Greek city of Samaria. He conquered territory east of the Jordan and then subdued Idumea to the south.
The Idumeans, basically the people known in the Old Testament
as Edomites, were given the choice of becoming Jews or exiles.
From these "half-Jews" eventually rose the greatest king the
Jews ever had, at least after David, Herod the Great. Josephus

reports that Hyrcanus "administered the government in the best manner for thirty-one years." It was at about this time that the book of Esther was written.

Aristobulus succeeded his father as high priest. His mother was expected to administer the government, but Aristobulus imprisoned her and three of his brothers. He let his mother die of starvation. He conquered a part of Galilee, but died within the year.

The widow of Aristobulus, Alexandra Salome, was much like Jezebel's daughter, Athalia, who ruled Judah for six years (2 Kings 11). Alexandra released her husband's brothers from prison and married the oldest, Alexander Janneus, making him both high priest and king. He was twenty-four, she thirty-seven. Psalm 2 seems to have been written for the wedding ceremony. With the help of hired foreign troops, Janneus expanded his territory eastward, and also south to the Egyptian border. His greatest campaigns were against cities along the Mediterranean coast of Palestine. Some of these had never been under Jewish control. After considerable trouble with Egypt, Janneus subdued most of them. His determination was to restore David's kingdom to its full extent.

Meanwhile, at home, opposition was growing against a high priest who was much more interested in leading foreign troops to war than in maintaining the temple and its sacrifices. Josephus reports that at a Feast of Tabernacles the people pelted Janneus with citrons while he was officiating at the altar. In revenge he had six thousand Jews put to death. He built a wooden screen around the altar. Many of the Jews could not forget that he had broken the law which required that a priest marry only a virgin. The law specified that the levirate did not apply to priests. A six years civil war resulted, in which Janneus is said to have killed 50,000 Jews, crucifying 800 men and cutting the throats of their wives and children while the men were hanging on crosses. Much of his non-Jewish territory had to be reconquered from time to time.

Upon the death of Janneus, Alexandra, although sixty-three years old, took over the government and ruled for nine years. She appointed their older son, Hyrcanus II, as high priest. He was a non-military type, incompetent, and perhaps feeble-minded, but he pleased the Jews, especially the pious Pharisees who had caused Janneus so much trouble. Alexandra also gave much more authority to the Jerusalem council or Sanhedrin.

To the nobles and priests who made up the council, she added a group of educated scribes, who much more represented the populace. Josephus says, "While she governed other peoples . . . the Pharisees governed her." Alexandra sometimes used her younger son, Aristobulus, as a general but took care to see that he did not get too much authority. However, the military minded were dissatisfied. Seeing Aristobulus as their potential leader, they got themselves appointed to various forts through the nation and waited for the death of the elderly queen.

When Alexandra died, the high priest, Hyrcanus II, was nominally in command. He was soon met in battle near Jericho by his brother, who easily defeated him and proclaimed himself high priest and king, Aristobulus II. Hyrcanus placidly retired as a private citizen, moving into the house formerly occupied by Aristobulus.

Janneus, after conquering Idumea, had appointed a local leader, Antipater, as governor. He had been succeeded by a son of the same name. The second Antipater was ambitious for power. He saw an opportunity to use the deposed Hyrcanus II as a puppet. Antipater convinced him that Aristobulus was plotting his death. He persuaded him to flee to Petra, the capital of the Arabian ruler, Aretas III. There, at the instigation of Antipater, Aretas offered to help Hyrcanus regain his throne. Of course, he would return to Aretas territory which Janneus had taken from the Arabs. With Arab assistance, Hyrcanus drove his brother back to Jerusalem. Many of the followers of Aristobulus deserted, and the king was forced to defend himself in the temple area.

Ever since Rome had defeated Antiochus III (the Great) in 191 B.C., she had been eager to expand eastward and to enjoy the wealth that conquest brought. After attempting to control Syria by threats, she finally had taken over. The military leader Pompey was put in charge. Pompey hoped to include Palestine in his province, since it had once belonged to Syria. When he learned of the troubles between Aristobulus and Hyrcanus, he sent a general to investigate. Both sides offered bribes. Aristobulus was the higher bidder. The general decided it was easier to disperse Hyrcanus and his Arab rabble than to take Jerusalem by siege. General allegiance was thus again given to Aristobulus.

When Pompey himself reached Damascus in 63 B.C., he was met by delegations from both Aristobulus and Hyrcanus asking for support. There was also a third group wanting to do away with the kings and military rulers and return to being a peaceful quiet people, loyal to the temple and not concerned with extending territory.

Pompey concluded that Aristobulus was untrustworthy. He arrested him and then took Jerusalem. Forces loyal to Aristobulus retreated to the temple, where twelve thousand lost their lives in the resulting massacre. Pompey allowed his curiosity to lead him into the Holy of Holies. He left the temple treasure untouched, but the Jews never forgave him for going where only the high priest was allowed. Pompey was so surprised to find the Holy of Holies empty that the belief grew among the Romans that the Jews were atheists, worshiping nothing.

Aristobulus and his sons were sent to Rome to be exhibited among Pompey's conquests. Hyrcanus was again made high priest with the title, not of king, but of ethnarch, under the control of Rome. Much of the territory conquered by his predecessors was not considered his, although Idumea, Galilee, and Perea were left under his supervision. Never again was any part of Palestine completely under Jewish control until the establishment of Israel in 1948.

ASSIGNMENT

1. Identify in some detail each of the Hasmoneans.
2. Why was the use of the word "king" opposed?
3. Identify: Antipater, Aretas III, Pompey.

SUPPLEMENTARY READING

Dentan—Pages 33-4
Enslin—Pages 27-37
Mathews—Chapters VI-VIII
Pfeiffer, R. H.: *History*—Pages 19-24
Schurer—Chapters 8-12
Snaith—Chapter VI
The Interpreter's Dictionary of the Bible—Article on Hasmoneans.

Chapter 11

Herod the Great

The real power in Palestine was Antipater. At the time of Julius Caesar's struggle for control of the Roman Empire, Antipater sent reinforcements to him in Egypt and won his friendship. He also persuaded the Jews in Egypt to support Caesar, who in turn befriended Jews wherever they were. Taxes were cancelled and the Jews were allowed to have their own law courts. They were not drafted for the Roman army. Those who volunteered for the army were put in separate companies and not required to fight on the Sabbath. Roman forces were withdrawn from Judea. Antipater, whom Caesar fully trusted, was made governor, or administrator, and a Roman citizen. The Jews still gave allegiance to the high priest, Hyrcanus II, but he lost much of his power. Both before and after this, Aristobulus and his sons made futile efforts to regain Judea.

The Jews hated both Antipater and Caesar. They were foreign conquerors. Antipater had been circumcised as a Jew, but the Jews never considered him one of their number. There had been hatred between Israelites and Edomites, stemming from the traditions of enmity between their reputed ancestors, the twins Jacob and Esau.

Antipater made his younger son Herod, twenty-five years old, prefect of Galilee, and his older son Phasael prefect of Judea. Many of those in Galilee were non-Jews, many others forced or half-Jews. There were numerous brigands. Herod straightened out his region, putting one of the brigand leaders to death. This won the gratitude of people in Galilee but gave the Jews in Jerusalem an opportunity to complain. They insisted that only the Sanhedrin had the right to execute people. Hyrcanus, as high priest, summoned Herod before the Sanhedrin. When he saw the situation, Herod hurried to Damascus to get support from the Roman governor. Only his father and brother prevented him from attacking Jerusalem with an army. Dissatisfaction among the Jews led to Antipater's being poisoned in 43 B.C.

Herod promptly avenged his father's death. The Romans appointed Phasael and Herod tetrarchs of the Jewish state, with the approval of Hyrcanus, who was still ruler in name. A son of Aristobulus, Antigonus, again attempted to take Palestine. He captured Phasael, who is reported to have committed suicide by dashing his head against the walls of his cell. Antigonus also captured Hyrcanus and bit off his ears. As a man with a disfigured body, Hyrcanus was no longer eligible to be high priest. He was taken to Babylon and treated fairly well there. Herod hurried to Rome to get help from Mark Anthony.

Antigonus became high priest for three years and called himself king. The Roman Senate appointed Herod king. After conquering the port of Joppa and pacifying Galilee, Herod took Jerusalem in 37 B.C. At Herod's request, the Romans executed Antigonus—the first captured king the Romans had ever put to death. To keep the support of Rome, Herod levied taxes on the wealthy and gave the money to Mark Anthony.

Herod had married Mariamne, a granddaughter of both Hyrcanus II and Aristobulus II, but the Jews despised him. His securing various favors for the Jews and reducing their taxes did not change this situation. He was still an Idumean and very friendly with the Roman government—it was the latter who eventually called him Herod the Great.

The women in his life caused Herod much trouble. His mother-in-law, daughter of Hyrcanus II, accused him of taking the throne from her family, although at one time, when he thought he had lost his own opportunity, he had tried to have her son declared king. The infamous Cleopatra of Alexandria had plotted to use Herod against her enemies and then murder him, but he was one of the very few men too clever for Cleopatra. She did her best to turn Mark Anthony against Herod. She kept up a correspondence with Mariamne and her scheming mother, constantly maligning Herod. After plots and counterplots, Herod finally executed his mother-in-law and his wife, although he loved Mariamne deeply and never quit grieving for her. Several other relatives were executed, including the plotting brother-in-law whom Herod had tried to make king and had even appointed high priest. Herod had him drowned in a swimming pool at Jericho.

When Anthony was disgraced and committed suicide, Herod went to Rome's top man, Octavian, later to be the emperor

Augustus Caesar. He did not fawn before him, but bragged about how loyal he had been to Anthony. He was loyal to his friends and would be glad to be a friend of Octavian. Octavian recognized his ability and loyalty, confirmed his kingship of Judea, and enlarged his territory. Herod skillfully pacified much land to the east of Palestine. This was added to his kingdom.

After a period of peace, plots and rumors of plots made life miserable for Herod. He had ten wives and numerous children. He executed the two sons of Mariamne; their Hasmonean blood had made them overbearing but popular among the Jews, who wanted a descendant of the Maccabees as king. Herod had exiled his oldest son, the child of the Idumean, Doris, whom he had married previous to Mariamne; he now called him home and named him his heir. However, the latter was too eager for his father to die. Herod had him executed five days before his own death, having already named another son, Antipas, his successor. Then, just before his death in 4 B.C. at the age of seventy, Herod changed his will again, dividing his territory among three sons, Antipas, his full brother Archelaus, and a half-brother Philip. Herod had driven himself feverishly in his many campaigns and toward the end of his life suffered greatly from an incurable disease.

Herod wanted to be known as a man of culture and as a builder greater than Solomon. He surrounded himself with men having a good training in Greek philosophy and rhetoric. Best known of these was Nicholas of Damascus, who wrote 144 volumes of world history. From this Josephus got most of the extensive biographical material about Herod which we use today.

Herod wanted to please his Jewish subjects. Therefore, in 20 B.C. he started to rebuild the Jerusalem temple. He began this as a repair job, but, when it was completed, so little of Zerubbabel's temple was left that it became known as Herod's temple. It was really only started by Herod and was in construction throughout the life of Jesus of Nazareth. It was probably considered completed in the year A.D. 64, but was destroyed by the Romans in A.D. 70.

Many other buildings were constructed in Jerusalem. They made the Jews proud but unhappy. Herod's first building was a palace 375 feet long at the north end of the temple grounds. Here he lived with Mariamne, but after her execution he could not help dreaming about her. He, therefore, made it into a fort, the Tower of Antonia, named for Mark Anthony. He then built a magnificient palace, larger than the temple complex itself and twice as large as the Antonia, at the western side of Jerusalem. A part of one tower of this palace still stands, known as the Tower of David. His system of bringing water from a distance to the city is still used today. In Jerusalem he built a theater and nearby an amphitheater. He constructed a new Jericho two miles south of the old city. In it he built a palace with luxurious pools, baths, and courtyards. He erected two forts near Jericho and others throughout his kingdom.

Herod beautified the city of Samaria, destroyed by John Hyrcanus and rebuilt by a Syrian proconsul. Since this was outside Jewish territory, he felt it safe to erect a great temple there in honor of his friend, the emperor Augustus. He renamed the city Sebaste in honor of the same Augustus.

Herod's biggest building enterprise was the city of Caesarea, again named for the emperor. This is now being excavated. Herod's territory had no satisfactory port. Roman ships debarked at the port of Acre (Persepolis), just north of Mount Carmel and a bit outside Herod's kingdom. This was a long distance from Jerusalem. Herod wanted his Roman visitors to have a better first impression of his nation. He, therefore, "went all out" in making an artificial harbor and an elegant city on the site of Strato's Tower. Of course, it had a temple to Augustus, baths, and a hippodrome. Begun in 22 B.C., the city was completed in 10 B.C. Later rulers made this the capital of Judea, and it came to be considered a Roman colony.

To develop good will for himself and for the Jews throughout the Roman Empire, and to express appreciation for kindnesses shown to him, Herod made lavish gifts. He presented parks, theaters, gymnasiums, baths, temples, paved streets, water systems to foreign cities, including Tyre, Sidon, Beirut, Ptolemais, Damascus, Antioch, even Athens. Despite all these monuments he built, many ruins of which are still in existence, and the reputation he achieved as the most distinguished non-Roman in the world, Herod the Great is far less known than a boy born in his kingdom shortly before Herod's death, Jesus of Nazareth. The story in Mt. 2:1-16 of the slaughter of the innocents in connection with the birth of Jesus makes it difficult for Christians to develop an unbiased evaluation of Herod.

ASSIGNMENT

1. Distinguish between Edomites and Idumeans.
2. Identify Phasael, Antigonus.
3. Who was Herod? By whom was he called "The Great"? Why? Analyze his abilities and his weaknesses. Today his name is a term of opprobrium. Why? What was his relation to the Hasmoneans? To the Jewish religion? Discuss in detail his building program. Discuss the women in Herod's life.
4. Identify Anthony, Octavian.
5. Outline the story of Hyrcanus II.

SUPPLEMENTARY READING

Dana—Chapter VIII
Dentan—Pages 34-5
Enslin—Chapter III
Mathews—Chapters IX and X
Perowe: *Herod the Great*
Pfeiffer, R. H.: *History*—Pages 24-33
Schurer—Chapters 13-15
Snaith—Chapter VII
The Interpreter's Dictionary of the Bible—Articles on Herod, Roman Empire, Rome

Chapter 12

The Other Herods
and the Procurators

Herod's will left Palestine badly divided. Archelaus was given
the principal part, Judea and Jerusalem, as well as the ancestral
Idumea to the south, and Samaria north of Judea. His full
brother, Antipas, ws given Galilee farther north, and the territory across the Jordan east of that of Archelaus; this region was
known as Perea. Philip was given several small sections north
and east of the Sea of Galilee that had been assigned to Herod
from time to time.

Herod's will was not final until approved by the emperor
Augustus. All three young men hurried to Rome, where Antipas tried to become the sole heir. Other delegates went to Rome
asking that none of Herod's sons be appointed, but that the
kingdom be ruled directly from Rome. Herod's will was not
liked, but finally approved, with the exception that Archelaus
lost some Greek cities located in his territory, and was made
ethnarch rather than king. The other two were appointed
tetrarchs. Hyrcanus II had been classed as an ethnarch by
Julius Caesar. The original Herod and his brother had been
classed as tetrarchs by their father. Tetrarch was the lesser title,
originally meaning ruler over a fourth, but loosely used, much
as our English word quarters is often used today. None of
Herod's sons was classed as a king, but they did not object to
being called that by their subjects. Each appreciated being
called Herod, and was glad to be reminded that he had inherited
Roman citizenship from Herod the Great. Archelaus called
himself Julius Herodes Archelaus.

Archelaus had trouble from the beginning. He was only
eighteen when his father died. Before he went to Rome, dis-

turbances broke out in Jerusalem during the Passover, after he had appointed a new high priest. He sent in troops and 3,000 Jews were killed. Rome had sent an officer to govern until the succession to Herod had been worked out. This official stirred up more trouble by robbing the temple at the time of the Feast of Pentecost. Bedlam broke loose. Several aspirants from different parts of the country tried to grab the throne.

The Syrian governor intervened. He brought an army into Palestine. In Galilee, he burned the city of Sepphoris, where an insurrection had taken place. He sold the inhabitants into slavery. Going to Judea, he crucified 2,000 ringleaders.

Archelaus was never popular. His marriage was contrary to more than one Jewish law. He launched an expensive building program. He even antagonized the Samaritans, who had taken no part in the earlier rebellion. In time, both Jews and Samaritans went to Rome demanding the removal of Archelaus. In A.D. 6 he was deposed and exiled to southern France. The emperor, Augustus, could not trust either of the other brothers. A Roman procurator was appointed in the place of Archelaus. To some extent Palestinian procurators were under the authority of the governor of Syria. The Syrian governor at once proceeded to take a census of the district, probably as a basis for taxation. This made him very unpopular. Procurators were changed from time to time. The fifth of these is the one we know, Pontius Pilate, who became procurator A.D. 26.

Because of his part in the crucifixion of Jesus, it is difficult to get an unprejudiced picture of Pilate. Imperial standards bearing the portrait of the emperor were by his order taken into Jerusalem at night. Such portraits were contrary to Jewish religious law. Jews flocked to Caesarea to demand their removal. These Jews were herded onto the racetrack and threatened with death. They bared their necks to the Roman swords, but Pilate did not dare to have them killed, so ordered the banners removed.

Pilate started an aqueduct to bring water twenty-five miles to Jerusalem and tried to pay for it from the temple treasury. He was attacked by a mob and had to use his soldiers to disperse it.

However, it was the Samaritans who caused Pilate's downfall. Someone claimed to be able to reveal worship equipment he said Moses had buried on Mount Gerazim. Crowds gathered to see this. Pilate discovered that they were armed and had his soldiers attack; they killed a great number. This led to his discharge from office after ten years of service. Only one procurator served longer.

Philip had few real Jews in his territory. There was little of the demand for freedom based on the idea that Rome was interfering with the reign of Yahweh. Near the sources of the Jordan he built a beautiful new capital, which he named Caesarea Philippi. With little trouble he continued as tetrarch until his death A.D. 34.

Antipas was less fortunate. He was clever and vainglorious—Jesus called him a fox (Lu. 13:32). He rebuilt Sepphoris, fortified it, and made it his capital. Later, he built a more magnificent capital on the shore of the Sea of Galilee and named it in honor of the emperor Tiberius. Part of it was on the site of an old cemetery. To the Jews, that made it unclean. Very few Jews were willing to live there.

As it was with his father, much of Antipas' trouble came from the women in his life. He married the daughter of the Nabatean Arab king, Aretas IV. On a visit to Rome, he met and fell in love with Herodias, the wife of one of his younger half-brothers, Philip—not the tetrarch Philip; Josephus calls him Herod. She was his niece, a granddaughter of Herod the Great, and determined to be a queen. It was she who, according to Mk. 6:13-29, brought about the death of John the Baptist. Antipas repudiated his Nabatean wife and married Herodias. This got him into trouble with his Jewish subjects, and also with Aretas, who molested him from time to time and eventually defeated him in battle.

Some time after the death of Philip, the new Roman emperor, Caligula, released his friend, Agrippa, from jail and gave him the territory that had belonged to Philip. Agrippa was a nephew of Philip and Antipas, and brother of Herodias. His father was one of the two sons of Herod the Great's favorite wife, Mariamne, whom Herod had executed. Agrippa was given the title of king. He was a young spendthrift whom Antipas had once helped by securing him the position of overseer of markets in Tiberias. He had been found guilty of taking bribes. Later he had been imprisoned for treason, having said that he wished the emperor Tiberius would die so that Caligula would be emperor. Now he held a title higher than that of Antipas. His sister, Herodias, was extremely jealous. She insisted that her husband go to Rome and demand the title of king. At the very time he did this, there reached the emperor a letter from Agrippa accusing Antipas of aiding the ruler's enemies. It was easily proved that he had stockpiled a large collection of arms. Antipas was exiled to southern France. Herodias chose to go with him. His territory was given to Agrippa.

Two years later, A.D. 41, Agrippa was also given the territory formerly ruled by his uncle Archelaus. The Roman procurator was recalled. For three years, Agrippa ruled practically the same territory that had been ruled by his grandfather, Herod the Great.

In Palestine Agrippa acted strictly as a Jew. In an anti-Jewish uprising in Alexandria, he had been stoned as a Jew. This made him a hero. He presented the temple with the gold chain the emperor had given him in exchange for the iron chain of his imprisonment. He financed daily sacrifices and made other donations to the temple. This brought him the praises of the Jews, who remembered that he could number Hasmoneans among his ancestors. To enhance this support, he put one of the early Christian leaders, James, to death, and imprisoned another, Peter (Acts 12:1-19).

Agrippa became too ambitious and lost the confidence of Rome, being suspected of seeking power beyond his own borders. At Caesarea he gave a great entertainment of races and other amusements. A group of non-Jews proclaimed him a god. He did not refute this. Shortly thereafter he died in great pain (Acts 12:20-23). The Jews interpreted this as the vengeance of Yahweh. Glad to be rid of Agrippa, Rome again sent procurators to govern Palestine. Their territory now included that formerly ruled by Antipas. We read of two of these procurators, Felix and Festus, in connection with the trial of the Christian apostle Paul.

When Agrippa died, his son, only seventeen years old, did not succeed him, but six years later was given territory east of the Sea of Galilee, practically what his great-uncle Philip had had. A little later, possibly in 61, parts of Galilee and Perea were given to him. Known as Agrippa II, he was used by Rome as a spokesman for the Jews. He was allowed to appoint the high priests and was in charge of the high priest's robes, a point upon which Jews and Romans had quarreled in the past. He blundered with the Jews and also with procurators. It was Agrippa to whom Paul appealed when he and Festus heard Paul state his position (Acts 25:13-27).

Rome insisted that Jewish religious prejudices should be

respected, but most of the fifteen procurators simply could not realize what such things meant to the Jews. To the Romans religion had no depth. Thus Romans had no fellow feeling toward the Jews. Rome's representatives were an aloof, administrative group. Some procurators were openly hostile. Others tried to placate the Jews but failed to understand them. Procurators often accepted bribes for allowing robbers to roam unmolested. In turn, they were plagued by ambitious Jewish leaders rising up to cause trouble.

Procurators had judicial, financial, and military authority. However, they could not depend upon their troops. These, known as auxiliaries, were to be raised locally, but, since Jews were exempt from military service, the troops were drawn from non-Jews, especially those in Samaria. Doubtless auxiliaries from other provinces were brought in. The famed Roman legions, composed of thoroughly skilled, Romanized men who served for twenty years, were not under the control of the procurator. He lived in Caesarea and seldom visited Jerusalem, except at the time of Jewish feasts, when it seemed wise to have extra troops there to maintain order.

The procurator Felix found many ways to antagonize the Jews. He persuaded Drusilla, the sister of Agrippa II, to divorce her husband and marry him. His drastic measures against a group called the Zealots gave rise to the Sicarii or Assassins. A famine made the Jews more irritating. They took their complaints to the emperor, who removed Felix from office. This made the Jews arrogant and unbearable. The next procurator, Festus, was unable to do much to help conditions. The two procurators who followed him continually stirred up hatred among the Jews. Agrippa II visited Jerusalem and, in a great oration, tried to ease the situation, but revolt seemed inevitable. The Jews had defeated the Selucid Syrians. Would not God help them defeat the Romans?

ASSIGNMENT

1. How was Herod's territory divided?
2. Distinguish between king, ethnarch, tetrarch, procurator.
3. Report the problems faced by Pilate.
4. What other procurators are mentioned in the New Testament?
5. Give in detail the story of Agrippa I.
6. Tell the story of Agrippa II.

7. Distinguish between auxiliaries and the Roman legions.
8. What Biblical references do we have to Archelaus, Antipas, Philip, Agrippa I, Agrippa II?

SUPPLEMENTARY READING

Enslin—Chapter IV
Mathews—Chapters XI, XII, and XV
Perowe: *Later Herods*
Pfeiffer, R. H.: *History*—Pages 33-40
Schurer—Chapters 16-19

Chapter 13

Down with the Roman!

The situation was out of hand. Leaders of both Pharisees and Sadducees opposed military action, but in A.D. 66 war broke out. Josephus returned from Rome and tried to reason with the revolutionaries, insisting that Rome was much stronger than Judah. At this point he failed.

The rebels played on religious sentiment. They proceeded to hold the temple and captured the Tower of Antonia. The procurator sent his army against them but was defeated with the loss of several thousand men. Jewish factions fought among themselves. At certain places the Jews were able to defeat the Roman garrisons, but in general many more Jews were killed. Where there were Gentile majorities, as in Caesarea, Damascus, and Alexandria, anti-Semitic attacks devastated the Jews. Only in the small territory of Agrippa II were Jews safe.

In October of the year 66, the legate of Syria attacked Jerusalem. He soon decided that he had inadequate forces and started north. At a pass he was surrounded by Jews. He fled, abandoning his equipment. This success united the Jews. They became organized. Even Josephus accepted appointment as governor of Galilee.

The emperor Nero chose his ablest commander, Vespasian, to crush the rebellion. In the spring of 67, Vespasian arrived in Palestine with 60,000 Roman legionaires. He soon captured Galilee and Josephus. However, a group of extremist Jews who called themselves Zealots escaped to Jerusalem. They plunged the city into a winter of civil war. Many of the Jerusalem leaders were assassinated. Vespasian allowed the Jews to kill off one another in Jerusalem, while he conquered territory on every side of it.

When Vespasian learned that the emperor Nero had committed suicide, he held things as they were for about a year. In

June 69 he expanded his holdings to include all of Palestine except Jerusalem and some segregated forts. At this time, a band of Zealots of Idumea invaded Jerusalem, which now had two mutually hostile tyrants.

In Rome a quarrel developed as to who was to be Nero's successor. Three men claimed the position. Roman soldiers in Egypt and the Middle East proposed Vespasian. He left his son Titus in charge in Palestine and in the summer of 70 arrived in Rome, where he secured the throne for himself.

Meanwhile, in Jerusalem, a third local leader rose to complicate the situation. This was further aggravated by a famine. In August Titus forced his way into Jerusalem. In the battle in the temple area, the temple was set on fire, contrary to the order of Titus. In time, the Jews were butchered and the city practically destroyed.

In his triumphal march in Rome the next year, Titus exhibited materials taken from the temple. Among these was the seven-branched candlestick. Later a triumphal arch was erected in honor of Titus. On this was carved a representation of the candlestick. The arch picturing the candlestick stands in Rome today.

The last Jewish fortification was not taken until A.D. 73. This might have seemed to be the end of Judaism, but, like the destruction of Jerusalem in 586 B.C., demolishing the city did not mean the end of the Jewish religion. A leading rabbi escaped from Jerusalem and secured permission to re-establish a school for the study of the Torah at Jamnia, west of the city. Sacrifices were no longer made. The temple was no longer the center of Judaism. The Torah, both written and oral, took its place. It was in Jamnia in A.D. 90 that the decision was made vetoing the Apocrypha and "sealing" the Jewish scriptures. The truth of Hosea's statement attributed to Yahweh was newly discovered:

I desire steadfast love and not sacrifice;
     the knowledge of God, rather than burnt offerings (6:6).

Fortunately, the synagogue had come to be more important than the temple in the lives of most Jews. The temple could be destroyed, but wherever there were ten Jewish males twelve years old there could be a synagogue.

Agrippa II had done his best to prevent the rebellion against Rome. Finally, he came to the assistance of Titus. Nero had already given him additional territory. After the war, he was given more land to the north; about A.D. 75, he moved to Rome, and his kingdom was incorporated into the province of Syria. The rule of the Herods ceased upon his death about twenty-five years later.

The homeland of the Jews was no longer a safe place for them. Many joined their relatives throughout the Diaspora. Other than the small group at Jamnia, the greatest center of Jewish scholarship now was Babylonia. This attracted many of the more sincere Jews. As a result, the Jewish population of Babylonia rose to nearly a million.

However, the Jews could not give up their ambitions. In 115, those in Egypt and a section farther west in Africa attempted a revolt against Rome. It cost the lives of many Jews. In 130, Rome rebuilt Jerusalem, but called it Aelia Capitolina. On the site of the temple, an altar to Zeus was erected. The Romans also forbade circumcision. It is not surprising that there rose up a "Messiah," Bar Kozibah, generally punned to read Bar Cocheba (or Kochbah), son of the star. After three years of guerrilla warfare, he was defeated. No Jew was permitted to enter Jerusalem upon pain of death. As much as 300 years later, Jews were allowed in Jerusalem only on the anniversary of its 586 B.C. destruction. They came on that day to weep for the loss of their temple. Recently, in a cave near the Dead Sea in Israel, a group of letters from Bar Cocheba to two of his leaders has been found.

Why did the Jews so despise Rome? Rome was proud of her justice, but was more tolerant of the Jews than of any other group in the Empire. However, the Jews were convinced that they were God's chosen people. Therefore, they should be ruled by no one else. Rome had no concept of freedom. She expected always to rule the world.

Rome gave considerable self-government. Each community of Palestine had its council. For Judea, there was the Great Council, or Sanhedrin. It was allowed to make numerous laws, hold trials, and execute its decisions. Rome apparently took away from it the right to put people to death. Rome kept control of the choice of men to serve as high priests, and part of the time even kept charge of the high priest's robes, which to Jews seemed to be a profanation of sacred things.

While the provinces were expected to finance the Empire, Rome seems to have spent most of the Palestine direct taxes, such as land taxes, for physical improvements in the province. It was the matter of internal revenue, or customs, that irked the Jews. These were farmed out to the highest bidder. He was known as a publican. Naturally, he abused his power. If necessary, bribing would cause the procurator to overlook excesses. On a short journey, numerous tax collection points were passed. Jews felt that this was taking what belonged to God. Jews who yielded to the temptation to make profit by thus working for the Roman government were considered robbers, no better than prostitutes.

The concept that out of a remnant Yahweh would raise up a deliverer, the anointed one or Messiah, maintained the conviction that soon God would intervene. Just which individuals considered themselves messiahs is uncertain, but many sought to overthrow Roman control.

ASSIGNMENT

1. What were the chief grounds for Jewish opposition to Rome?
2. Identify: Nero, Vespasian, Titus, Aelia Capitolina, Bar Cocheba.
3. Explain the terms: Sanhedrin, publican, messiah.

SUPPLEMENTARY READING

Mathews—Chapter XVI
Pfeiffer, R. H.: *History*—Pages 41-5
Schurer—Chapters 20-1
Yadin—Chapter 8

Chapter 14

Roman Life

Roman civilization was much later in developing than was Greek. It tended to be crude, with little interest in art or philosophy. Of course, there were Roman farmers and merchants, but military service was the life most preferred. Romans were tough, cruel soldiers; however, as their empire developed, they saw something desirable in Greek life and were eager to imitate it.

Religion of the Romans did not greatly differ from that of the Greeks. A multitude of gods had developed from their deifying the simple but little understood natural processes underlying the ordinary experiences of life. When contacts were made with Greek culture, similarities were recognized between Greek and Roman gods, and they were often equated. Romans had local deities with their little shrines at which food and flowers were offered. Worship of more general gods dealing with weather, harvests, or success in battle was encouraged by the government. Giving gifts to such gods was considered a patriotic act. The gods were to be brought into alliance with the emperor. The genius of the emperor was considered divine. In time, the emperor himself came to be thought of as a god to be recognized or worshiped by all loyal Romans.

Religion had little relation to anything moral or spiritual. Prostitution in the name of religion was common. Religions that furthered the power of the state were given the protection of the government. Other religions in the Empire were tolerated, but were unlicensed, and might at any time be forbidden.

Roman life was dominantly urban. Rural people were called *pagani*. The fact that our word pagan comes from this root indicates the contempt in which they were held. Cities of the Empire were knit together by an extensive system of Roman roads.

Pompeii, completely covered by lava erupted from Mount Vesuvius in A.D. 79, gives an understanding of life in the smaller Roman cities. Excavations of parts of Rome and its suburbs reveal the capital. Rome itself was crowded with tenement buildings six or seven stories high, some higher. Because a number of these, very flimsily built, collapsed, Augustus ordered that none were to be built more than sixty-five feet high. Streets were narrow, dark, ill-smelling. Street lights were unknown.

The typical one-family residences, more common in the smaller cities, were brick or concrete houses close to the street, having no front windows and but one entrance, closed by double doors which opened onto an uncovered court, serving as a reception room and used chiefly by the men. Behind this was a second uncovered court, with rooms on either side. Sometimes there were two stories of such rooms. Houses and rooms in Greece and farther east tended to be smaller than those of the Italian peninsula.

For the tenements, water was available on only the first floor. Few were connected with public sewers. The wealthier had good plumbing with beautiful baths and fountains, and had a few rooms heated by furnaces. Window glass was unknown, although the wealthiest houses made some use of translucent stones. Oil lamps, some of greatly complicated design, provided light. Cooking was done on an open hearth, or in earthen or stone ovens.

Furniture was scarce. The couch was the staple article. Couches were placed on three sides of a table at an angle, or around a U-shaped table. People reclined on their left arms at meals. On these couches people received visitors, read and wrote, as well as slept.

Roman attitude toward marriage was much inferior to that of the Jews. As with Jewish people, parents selected mates for their children. There was no courtship. The wife's parents provided her with a dowry, which was supposed not to become the possession of her husband. With all groups, religion played a part in the marriage ceremony. But with the Romans, the wife had fewer rights. She was the property of her husband. Having a mistress as a more real companion was not rare. Divorce was practiced extensively. Eventually, some women came to live independent lives. Infants had no rights. They were often exposed to die or were sold as slaves. So many leading families had no children that leadership in time was left to former rabble and slaves, despite attempts to counteract this tendency by making bachelors pay high taxes and giving awards to big families.

Slave labor was a part of Roman life. This resulted in long hours and low wages for free workmen, bringing about extreme poverty. It tended to develop a group of shiftless unemployed, supported by charity, gambling, and theft. To keep them from becoming trouble-makers, the government provided "bread and circuses." Roman genius for organization developed trade unions. These helped their members find employment, and provided death benefits for widows and orphans and the burial of members. Each guild had its own patron deity.

Although the Romans were far inferior to the Greeks in science and philosophy, by copying the Greeks and by trial and error, they developed medicine and surgery. Lawyers and teachers were respected but not held in high esteem. Beyond reading, writing, and arithmetic, the schooling could scarcely be called practical. Its chief aim was to teach Roman youths to make flowery, artificial orations in the Greek language.

Neither Romans nor Greeks respected labor. Here they differed from the Jews. To be idle was a sign of aristocracy, of social achievement. However, beginning with the emperor Augustus, Rome was able to enforce peace upon most of her Empire, resulting in an improvement in economic conditions. This tended to develop a self-respecting middle class.

Rome cleared the Mediterranean of pirates. With her roads, her system of coins, general adoption of one language—Greek—travel and commerce greatly increased. Ships large enough to carry several hundred passengers plied the Mediterranean (Acts 27:37). Division of labor developed—commercial agriculture and stock-raising, milling, baking, the work of the smith, the fuller, and the wine-maker. Wholesale and retail merchandising developed. Systems of accounting and commercial records came into use. Deeds for real estate and personal property were recorded. Banking became an extensive and well-advanced business. Notes and mortgages were negotiable. Checking accounts and interest-bearing savings accounts were used. Money could be borrowed at eight to twelve per cent interest. Travelers could use letters of credit.

Roman organization, law, order, system, made a practical appeal to Jews, and even more to the early Christians. Jews lived by tradition; Romans planned, experimented, changed. This suggested the idea of improvement. At this point, the

Romans had something of the spirit of Hebrew prophets, rather than of Jewish priests. Paul may have had in mind such a developing background for the spread of Christianity when he wrote, "When the time had fully come, God sent forth his Son" (Gal. 4:4).

On the other hand, recreation had degenerated. Amphitheaters, such as Herod built even at Jerusalem, were generally used for gladiatorial combats. Men were mangled by their opponents' deadly weapons, or torn by wild beasts. The arenas were soaked in human blood. The Romans were thrilled at seeing agony and bloodshed. As many as 10,000 people were forced to take part in one such entertainment. Both Greeks and Jews opposed these debasing exhibits. Chariot races, which were also often quite bloody, were another part of Roman amusement. Prostitution and drunkenness were common. Gluttony resulted in many eating places having "vomitoriums" where one might lose his food before gorging himself again.

Continued warfare had made the Romans coarse, cruel. Selling prisoners into slavery, kidnaping, and enslaving people for debt, decreased respect for human beings. Recklessness of despair degraded the poor, especially when they noted the luxury and ease of the rich. Graft in public office had become common. Pornography decorated the walls of houses in Pompeii and Rome.

This could not be completely accepted in the face of a growing appreciation of Greek esthetics, art, and beauty. Sculpture and other objects of art stolen from Greece influenced the interests of Roman people. Protests against cruelty, bloodshed, mistreatment of children, abortion, the degeneration of the home, were being heard in increasing tempo. Some Romans were discovering the satisfaction of moral living. Jews throughout the Empire lived by higher standards than most Romans. Their influence was not unfelt. On the other hand, the fact that Romans were controlling the "world" caused many Jews to question the value of their own morals—if the heathen rule, why not be heathen?

ASSIGNMENT

1. In what ways did the Roman outlook differ from that of the Greeks?
2. Describe the life of common people in Rome.
3. Describe the religion of the Romans.

4. What is meant by "the genius of the emperor"?
5. Aside from conquering Palestine, what influence did Rome have on the Jewish people?
6. What influence did Jews have on Roman thought?
7. What did Rome contribute to the spread of Christianity? What influence did Rome have on Christian thought?

SUPPLEMENTARY READING

Church
Dana—Chapter X
Carcopimo
Johnston

Chapter 15

Am-ha-arez

In contrast to the urban emphasis of Roman life, the Hebrews were basically rural. Their minds turned toward the cities, for it was there that they might be protected from enemy armies. In their constant need for protection, their dream of a desirable future life was a city, the new Jerusalem. But it was pictured as a park city, with trees and rivers. Romans thought of their origin as the building of the city of Rome by two brothers, Romulus and Remus. The Hebrew heroes were shepherds— Abraham, Moses, David. Their thinking went back to a garden —the Garden of Eden.

Most Jews were farmers or herdsmen. They raised grapes, figs, and other fruit, olives, and grain. God was thought of as giving them their crops. Their great religious festivals were celebrations of thanksgiving for the products of the field. They lived in villages and towns, but their employment was in the open country, wresting the necessities of life from the stony hillsides. Along the Sea of Galilee, fishing was a major industry. Cities were crowded but small. No one was much more than a quarter-mile from the country.

Each man was supposed to have inherited land from his father. He had been expected to secure from it enough food for his family. As cities and the total population increased, food became insufficient. Poverty led to outbursts of robbery and insurrection. It was easy to stir up people in opposition to those they could blame for their unhappy situation. It also enhanced the expectation of a messiah who would change the government, "fill the hungry with good things" and deprive the rich of their luxuries (Lu. 1:53).

Palestine was largely self-supporting. Trade and commerce were limited. Jews were afraid of the sea. Almost none of them were sailors. About the only imports were wood and metal articles and a limited amount of luxury goods. There was some export of fish, olive oil, wool, wheat, balsam, honey, and figs.

Throughout the intertestamental period, Jews of the Dispersion were so influenced by the Greeks that they came to be known as Hellenists. Palestinian Jews opposed it but were nevertheless influenced by the Greek culture. After 63 B.C., Roman influence was felt. Greek and Roman forms of recreation drew the curious and the unorthodox. The Greek language was heard on the city streets. Latin was used by some of the Romans stationed there. Well-educated Jews spoke Greek. Merchants knew a smattering of it. But most people felt that Greek was foreign and evil. Its letters looked strange. Aramaic was their language. True, it was not the sacred language in which the scriptures were written, but it looked like Hebrew and was closely related to it. However, pious Jews often gave their sons Greek names, as Philip and Andrew.

Greek clothing was seen. Temples to Greek gods and Roman emperors were found in neighboring cities that were not primarily Jewish. Roman coins, including those with pictures of the emperor, were used even by those who hated Rome the most (Mk. 12:13-17).

Association with all things foreign must be kept to the minimum. Religious rules, in increasing number, were made regarding relations with Gentiles. Most such relations were considered defilement, which could only be erased by a cleansing ceremony. The Jews were Yahweh's people and must associate with no others. Hebrew culture, especially that of the people of the land, Am-ha-arez, was religiously inspired.

Outside the major cities, the only public buildings were the synagogues. Inside the gate of each town was an open square where selling and buying and visiting were done. Most Jews lived in small private houses. These were considered one-family dwellings, but the family often included several married sons, their wives and children. Houses were made of field stones, chinked with mud in which straw had been mixed. Lumber was very scarce. Tree trunks rested on the walls, supporting the flat roof, which was made of thatch and clay. Only the wealthier houses had tile roofs. Windows of latticework opened on the streets. Plumbing was almost unknown, but foul or ill-smelling material was required to be removed quickly. Many houses on hillsides had roofs extending over a lower level where the animals were kept at night. Sometimes the mangers were used to cradle babies during the day.

Barley bread was the chief food of Am-ha-arez; the rich had bread made from wheat. It was thin round loaves sometimes called "circles of bread." Parched grain was also common. Beet and cane sugar were unknown, but honey was used extensively. Sheep milk and goat milk were much more common than cow's milk. Since it soured quickly, milk was generally used in the form of curds. Eggs and meat, generally mutton or goat meat, were luxury items. Pigeons were cheap, but fish was the usual substitute for meat.

Broad beans, lentils, and cucumbers were common. Onions, endive, and lettuce were also used. Various bulbs and roots were eaten. Locusts were enjoyed; the Talmud mentions 800 edible varieties. They were boiled, powdered, candied, or pickled. Food was highly spiced; a great variety of condiments was used. Olive oil was employed for cooking. Fruit included not only grapes, dates, and figs, but melons, apricots, pomegranates, and mulberries. Nuts included walnuts, almonds, and pistachios.

Ruling the synagogue and ruling the village were the same thing. A council of elders was elected in each synagogue. These made local regulations and tried offenders in addition to conducting the religious services. They established a school in which boys memorized the law and learned to read the scriptures, that they might become men of Yahweh and good citizens. Josephus brags, "We take the most pains of all in the education of children." The teacher was the best-educated man of the community, called "my great one" or rabbi. He secured little, if any, of his living from his teaching, but had some trade, such as carpenter, mason, or potter. However, since teaching was so important, it eventually became evident that it was inefficient to require a well-trained teacher to spend his time in other activity. It was felt that one should not charge for teaching the scriptures. This was solved by paying the rabbi for teaching a class in arithmetic or some other non-scriptural subject.

Manual labor was considered honorable, a sharing with God in creation. Rank or aristocracy was largely absent from villages. In cities, position, wealth, or education brought distinction, but this was not necessarily handed down from father to son, with the exception of the position of priest.

Some wealthy Jews had slaves, but they were treated to a considerable degree as members of the family; owner and slave often worked together. Many religious leaders opposed slavery.

Jews held women in more respect than did other people of intertestamental times, but their place was considered to be almost entirely in the home. Seldom were they taught to read or write. They had no part in the synagogue service but might sit behind a screen or in a balcony. They were not expected to observe some of the rules of the Torah. However, in the home service noting the beginning of the Sabbath, it was the mother who lit the candle of joy.

Families tended to be large; children were considered a great blessing. Boys, essential for caring for ageing parents and carrying on family traditions, were welcomed much more than girls, but there was no thought of exposing either to death. It is stated in the Talmud, "The birth of a male child causes universal joy— but the birth of a female child causes universal sorrow." The only inheritance a woman received from her father was her dowry. Even it became the property of her husband, although she was generally allowed to have one-tenth of it for pin money.

Marriage was almost universal. Very little polygamy was practiced in intertestamental times, but some wealthy men probably had more than one wife. Women could not secure divorce; men could. However, as compared to the Romans, there was little divorce, although Roman influence was increasing this. The fact that a man might divorce a wife who gave him no sons reduced the amount of polygamy.

Marriage was arranged by parents. The groom agreed to make a definite contribution to the parents of the bride to compensate them for rearing her. The service of betrothal was almost entirely between the groom and the bride's father. After that, the young people might live together. Generally, this was followed later by a public wedding. This was often marked by feasting and rough hilarity.

Family life was on a much higher level than among either Greeks or Romans. Old age was highly respected as a sign of God's approval. Religion was expressed in the home by thanksgiving at meals and by discussion about the Torah as food was being eaten, by other prayers, and by Sabbath observance. Dietary restrictions of the written and oral Torah were carefully followed. People generally sat on the floor for meals, with the food on a covering on the floor or on a low table.

The thinking of the Jew centered about God, but he emphasized obedience more than thinking. Jewish leaders established great numbers of regulations, They insisted that righteousness was impossible except through unbroken observance of all these detailed rules. The busy farmer or carpenter, fisherman or mason, could not live by all these dictations. His education did not provide him knowledge of all these details. Thus he was often despised by Jewish leaders. Yet, it was these people, Am-ha-arez, who were the children of God, the backbone of Judaism.

ASSIGNMENT

1. In what ways did the religion and philosophy of the common people of Palestine differ from those of Rome?
2. What were the beliefs and hopes of Am-ha-arez?
3. In what ways did the life of the common people of Palestine differ from those of Rome?
4. In what ways did education in Palestine differ from that in Rome?
5. What were the imports of Palestine? the exports?
6. What was the Jewish attitude toward women? marriage?
7. Describe Jewish family meals.

SUPPLEMENTARY READING

Dana—Chapter VII
Daniel-Rops
Enslin—Pages 126-8
Mathews—Chapter XIII
Toombs—Pages 47-8

Chapter 16

The Rise of the Sects

During the intertestamental period, Jewish leadership split into a number of sects.

The best-known of these is the Pharisees. The term appears ninety-nine times in the New Testament. The word seems to mean "separated," but from what they considered themselves separated is a problem. They were descendants of the Hasideans of the time of the Maccabean Revolt. It will be recalled that the Hasideans joined in the revolt to secure the temple from the Syrian Greeks, but, after that was done, they would have nothing to do with continuing the revolt, which grew into a demand for political independence. It has been suggested that the term Pharisee comes from the Hasideans separating themselves from Judas Maccabeus. Some have suggested that the name refers to separation from the common people, but Josephus reports, "The Pharisees have the multitude on their side." They also emphasized being separate from Greeks and other Gentiles. Some have suggested that the Pharisees believed they had separated themselves from sin. Their great emphasis was upon the Torah. The oral Torah was their child. Therefore, they proclaimed that they were separating, or distinguishing, the meaning of the law. It could also mean separated from the priestly emphasis in Jewish life.

In Chapter 7 we discussed the oral Torah, which eventually came to be written in the Talmud. These detailed regulations about Sabbath observance, ceremonial washings, and tithing, came to be considered "the tradition of the elders" (See Mk. 7:3). These disgusted Jesus, and have given us an undesirable impression of the Pharisees. Apart from this artificiality, the Pharisees probably were closer to the teachings of Jesus than were any other group.

Although Josephus mentions the Pharisees in connection with the second Maccabean leader, Jonathan, at another place he says that they first appeared during the time of John Hyrcanus. They opposed the political ambition of Hyrcanus and his successors, especially Alexander Janneus. Josephus reports that on his deathbed, Janneus urged Alexandra to make peace with the Pharisees. During her reign the country prospered. For this the Pharisees got considerable credit. These non-priestly or lay scribes, whom Alexandra added to the Sanhedrin, generated new thought and life. However, they did not like any of the Hasmonean line and were inclined to welcome Herod's taking over. They endeavored to stay clear of politics, but could not help despising the Romans and wanting Palestine for the Jews alone. This caused them to be energetic in their expectation that God would raise up the Messiah.

The Pharisees endeavored to be the voice of Moses. When the regulations attributed to him in the Torah did not fit the intertestamental period, the Pharisees modernized them, although they insisted that God had foreseen their current situation and had given detailed instructions to Moses. It is these instructions that became the oral Torah. They were sure that they were simply rediscovering old truths. They were making religion operative in everyday life. They felt that they were putting a hedge about the law in such a way that it would be almost impossible to break the rules of Moses. In reality, they did soften some of the harsh regulations of the Torah. The old law said that a woman guilty of adultery was to be stoned to death. The Pharisees accepted this, but insisted that it be done only when two eyewitnesses testified to her guilt.

The Pharisees were flexible. They had no trouble in reading into the Torah concepts that had developed in Judaism at a later period. They thus accepted the idea of a physical resurrection, of angels and demons. There are those who think that the term Pharisee comes from a word for Persian, that the Pharisees were so named because they held ideas that had penetrated Judaism from the Persian Zoroastrianism.

The Pharisees were not fatalists but still believed that God has a hand in man's fate. God has set up rules whereby men may have a good life, but each man must himself choose to obey these rules.

To the Pharisees the scriptures were more than the Torah. It was they who urged the inclusion of the Prophets, and later the Holy Writings. They were interested in the Messianic hope. They approved new rites in temple worship and new festivals (Hanukkah and Purim).

Pharisees took great pride in their group. They found in Num. 15:37-38 an edict "to make tassels on the corners of their garments." Jesus criticized them for overdoing this: "They make their phylacteries broad and their fringes long" (Mt. 23:5). They felt far superior to Am-ha-arez: "This crowd, who do not know the law, are accursed" (John 7:49). Jesus was included in "this crowd." However, the Pharisees did make some attempt to raise the religious standards of the masses whom they taught in the synagogues. They saw to it that the Torah was read and interpretatively translated into Aramaic at each synagogue service.

Other sects arose, but after the destruction of Jerusalem A.D. 70, they disappeared. Phariseeism and Judaism came in time to be synonymous.

Contrasted to the Pharisees were the Sadducees, mentioned fourteen times in the New Testament. This was a small, unpopular, haughty, aristocratic group of wealthy people, proud of their blood and position. They probably claimed to be descendants of Zadok, whom Solomon had made the chief priest. It is possible that they were named for some later Zadok. Some scholars argue that the term comes from a word meaning righteous ones. The Sadducees probably originated as a group loyal to the Hasmonean high priests.

The Sadducees felt that they were conservative. They did not believe in a resurrection, in angels or demons. None of these is mentioned in the Torah; therefore, they were considered modernistic ideas. To the Sadducees, the Torah was the only religious authority. It was to be accepted literally. The priests could guide people in their interpretation of the Torah without authority coming from Moses. Josephus reports their teachings, "that to act what is good, or what is evil, is at man's own choice."

The Pharisees opposed the presence of Greeks and Romans. The Sadducees were more interested in peace and financial profit than in keeping their religion strictly pure. Therefore, they became the appeasement party—the Romans are here, so let's make the most of it. The Romans appreciated this and rewarded the Sadducees by giving them the most respected and remunerative position in Palestine, that of high priest. From their control of the temple, selling sacrificial animals, collecting from each worshiper a fee which must be paid by a coin which certain Sadducees were willing to sell at a profit, they enhanced their wealth. In charge of the priesthood, they held most of the seats in the governing body, the Great Council or Sanhedrin. Because the Sadducees controlled the temple, the Pharisees lessened their interest in it and emphasized the synagogue.

Somewhat between the Pharisees and the Sadducees was a third group never criticized in the New Testament, the Essenes. Josephus says of them that they were fatalists, believing that "All things are best ascribed to God." Because of the knowledge about the Hebrew scriptures and the thinking of intertestamental times revealed in the recently discovered libraries of the Essenes, they will be discussed in detail in the next chapter.

Josephus tells of what he calls "the fourth philosophy," the home rule party. These are probably limited to the group we have come to know as the Zealots, extreme patriots. Their motto was: "The sword, and that not sparingly; no king but Yahweh." They refused to call any man "lord," and proclaimed great zeal for the Torah. Just when the group came into being we do not know. Josephus says that Judas the Galilean was the founder, but it may be that he put new life into an older movement. They found for themselves a pattern in stories of zeal of Old Testament characters, Simeon and Levi (Gen. 34:25), Phinehas (Num. 25:6-8), and Elijah (1 Kg. 18:40 and 19:14). Spiritually, the Zealots were descendants of the Maccabees. Judas led a revolt in A.D. 6 against the taking of a census by the Syrian governor. Other than this reference, Josephus tells only of the part taken by Zealots in the revolt of A.D. 66. They were largely individuals who sought out and killed Romans in Palestine, never fearful of losing their own lives. One of the disciples of Jesus is listed as Simon the Zealot (Lu. 6:15); he is also called Simon the Cananean (Mt. 10:4).

ASSIGNMENT

1. Who were the Hasideans? What have we had about them?
2. Who were the Pharisees? What does the term mean? What were their special emphases? What was their strength? Why is the new Testament so critical of them?
3. Who were the Sadducees? What does the term mean? In what major ways did they differ from the Pharisees? What

was their attitude toward Rome? Why? What reward did this bring them?

4. Describe the conflict between the Pharisees and Sadducees.
5. Identify the Essenes.
6. Give the history, aims, and methods of the Zealots.

SUPPLEMENTARY READING

Bruce—Chapter VI
Yadin—Chapters 9 and 10

Chapter 17

The Qumran Community

The Zadokite priesthood disappeared when Antiochus IV (Epiphanes) gave the position of high priest to the highest bidder, Menelaus, a man not of the priestly family. This gave rise to an opposition party, the Hasideans, the pious, "every one who offered himself willingly for the law" (1 Macc. 2:42). They first joined the Maccabees to regain the temple. When that had been achieved, the Hasideans withdrew their support from the Maccabees, who were ambitious for political control. Although Josephus at one place says that Judas was appointed high priest, he says at another place that for a period of seven years there was no high priest.

Judas' brother Jonathan was appointed high priest by a Syrian ruler, but it was only his brother Simon who received enthusiastic approval of the Jews as the holder of this office. They proclaimed that he (and his descendants) "should be high priest until a faithful prophet should arise . . . and take charge of the holy things." This official statement engraved in bronze goes on to promise punishment to any priest who "should act contrary to these decisions." The Maccabee brothers were not of the Zadokite line. It evidently was recognized that some priests did not approve. Although the Hasideans officially cooperated, they were not happy with the situation.

From this Hasidean unhappiness sprang a separatist group who became the Essenes. They are not mentioned in the Bible, the Apocrypha, or the Talmud. In the first Essene writing found (in Cairo in 1896) this unhappiness is reported in the statement: "They came to understand the iniquity and to know that they were guilty men; but they were like blind men or like those who grope for the way for twenty years."

This same quotation continues: "And God recognized their works, that they sought Him with a whole heart and so raised up from them a Righteous Teacher to make them tread in the way of His heart and to instruct the last generations that which He would do in the last generation against the congregation of the false."

These twenty years are roughly from the 160's to the 140's B.C. The Righteous Teacher, the organizer of the Essenes, began his ministry late in the reign of Jonathan (160–142 B.C.) or early in the reign of his brother Simon (142–134 B.C.). He was a Zadokite priest of the Hasideans, the hyper-orthodox group who had lost control of the temple. They believed that the priests at Jerusalem were false, the sanctuary defiled, and the calendar in error.

Evidently the Hasideans split at this time into the Pharisees and the Essenes. The former made an effort to cooperate. The latter soon found their leader being persecuted by the powers in control. This leader of the Essenes, called in their literature the Righteous Teacher or Teacher of Righteousness, or the true teacher, believed that he was the "faithful prophet" suggested in the acclaim given Simon. His followers went so far as to call the official high priest the Wicked Priest.

The self-denying attitude of ancient Nazirites and Rechabites was reflected in the Essenes. They felt that they were a new Israel, a remnant of the old Israel. They believed they had a new covenant with God. They are sometimes called the Covenanters.

The Essenes took an apocalyptical turn of mind. They were sure that they were living in the last ages, that they were appointed by God to prepare for the coming of the Messiah. They recalled the admonition of Second Isaiah, "In the wilderness prepare the way of the LORD" (40:3). They felt they should withdraw from "the world." Therefore, a considerable number of Essenes moved to a desert location overlooking the north end of the Dead Sea. This was on a marly terrace below the cliffs at a point where the Wadi Qumran cuts a deep gorge to the sea. It is now called Khirbet Qumran, the modern Arabic term for Qumran ruin. It was the site of an Israelite fortress town from the ninth to the sixth centuries B.C., listed in Joshua 15 as "City of Salt." Here the Essenes reconstructed an ancient Israelite aqueduct and cistern. This was near the end of the reign of Simon or early in the reign of his son John Hyrcanus.

The group grew, and rooms and cisterns were added to the walled community center. Doubtless many members lived in huts or tents nearby. In 31 B.C., during the reign of Herod the Great, an earthquake broke a crevice through the center of the buildings and dropped the eastern side of the complex nearly two feet. Josephus reports that in this earthquake 30,000 men of Judea were killed.

The site was abandoned until the early years of Herod's son Archelaus, about 1 B.C., when much of the settlement was rebuilt. The community continued to thrive during the life of Jesus. In the Jewish revolt, Vespasian attacked Qumran with his Tenth Legion early in the summer of 68, after he had conquered Jericho eight miles to the north. Part of the burned buildings were restored and for some time used as a Roman fort.

The Essenes made much of their library, their most precious possession. Every member of the Qumran community seems to have been expected to spend one entire night of every three studying the scriptures, although the statement could possibly mean a third part of every night. They made numerous copies of the books of the Bible in their scriptorium and wrote various books of their own. They evidently feared the coming of Vespasian. In preparation they rolled many of their scrolls tightly, sewed them in linen wrappings, and placed them in jars which they made for the purpose. These were carefully sealed and hidden in caves within a mile of the community center. Apparently this was not completed when it was learned that Vespasian was approaching. Most of their library was, therefore, quickly dumped into a nearby cave, now known as Cave 4. Approximately four hundred manuscripts have recently been found in this cave, most of them in badly deteriorated condition, broken into several thousand fragments. A large part of these manuscripts are copies of books of the Old Testament. Not all are in Hebrew; some are in Aramaic; others are parts of the Greek Septuagint.

Whether the members of the community were all killed, or escaped, is not known. Evidently they never got back to reclaim their precious library.

Some time during the winter of 1946–7, three Arab shepherds, cousins, noticed a small opening in a cliff overlooking the northwestern coast of the Dead Sea. They discussed investigating it together, but the next morning the youngest slipped away by himself and managed to crawl through the opening into a small cave. Here he found lined up against the wall "about ten jars," twenty-five to thirty inches high and about ten inches wide. Opening one, he found, not gold or jewels, but tightly rolled scrolls of leather. Although disappointed, the cousins took these to an antique dealer in Bethlehem.

In turn, the Syrian Orthodox Metropolitan of Jerusalem purchased four of the scrolls. He took them to the American School of Oriental Research in Jerusalem, where it was soon discovered that one of the scrolls was a practically complete copy of the entire book of Isaiah, a copy made not later than 100 B.C. This was determined by the shape of the letters used. Later this date was confirmed by the Carbon-14 radioactive time clock test.

Other scrolls were purchased by the Hebrew University at Jerusalem. The Syrian Metropolitan took his scrolls to America, where they were offered for sale for $1,000,000. Eventually they were purchased for the Hebrew University for a fourth of that amount. These were added to three scrolls which Jewish scholars bought from the Bethlehem dealer about the time the Syrian Metropolitan secured those just described.

War between Israeli and Arabs in Palestine in 1948 made research difficult. However, an intense search for more cave treasures was initiated by both archaeologists and Arab bedouin. Eleven caves with hidden manuscripts have been found in the Qumran region. In only one were the scrolls in as good condition as those found in "Cave 1." Many other caves holding a variety of written material and other relics have been found in southern Palestine. Among these is a list of names and numbers written about the time of Jeremiah. This is a palimpsest, that is, something written over an earlier writing. This list had been superimposed on a letter written about 750 B.C.

Discovery of the scrolls led to the examination of the community center. This had been thought to be only a Roman fort. Excavation revealed not only cisterns, but a pottery, grain mill, bakery, kitchen, laundry and forges. Of special interest is the scriptorium where the scrolls were copied. In it were found a long narrow table, a bench, and inkstands with dried ink in them. Another room seventy-five by fifteen feet was the assembly and dining room. Adjoining it was a pantry containing several hundred bowls, plates, cups, and jars.

The dating of the Qumran community is greatly helped by coins found in the ruins. No coins minted earlier than the reign of John Hyrcanus (134–105 B.C.) have been found. By 1957 eighty-six coins of the time of Alexander Janneus (103–76 B.C.)

were identified, with a few more of the Hasmonean era (76–37 B.C.). The absence of pre-Hyrcanus coins indicated that the settlement could not have been made much before the time of Hyrcanus. Among the coins found in the ruins of the pre-earthquake buildings are only five from the time of Herod.

Under the floor of the post-earthquake construction, but above the debris of the pre-earthquake period, three jars containing 558 silver coins have been discovered, hidden by someone who did not want members of the community to know about them. Most of these are from Tyre, dating from about 100 B.C. until the beginning of the Christian era. In the post-earthquake ruins, seventy-three coins were found minted in A.D. 67, only five in 68. In the ruins of the later Roman construction were found a number of coins minted in Caesarea and other coastal cities in 67 and 68, and later. One such coin had been stamped with the Roman numeral X by the paymaster of the Tenth Legion.

The Qumran literature refers to other Essene groups in camps and settlements in villages of Judea, but it is about the Qumran group that we learn the most. They had retreated to the desert "to separate themselves from the abode of perverse men," to avoid the pollution of "the children of darkness." Here they lived in vigorous simplicity. Those who wished to join the fellowship must spend one year of probation outside the immediate group and another year of testing as probationary members within the settlement.

Philo and Josephus wrote about the Essenes. Two other writers, Pliny the Elder, and Hippolytus, also give us some information. Pliny even locates the Essenes at Qumran, although he does not name the community. However, since they were not mentioned by name in our Bible, we paid little attention to the Essenes. Now, not only their libraries but relics of their community center give us additional information. A number of things which we had thought unique to the Christian religion, or taken over from the Greeks, we now learn were believed or practiced by the Essenes. To some extent they were a bridge between Judaism as we know it and Christianity. Many scholars are convinced that John the Baptist spent some time with the Essenes; a few even argue that Jesus' teachings suggest that he too had some experience with this fellowship.

Josephus tells of the self-appointed poverty and community of goods. They were the congregation of the poor who expected to inherit the earth. They believed that Ps. 37:9 referred to them:

> The wicked shall be cut off;
> but those who wait for the LORD shall
> possess the land.

They had a very definite sense of community, waiting the destruction of the old world by fire. They made much of reading the scriptures, not only the Torah but the sayings of the prophets, and also the Psalms. They believed in angels, and in immortality and the resurrection of the body. They were strict in matters of Sabbath observance.

They had their own gardens and date-palm groves. Some members worked outside the community as masons, carpenters, etc., but all earnings were put into a common treasury. Scriptures and other writings were carefully copied. Probably some income was secured from the sale of scrolls thus made. At noon and in the evening they assembled for a simple common meal. During the meal sermons were preached from a platform at one end of the hall. Luxuries were avoided. Meat was eaten only at certain banquets held in anticipation of a great banquet with the coming Messiah or Messiahs. Cleanliness, avoiding evil, was symbolized by frequent bathing and wearing white clothing.

About two miles south of Khirbet Qumran, a supplementary settlement was established. This is the oasis of 'Ain Feshkha. This seems to have been a center for cultivating vegetables and fruit, and tending flocks. Coins found there indicate a history similar to that of Qumran. It was later occupied by insurgents of the war of A.D. 132–135.

In general, the Essenes refused to take part in war, but kept looking forward to "The War of the Sons of Light against the Sons of Darkness" in connection with which the Messiah would purify Israel and conquer the entire world. The temple priesthood was considered corrupt; the priests were accused of introducing Greek practices into temple worship. Therefore, the Qumran Essenes would not participate in temple services. They had their own priests and may have made their own sacrifices in connection with their occasional sacred banquets. They did send gifts for use in repairing or ornamenting the temple. They preserved documents pertaining to priestly service and expected in time to take over the temple.

Did the Essenes marry? Philo and Pliny say, No. Josephus

says that only one small branch of the Essenes married, and that only for procreation. The major group, Josephus says, "adopt the children of others while they are still pliable and docile." They probably believed that marriage was good, but since they were living so near the end of the present age, time should be spent preparing for the great cataclysmic event. The Christian apostle Paul expresses much the same idea in 1 Cor. 7:8-9. The Qumran settlement has a main cemetery of eleven hundred graves. All bodies seem to be those of men. However, there are two small adjoining cemeteries in which bodies of women and children are found buried. There were several small groups of Essenes living in the general neighborhood of Qumran but not in or adjoining the walled settlement. It is possible that among these was a branch of Essenes who did marry. Probably those who lived among other people in cities and villages married. In their literature are definite references to families after the Sons of Light have defeated the Sons of Darkness.

One of the most exciting and also disappointing discoveries was made in Cave 3. This was two copper scrolls which evidently had been one piece of metal about a foot high and eight feet long. The copper had become completely oxidized, so the scrolls could not be unrolled. Finally they were cut into small strips and the letters deciphered. There were about 3,000 letters punched out in the copper. The text proved to be directions for hidden treasure. One sample reads: "In the cistern which is below the rampart on the east side in a place hollowed out of rock, six hundred bars of silver." Some sixty locations are mentioned as the burial places of two hundred tons of gold and silver. It has been suggested that these are the hiding places of the temple treasury at the time of the revolt of A.D. 66. More likely they are imaginary, possibly a message written in code.

The last forty years of the Qumran community were at the same time as the early Christian development. Both are outgrowths of orthodox Judaism. Naturally they developed certain elements in common. Their vocabulary was similar. Many practices and concepts not found in the Old Testament but found in early Christianity are also found among the Essenes. Symbolic cleansing by water and having a common meal suggest factors in common, but the significance of each of these differed greatly. Men of Qumran were expected to love all the Sons of Light, but to hate the Sons of Darkness. Christians were to love all, even their enemies. Both groups were much interested in the Messiah, but their understanding of the Messiah differed greatly. The Essenes were concerned about themselves and gaining power. Only Jews were admitted to the group. They had no concept of saving the world. There was no thought of taking good news to all mankind.

Doubtless some Essenes saw in Christianity an improvement over orthodox Judaism greater than their own, and became Christians. Very likely they contributed ideas and practices to the early church. Acts 6:7 reports that "a great many priests were obedient to the faith." If these were temple priests, would not the author of Acts have had more to say about them? May not these have been Essene priests? Not all the Essenes lived at Qumran. Others scattered throughout Palestine would have contacts with Christians.

ASSIGNMENT

1. What does Josephus tell about the Essenes? What other information did we have about them previous to 1947?
2. Give the history of the Qumran community.
3. Describe the community center and life at Qumran.
4. At what points did the Essenes differ from the Pharisees?
5. How did the Essenes consider themselves? What were their objectives?
6. Identify the Righteous Teacher; the Wicked Priest.
7. Tell the story of the discovery of the Dead Sea Scrolls.
8. What did the Essenes have in common with the early Christians? What were their major differences?
9. Identify 'Ain Feshkha; the copper scrolls.
10. What contributions to an understanding of Christian origins has the discovery of the Dead Sea literature made?

SUPPLEMENTARY READING

Black—Pages 173-91
Burrows: *Dead Sea*
Burrows: *More Light*
Cross
Fritsch
Gaster
Howe
Howlett
Stendahl
Van der Ploeg

Chapter 18

The Zadokite Document

Two tenth- or twelfth-century copies of parts of the so-called Zadokite Document were found among old books in the genizah or storage room for wornout or otherwise discarded scrolls and books in the attic of a synagogue near Cairo, Egypt, in 1896. A connection with the Essenes was not recognized. The people mentioned in the writing were listed as sons of Zadok—therefore the name given to the material. However, in Cave 4, seven copies of various versions of this writing have been found. Others have been found in Caves 5 and 6. Some of these contain material not in either of the Cairo documents. The Cairo copies were probably based on one or more of the scrolls discovered near Jericho about A.D. 800.

This writing is also called the Damascus Document, and its people the Covenanters of Damascus. In it the group is spoken of as being exiled "in the desert of Damascus." The writer considered this a fulfillment of the prediction of Amos that Yahweh "will take you into exile beyond Damascus" (5:27). The Zadokites were thought to be a group of reformers who withdrew from Judea to Damascus but later returned to the cities of Israel.

Following the Qumran discoveries the question arose: Where were the Essenes after the earthquake of 31 B.C. and their re-establishment of the Qumran community? The answer naturally came: In Damascus. However, in the Zadokite Document we read that they "entered the new covenant in the land of Damascus . . . to seek every one the peace of his brother . . . and to keep away from harlots." This would have been no reason for leaving Qumran, for where else would they have found more peace and fewer harlots? Evidently "Damascus" is a figurative term for the desert in which the Qumran community was established, just as the New Testament apocalypse, the Revelation to John, calls Rome Babylon.

Why should this desert region be called Damascus? The term Damascus never appears in this document alone, other than in the quotation from Amos. Rather the expression is "the land of Damascus" or "the wilderness of Damascus." The Nabatean Arabs captured Damascus in 87 B.C. Nearly all the land east of the Jordan was Nabatean desert. The desert around Qumran was considered not a part of Judea proper. It seemed much more to be a part of the desert called the wilderness of Damascus. Going to Qumran was getting away from the cities of Judea and their harlots in order to find "the peace of his brother." The Essenes may also have been influenced by the statement of Zech. 9:1 that "The work of the LORD will rest upon Damascus." It might be added that fragments of the Zadokite Document have been found which, the handwriting indicates, were written a number of years before the earthquake.

We are still left with the question: Where were the Essenes between the earthquake of 31 B.C. and the re-establishment of the Qumran settlement in 1 B.C. or a bit earlier? The answer seems to be Jerusalem, and possibly other cities of Judea. Since the time of Alexandra, Zadokites of the Pharisees held the high priesthood. Herod the Great was tolerant. With Qumran destroyed, the Essenes felt that perhaps it was the will of God for them to return to the Jewish cities, where life would be less harsh. They could be on hand when the last days came, that they might be judges of the nations. However, their community type of life was much more difficult in the city. Personal purity, which could be maintained in the desert, was almost impossible in the city. It was hard to hold to the standards and practices of Qumran. The desert community life more and more seemed utopian. Herod became less tolerant in his old age. His son Archelaus made life difficult. Before his position had been confirmed at Rome, he had killed 3,000 men in Jerusalem at Pentecost. Some time later the temple was robbed by a Roman officer from Syria. This all seems to have resulted in a second migration to Qumran. It must be recalled that many Essenes never lived at Qumran.

The first part of the Zadokite Document, sometimes called "Admonition," tells of God's saving plan in history and gives exhortations. It tells indefinitely of the migration "from the land of Judah to sojourn in the land of Damascus." Belial, or Satan, was rampant in Israel. Sins of the Jews are catalogued with numerous Biblical references forbidding such deeds.

The second part, "Injunctions of the Law," sometimes simply referred to as "Law," includes high standards that we generally consider Christian: "Love each man his neighbor like himself"; do not "nurse grudges from day to day." On the other hand, on a par with these, are laws "to distinguish between clean and unclean," and also "to keep away from unclean things." One is "to cheat not his own kin." How about other people? Those who disobey the Law "shall hope for healing, but the blemish shall cling to them."

Much of the document is an interpretation of scriptures. Extensive symbolism is found. For example:

> Concerning them has God said: "Their wine shall prove the poison of serpents and the cruel venom of asps" (Deut. 32:33). The "wine" in question is their conduct; the "serpents" are the kings of the nations; and the "venom of asps" is the chief of the Grecian kings who will come to wreak vengeance upon them.

All those who follow the Law of God "shall rejoice and their hearts shall be strong, and they shall prevail over all that dwell in the world."

Community regulations, found in the second part of the writing, give one code for Essenes who live in cities, and another code for those who live in camp communities. City Essenes were allowed to possess property as individuals. This property could include slaves. Sacrifices might be made at the temple.

Parts of the code deal with moral matters, forcing others to take an oath, failing to report knowledge of theft. Rules regarding testimony and judges are given. Ritual laws are specified: "No one is to bathe in dirty water, or in water which is too scant to produce a ripple," Sabbath rules were strict: "No one is to indulge in ribald or empty talk. No one is to claim repayment of debts. . . . No one is to talk about labor or work to be done the next day." "No one is to do any work on Friday from the moment that the sun's disk stands distant from the gate by the length of its own diameter; for this is what Scripture implies when it says explicitly, 'Observe the Sabbath day to keep it holy'." Holy places must not be defiled. Relations with heathen were sharply restricted. Unclean food must not be eaten. If a person desecrates the Sabbath because of a mental condition "he is not to be put to death. In that case, it is the duty of men to keep him under observation. If he recovers, they are to watch him for seven years, and only thereafter may he be re-admitted to public assemblies."

Every camp having ten or more men must have an overseer who is "to enlighten the masses about the works of God. . . . He is to tell them in detail the story of things that happened in the past." "He is to examine every new adherent to his community regarding his conduct, intelligence, strength, valor, and wealth." He must have a priest to interpret the law, especially the law of bodily blemishes. "If the priest be feeble-minded, that official [an overseer] must simply keep him under lock and key at all times." No member is to have any traffic with outsiders "except in spot cash transactions."

Every member is to be registered as priest, levite, layman, or proselyte. "It is in this order that they are to be seated at public sessions, and in this order that their opinions are to be invited on all matters."

"The priest who holds office over the masses is to be from thirty to sixty years old, versed in the Book of Study and in all the regulations of the Torah." The overseer "is to be from thirty to fifty years old, adept in human relations."

"No one is to take oath by EL or by AD"—at this point only the initial letters for the words "God" or "Lord" are given, although this is not observed elsewhere. "Nor is he to make mention in this connection of the Law of Moses, for the name of God is spelled out in that Law." Despite this prohibition of oaths, each member swore upon being accepted into the fellowship to "return to the Law of Moses."

ASSIGNMENT

1. Why is this also called the Damascus Document? Tell the story of the discovery of this writing? When were these copies made?

2. The Zadokite Documents are compilations. What is the nature of each of the parts?

3. What is the evidence that the Zadokite Document was to be used by more than the people of Qumran?

4. In what ways is the moral code similar to that of Christianity? Different?

5. What is the problem raised by the term "Damascus" in the Zadokite Document? What is its solution?

6. Discuss the matter of rank and precedence indicated.

7. Discuss the matter of oaths.

8. What attitude toward marriage is shown in the Zadokite Document? What did Josephus say about this?

SUPPLEMENTARY READING

Burrows: *Dead Sea*—Pages 187-202, 349-64
Burrows: *More Light*—Pages 191-3, 324-6
Charles: *Religious Development*—Pages 234-6
Charles: *The Apocrypha*—Vol. II, Pages 799-834
Gaster—Pages 61-86, 98-105
Pfeiffer, R. H.: *History*—Pages 57-8

Chapter 19

The Manual of Discipline

Among the first Dead Sea Scrolls discovered is The Manual of Discipline or Rule of the Community. It has eleven pages or columns written on five sheets of leather. It is about six feet long and ten inches high. This copy has numerous erasures, corrections, and additions. Evidently at least the beginning of the Manual is missing.

Ten fragmentary copies have been found in Cave 4. These vary to some extent. Evidently the Manual went through a process of revision. It seems to be an older set of regulations than the Zadokite Document. It is a composite work. Some consider one part the first draft of a Qumran constitution. The manual begins with rules for the ceremony of initiation and an annual re-commitment.

Those who join the community are to bring it "all their knowledge and strength and wealth." This property was to be turned over to the council. All their sins must be confessed, and Belial, the evil one, cursed. Imprecations are expressed for anyone who enters the organization with the taint of idolatry in his heart. "God will cut him off from the midst of all the Sons of Light when he turns away from following God." One must "commit himself by a binding oath to abide with all his heart and soul by the commandments of the Law of Moses, as that Law is revealed to the Sons of Zadok." The vows were to be renewed "year by year so long as Belial continues to hold sway." Every member pledges to love all Sons of Light and hate all Sons of Darkness. Each must rigidly observe the special calendar of the community.

"God created man to rule the world and appointed for him two spirits . . . spirits of truth and perversity. The origin of truth lies in the Fountain of Light, and that of perversity in the Wellspring of Darkness." "There is an Angel of Darkness;

all men's afflictions and all their moments of tribulation are
due to this being's malevolent sway. . . . Howbeit, the God
of Israel and the Angel of His truth are always there to help
the Sons of Light." "Between the two categories, He has set
an eternal enmity." At the "time of visitation" God will destroy
perversity.

Members are instructed "to abide by the decision of the
Sons of Zadok, the same being priests that still keep the Covenant. . . . It is by vote of such that all matters doctrinal, economic, and judicial are to be determined." Members "are to
keep apart from the company of the froward," and "unite in
a bond indissoluble forever."

"No one is to go into water to attain the purity of holy men.
For men cannot be purified except they repent their evil." "No
man is to bring a charge publicly against his neighbor except
he prove it by witnesses."

As in the Zadokite Document, rank is emphasized. "Everyone is to obey his superior in rank." "When they sit . . . they
are to take their places according to their respective ranks."
"No one is to speak in advance of his prescribed rank." Each
member receives his rank "according to his knowledge and his
deeds." Individuals are re-examined each year and may be
promoted or demoted.

"Together they shall eat and together they shall pray; together
they shall counsel." No one is to eat or drink until the priest
has invoked a blessing. "The general members of the community are to keep awake for a third of all the nights of the
year reading the Book, studying the Law, and worshipping
together."

When a candidate "comes to present himself to the general
membership, everyone is to be asked for his opinion about him."
Admission "is to be determined by general vote." He is to
"bring with him all his property and all the tools of his pro-
fession." "Not until the completion of a second year among the
members of the community is the candidate to be admitted to
the common board." At this time he is to be subjected to a
further review by the general assembly "who may reject him."
If a man "lies on the matter of his wealth," his food ration is
to be reduced one-fourth. Reduction of food ration was the
penalty for a number of offenses. Anyone who "goes to sleep
at a public meeting" is to have his rations reduced for thirty
days. If a man "spit into the midst of a public session" or

"indulges in raucous, inane laughter" he will meet the same punishment.

One rule specifies that the man who harbors "a grudge against his neighbor without legitimate cause" is to have his rations reduced for six months. Someone has inserted in the manuscript above this the words "one year." If a man "slanders the entire group" or "complains against the basis of the community" "he is to be expelled, never to return." If a man "betray the truth and walk in the stubbornness of his own heart" but repents, his rations are to be cut for two years. The first year he must eat alone; the second year he may eat in the same room, but "occupy a place behind all the other members."

The section sometimes called the constitution for the Essenes specifies "In the formal congregation of the community there shall be twelve laymen and three priests schooled to perfection in all that has been revealed of the entire Law. Their duty shall be to set the standards." After two years of preparation, these men will "go into the wilderness to prepare the way" as directed in Isa. 40:3. If one of these fifteen men "transgresses in a single word of the Law of Moses . . . he is to be excommunicated, never to return." "The priests alone are to have authority in all judicial and economic matters, and it is by their vote that the ranks of the various members of the community are to be determined." These men are to be in charge "until the coming of the Prophet and the Messiahs of Aaron and Israel." This indicates an expectation of a priestly Messiah and a military Messiah, the Prince of Israel.

All members are to have no contact with men of bad reputation. They must "bear unremitting hatred toward all men of ill repute." They are "not to lust after anything that God has not commanded."

The Manual of Discipline ends with a psalm of praise in which the entire Qumran calendar is outlined with the insistence that on every occasion the individual will praise God.

Another writing, which apparently had become detached from the copy of the Manual of Discipline first found, has been called "The Rule of the Congregation." The Manual of Discipline probably applied purely to the Qumran community; the Rule of the Congregation, to all Essenes. The latter mentions marriage, women and children, while the former implies a celibate life.

"This is the order for the whole congregation of Israel at the end of days." For ten years youths must be taught the Book of Hagi. We know nothing of this book save that it is mentioned in the Zadokite Document that leaders and priests shall be instructed in it. At twenty a young man may become a member of the congregation; he is ready for marriage and the responsibilities of adulthood. Age requirements for various positions are given. Positions are appointed by lot, but "No simpleton shall enter the lot to take a place over the congregation." "Anyone afflicted in his flesh . . . shall not enter to take a place in the midst of the congregation of men of renown."

Reference is made to a great feast at which all will be gathered. "Let not any put forth his hand on the first of the bread or the wine before the priest," who seems to be the Levitical Messiah. After the priest, "next the Messiah of Israel shall put forth his hand on the bread." This would seem to be the great banquet to be observed after the coming of the two Messiahs, but the last sentence of the Rule of the Congregation reads, "According to this statute they shall do for every meal when there are met as many as ten men." This suggests that these are rules to be obeyed in connection with each meal, although this would require that the Messiah be impersonated or symbolized.

Evidently in the same scroll containing the Manual of Discipline and the Rule of the Congregation was a group of benedictions. We do not know how they were to be used. The introductory statement says that they are "words of blessing for the wise man, that he may bless those who fear God, . . . who walk perfectly in all the ways of his truth."

ASSIGNMENT

1. Where and when was the Manual of Discipline first found?
2. What does the Manual of Discipline reveal about admission into the Essene organization?
3. What two spirits did the Essenes believe God appointed?
4. What type of organization did the Essenes have?
5. How were members who failed to observe all the rules punished?
6. What were the rules for social relations?
7. What was considered misconduct?
8. What was the Essene Messianic expectation?
9. With what does the Rule of the Congregation deal?

SUPPLEMENTARY READING

Chapter 20

Qumran Copies
of the Scriptures

Approximately two-thirds of the Qumran scrolls found are portions of the Hebrew scriptures. These were held in great respect. In general, they were much more carefully copied than were the other writings.

The twentieth century bedouin shepherds were not the fiirst men to discover Dead Sea scrolls. Doubtless scrolls were preserved in jars in many places and times, but only in the Dead Sea region is Palestine dry enough to preserve scrolls many centuries. The prophet Jeremiah instructed his secretary Baruch concerning certain deeds, "Put them in an earthenware vessel that they may last for a long time" (Jer. 33:14).

In the Pseudepigraphic "Assumption of Moses," directions are given to "preserve the books which I shall deliver unto thee [evidently the Pentateuch]; and thou shalt set them in order and anoint them with oil of cedar and put them away in earthen vessels in the place which He made from the beginning of the creation of the world" (1:17). Was this a cave? Was this instruction written by one of the Qumran group?

Writing a little after A.D. 200, Origen tells of an edition of the Psalms "which was found together with other Hebrew and Greek books in a jar near Jericho."

Writing about A.D. 800, Timotheus I, Patriarch of Selucia, says that "some books were found ten years ago in a rock dwelling near Jericho." He says that an Arab hunter followed his dog into a cave. There he "found a chamber in which there were many books." These, he explains, were "books of the Old Testament and others in the Hebrew script." He says they contained statements quoted in the New Testament from the Old Testament but missing from copies owned at that time by either

Jews or Christians. Probably among the non-Biblical writings found at this time was the Zadokite Document, copies of which were later discovered in Cairo.

A few years later a Jewish writer, Zirqisani, refers to a group he calls the Cave Sect "because their books were found in a cave." He says the sect had its own calendar and some of its books dealt with exegesis and discussion of the Bible. This sect was apparently our Qumran friends. There is extensive indication that these writings influenced a Jewish sect which arose in the eighth century and still exists, the Qaraites.

In the Pseudepigraphic Letter of Aristeas, we have some description of a Hebrew copy of the Torah, "valuable parchments [or skins], in which the law was inscribed in gold in Jewish characters, for the parchment was wonderfully prepared and the connection between the pages [or sheets] had been so effected as to be invisible." Each page of the scroll was ruled horizontally with faint parallel lines (176). The tops of the letters touched these lines, rather than the bottom of the letters.

Practically all the Dead Sea scrolls were partly disintegrated when found. Most of them are only a handful of scraps. Assembling these is the tedious task of working the world's most complicated jigsaw puzzle. These are puzzles of which many parts are lost; those remaining, have become mixed up with parts of other puzzles. Much work remains to be done.

Among the scrolls and fragments so far identified are at least parts of every Old Testament book except Esther. We also have a number of the Apocrypha, and some of the Pseudepigrapha. A dozen or more copies of some Old Testament books have been identified. The books most commonly found are Deuteronomy, Isaiah, and the Psalms. Perhaps the greatest single contribution to Biblical scholarship is the fact that at many places where our Septuagint differs from the Hebrew text from which our English Bibles have been translated, the Masoretic text of about A.D. 900, the wording of the Dead Sea scrolls is in closer agreement with the Septuagint than it is with the Masoretic copies. Evidently the Septuagint translators were more accurate than we had thought, while those making copies of the scriptures in Hebrew made variations of their own.

It is also to be noted that one Qumran scroll often differs from another. For example, Jeremiah appears in two forms, one very similar to the Septuagint, the other to the Masoretic text. Evidently no standardization of scripture had been developed when the Dead Sea scrolls were made. Some readings are in accord with the ancient Samaritan copy of the Pentateuch proudly exhibited by the Samaritans today in Nablus, Jordan.

Some parts of the scrolls found—for example, a portion of 1 Samuel—are in a script which indicates writing earlier than the Essenes. These were probably older master scrolls from which the Essenes made their copies. The 1 Samuel portion was written some time between 400 and 200 B.C.

Evidently the men of Qumran considered the first two sections of our Old Testament, the Law and the Prophets, as divinely inspired. This probably does not apply to the third section, the Writings. The absence of Esther suggests this, as does the rather careless way in which Daniel was copied, although Daniel seems to have been a favorite book—at least seven copies have been found. None of the stories of Daniel given in the Apocrypha has been identified at Qumran. However, fragments of other Daniel stories have been found. One is the prayer of Nabonidus in which he tells how Daniel helped him. Another has Daniel recounting Biblical history from the Flood to Hasmonean times and predicting what will happen in the future.

The first twentieth century Qumran discoveries contain what is probably the most complete manuscript of the more than five hundred so far identified. This is the Isaiah manuscript known as 1 Q Isᵃ. It is 17 leaves sewn to each other with linen thread. It is divided into 54 pages or columns, containing all 66 chapters of Isaiah. The sheets vary in length from 10 to 25 inches. The total length of the scroll is approximately 24 feet. It is about 10 inches high or wide. The scroll had been extensively used before it was buried. Tears in it had been carefully repaired.

The scribe made numerous mistakes but discovered and corrected most of them himself. However, several omitted passages were inserted by a later scribe whose handwriting differed considerably. Chapter divisions are about as we already knew them. Chapters and paragraphs are indicated by leaving a space or complete line.

The Qumran Isaiah spelling is much more phonetic than classical Hebrew and helps scholars understand something of Hebrew pronunciation at the time it was copied. Grammatical forms and endings often differ from the text we have been using. A careful examination of 1 Q Isᵃ indicates it was copied by eye. The second and much less complete Isaiah text found in Cave 1 and known as 1 Q Is^b evidently was copied by ear —some one read an earlier copy aloud to the scribe, probably to a group of scribes.

The 1 Q Is^a has numerous places where a word or phrase used in the Masoretic text is missing. At other places words are added to the text with which scholars have been familiar. The translators of the Revised Standard Version of the Bible published in 1952 felt that in general the Masoretic text is superior to those newly discovered. However, they adopted thirteen readings from 1 Q Is^a.

Isa. 21:8 now reads "He who saw cried, 'Upon a watchtower I stand.'" The Masoretic text had interchanged two consonants, giving the word for lion. This did not make sense. The King James translation made it read, "He cried, A lion. My Lord, I stand continually upon a watchtower." The American Standard Version reads, "He cried as a lion."

Based upon the Masoretic text, both King James and American Standard Versions read Isa. 14:4, "How hath the oppressor ceased! the golden city ceased!" The "golden city" did not seem to fit here. In its place the Greek Septuagint, the Latin Vulgate, and the Syriac could be read, "the insolent frenzy." This is the term found in the Qumran Isaiah. Therefore, it has been adopted in the Revised Standard Version.

Further study of the Isaiah scrolls and those of other Old Testament books will be reflected in forthcoming translations of the Hebrew scriptures.

ASSIGNMENT

1. Describe the Dead Sea scroll discoveries previous to the twentieth century.
2. Describe the Hebrew formation of scrolls.
3. Identify: Masoretic text; Samaritan Pentateuch.
4. What suggests that the men of Qumran did not consider the third section of the Old Testament to be divinely inspired?
5. Describe 1 Q Is^a. Why is this title given?
6. Explain one change made in the Revised Standard Version Bible due to the Qumran Isaiah.

SUPPLEMENTARY READING

Bruce—Chapter VI
Yadin—Chapters 9 and 10

Commentaries
on the Scriptures

Cave 1 included an excellent sampling of Essene literature—two copies of Isaiah, the Manual of Discipline, the Thanksgiving Hymns, the War Scroll, the Genesis Apocryphon (see Chapter 31), and the Commentary on the Book of Habakkuk. The latter is a small scroll, not more than eight inches high and five feet long. The bottom of the scroll has disintegrated. This causes a part of each column to be missing.

The book of Habakkuk was written about 600 B.C. The Babylonians, using large numbers of Chaldean soldiers, had conquered Nineveh, the capital of Assyria. People of Judah were happy that their great enemy had been defeated. However, Habakkuk realized that a power strong enough to defeat Assyria would have no trouble destroying Judah. He complained to Yahweh about this and raised the question, Why does God allow good people to suffer? Then there came to him the assurance that God was using the Chaldeans to punish the people of Judah for their sins; that God and righteousness will eventually win.

The Essenes found references throughout the Old Testament which they adapted to apply to their own situation. Philo, who at this point found them kindred spirits, wrote that the Essenes "philosophize on most things by constructing them symbolically." The Dead Sea caves have revealed several examples of Essene interpretation of scriptures. The most extensive is the Commentary on Habakkuk. Here the purpose of the original author seems to have been discounted. Habakkuk is considered a prediction of the Essenes. In withdrawing from "the world" to Qumran, the Essenes probably believed that they were following the thought expressed in Hab. 2:1, "I will take my stand to watch, and station myself on the tower, and look forth to see what he will say to me." We do not have the commentary on this verse.

The first column of the commentary is missing. What we have begins by quoting a phrase from the fourth verse of the first chapter of Habakkuk, "The law is slacked," and sees in this a reference to the Jews who seem to reject the Torah. On the second clause of this verse, "For the wicked surround the righteous," the author sees a reference to the Essene "Righteous Teacher" who is tormented by the Wicked Priest.

When Habakkuk quotes Yahweh as saying, "I am doing a great work in your days that you would not believe if told," the Essene writer sees a reference to the man of the lie who did not heed the Righteous Teacher, "the priest into whose heart God put wisdom."

When Habakkuk has Yahweh continue, "I am rousing the Chaldeans," the Essene sees reference to the Kitteans. Identifying the Kitteans, or Kittim, is not easy. The term is used several times in the Old Testament in reference to various people of the Mediterranean. Although a few scholars feel that the Habakkuk commentator refers to the Syrian Greeks, the majority are sure that the reference is to the Romans. The Kitteans threaten soon to conquer all nations. Jerusalem is especially threatened. The commentator finds references to the Kitteans in each of the verses of Hab. 1:6-11, as well as in later statements.

Habakkuk's question as to why Yahweh did not interfere "when the wicked swallows up the man more righteous than he" is immediately seen to refer to those who did not help the Righteous Teacher "against the man of the lie." When Habakkuk comments that men are treated with no more respect than fish, and mentions that sailors sacrifice to their nets, the commentator sees an analogy to soldiers of the Kitteans (Romans) sacrificing to their standards.

When Habakkuk felt that Yahweh ordered him to write an explanation of why he permitted the Chaldeans to rise, the Essene interpreter sees a reference to "the last generation," which to him means the Essenes. The well-known phrase, "so that he may run who reads it," "means the Righteous Teacher to whom God has made known all the mysteries." Of course, the often quoted statement, "The righteous shall live by his faith," is taken to refer to the Essenes. The statement, "Wealth is treacherous," "means the Wicked Priest, who . . . forsook God and betrayed the statutes because of wealth." The question, "Will they not suddenly arise, those who torment you," "means the last priests of Jerusalem, who assembled wealth and booty from the sport of the peoples," but "it will be delivered into the hands of the army of the Kitteans."

"Woe to him who builds a town in blood and founds a city in iniquity!" is said to refer to "the preacher of the lie." Is this the Wicked Priest, or some associate of his? After finding several other references to the Wicked Priest, the commentator explains "the violence done to Lebanon" as meaning "to the council of the community," perhaps because "Lebanon" means white and the Essene council wore white clothing.

The Righteous Teacher, an extremely important man akin to the Hebrew prophets, is the hero of the commentator, but he never definitely explains who this teacher is. He is referred to in the Zadokite Document, and apparently in the fragmentary commentary on Psalm 37. He may be the author of the Essene psalms found in the Qumran region. He probably was the founder of the Essene sect, the man who dared to denounce the high priest to the people. He was considered especially gifted in unlocking the scriptures for his people.

The Wicked Priest is also never definitely named. He is referred to in the Psalm 37 commentary as well as in the Habakkuk commentary, and would seem to be the high priest of the Jerusalem temple. The conflict between the Righteous Teacher and the Wicked Priest is considered the eternal conflict between good and evil, light and darkness.

The prophecy of Habakkuk has appended to it a psalm as a third chapter. For many years scholars have felt that this was not a part of the original writing. This tends to be confirmed by the fact that it is not used in the Essene commentary. Comment on this third chapter has not been torn off the scroll, as there is considerable unused space at the end. However, Essene commentaries do not generally deal with entire books of the Bible. The third chapter of Habakkuk could have already been considered a part of the book of Habakkuk before the Qumran commentary was written.

Other Essene commentaries on Old Testament writings are fragmentary. Parts of a commentary on Psalm 37 give comments on fifteen verses, which differ at a number of places from the Masoretic text. Here again it was believed that the original writing looked forward to a conflict between a Wicked Priest and a priest "who expounds the Law correctly," the Righteous Teacher. We had not been told elsewhere definitely that the Righteous Teacher was a priest. This conflict would result in building a congregation "resting on a firm foundation," the poor who will inherit the earth. The sect is called "Those who Return to the Law," and "The Community of His Elected Ones." It is they who adhere to the "Appointed" calendar.

Commentary on four verses of the first chapter of the prophecy of Micah maintains that Micah foresaw that Jerusalem priests would lead God's people astray, but once more God's glory will move to Jerusalem. Part of the interpretation is made by playing upon Hebrew words that sound somewhat alike.

Several fragments of a commentary of the prophecy of Nahum have been found. That which has been published deals with three verses of the second chapter of Nahum. The commentator thought that Nahum had foreseen an event of 88 B.C. told about by Josephus. Some Jews joined the Syrian king Demetrius III in an attack upon Alexander Janneus. Janneus was defeated, but received re-enforcements and Demetrius withdrew. Janneus crucified eight hundred Jews and cut the throats of their wives and children. The commentator says that "Seekers after Smooth Things" invited Demetrius to Jerusalem. Who these were, and the identity of the "Lion of Wrath" who "hangs men up alive", are problems yet to be solved. There is considerable evidence to suggest that the "Lion of Wrath" and the "Wicked Priest" are the same person, that these terms refer to Alexander Janneus.

One fragment is commentary on Gen. 49:10, which is taken to foretell the Essene community and its expectation of a Messiah of righteousness. Another fragment contains 2 Sam. 7:11-14, which is made to refer to "the interpreter of the law in the latter days." Amos 9:11 is quoted as further evidence.

A number of scroll fragments contain commentary upon parts of the tenth and eleventh chapters of Isaiah. The commentator believed that Isaiah had expected a great war with the Kitteans. A son of David will arise; "over all the nations shall he rule, and Magog"—but the next words are missing leaving us uncertain as to what was said about Magog.

Another non-Biblical Qumran writing is the Oration of Moses. This parchment had deteriorated into forty-nine fragments. Numerous words have been lost. It is a paraphrase of Moses' farewell address given in Deuteronomy, in which some passages from Leviticus are incorporated. The sabbatical year of rest for fields and release of debts is prescribed. The Oration includes a non-Biblical legend about the calendar date of the Day of Atonement. This Oration is possibly the Testament of Moses mentioned in some lists of pseudepigraphic books.

ASSIGNMENT

1. On what Old Testament books have Essene commentaries been found?
2. What was Philo's comment on the Essenes' use of the Hebrew scriptures?
3. What was the theme of the original Habakkuk? At what points did the Essenes twist the original meaning to serve their own purposes? What does the commentary reveal about the beliefs of the Essenes? Comment on Habakkuk 3.
4. Who were the Kitteans?
5. How does Josephus help us set the earliest possible date for the writing of the Nahum commentary?
6. What is the general theme of other Essene commentaries on Old Testament writings?

SUPPLEMENTARY READING

Burrows: *Dead Sea*—Chapters VI-X, and Pages 365-70
Burrows: *More Light*—Pages 400-4
Gaster—Pages 229-71
Sloan: *Old Testament*—Pages 267-70
Van der Ploeg—Pages 165-70
Yadin—Chapters 11 and 12

Chapter 22

The Essene Hymnal

NOTE. —Read the Thanksgiving Psalms.

Every religion has its poetry, its songs. We are not surprised to find poems or psalms here and there in the Qumran writings. In connection with the scrolls discovered in the general Qumran region about A.D. 800, Timotheus was told that more than two hundred psalms of David had been found. This collection probably contained numerous Essene psalms.

In the first twentieth-century discovery, one of the major writings was The Thanksgiving Hymns. When this collection came into the hands of scholars, it was composed of three folded sheets and seventy fragments, stiff and thickly stuck together. These fragments ran from a few letters to twenty lines. Some parts were so darkened and decayed that they could be read only with the aid of infra-red photography. A few fragments of similar psalms have been found in Cave 4.

This Thanksgiving "scroll" was the work of two scribes. The first had beautiful handwriting and did his work carefully. The scribe who copied the latter part of the Thanksgiving Hymns wrote carelessly. The fragments must have been the first part of the book, as they are in the better handwriting. The original scroll was about a foot high and probably ten feet long.

Words and lines are missing from the best part of the scroll. It is impossible to know how many psalms were in the original collection. Scholars feel that they have thirty-two definite individual hymns.

The writing is a patchwork of phrases from the Biblical psalms and prophets, but the mood and theological structure are much different. The theme of predestination frequently appears. Josephus noted that the Essenes held that fate governs all things.

The psalms are individualistic. Many of them begin, "I give

116

thanks unto Thee, O Lord." The author is grateful for deliverance of himself and members of his sect from their enemies. There is no mention of delivering Israel from Egypt or the Canaanites. He is grateful that God has delivered his soul from all works of unrighteousness, that God has watched over his soul, that he has been delivered from the pit, from the slough of hell. He thanks God for having been his strong wall, that he has not forsaken him although the writer dwells among an alien people, in the congregation of the false. He is grateful that God has braced him for all the battles that Wickedness wages against him. He expresses thanks for having been given insight into God's truth and knowledge of his wondrous secrets, as well as ability to tell forth God's wonders day and night. He is glad that God has not let him rely upon worldly wealth.

God, the creator of the world and of men, is pictured less anthropomorphically than in the Old Testament. He is completely sovereign and just, foreseeing all the deeds of men. Some men have been predestined from birth for good, others for evil. Although man is frail, sunk in sin, God by his grace saves some, the Elect who have the spirit of truth. For all others there is no hope, regardless of their righteous acts.

The author seems to belive that no one outside his group is among the Elect. They are the only ones who have true knowledge of God. As elsewhere in the Qumran writings, the conviction is expressed that the battle between the good and the evil is about to take place. After this, the Elect will have fellowship with angels and heavenly spirits.

The Thanksgiving Hymns describe the Qumran associates as poor and simple-minded, but "perfect in the way" sons of God's good pleasure, sons of truth and of grace. As a council of the holy ones, they have a convenant of grace.

Were the Thanksgiving Hymns all written by one man? The similarity of the separate psalms suggests this. Who was the author? No name is given. Many scholars argue that he was the Righteous Teacher himself, the founder of the sect. This term does not appear in the Hymns. One would not expect the author to give himself such a title. The autobiographical items in the hymns correspond closely to things written about the Righteous Teacher elsewhere. He calls himself a spiritual leader, a teacher, an interpreter of knowledge to the community. He feels that he has a divine gift of illumination, has received a divine revelation of secrets. He says that he has been persecuted by enemies, preachers of the lie who have forced him into exile. God has rescued him from suffering and sorrow. The author pictures himself as a humble, religious man, delighting to praise God continually.

The last two columns of the Manual of Discipline are a different type of hymn, probably one to be used by those who were being initiated into the brotherhood. The initiate promises to render to God "the blessing of my lips" at all times of day and every season, at mealtime, upon going to bed and rising, in time of fear and distress, and in time of deliverance. He promises to pursue all men with good, not to engage in strife. He will abstain from coarseness and deceit, and will teach others sound doctrine. Knowledge and light come from God; the rock beneath his feet is the truth of God. Sound wisdom and prudent discretion are given to God's chosen. Everything that is, is ordained by God. The hymn concludes by thanksgiving to God for bringing the singer from the dust to knowledge and righteousness.

ASSIGNMENT

1. Describe the Qumran scroll of Thanksgiving Hymns.
2. What theme runs through these hymns?
3. How is God described in these hymns?
4. Who were the Elect? How are the Qumran associates described?
5. What suggests that these hymns were written by the Righteous Teacher?
6. What is the theme of the last two columns of the Manual of Discipline?

SUPPLEMENTARY READING

Burrows: *Dead Sea*—Pages 384-9, 400-15
Gaster—Pages 116-225
Mansoor
Yadin—Chapter 13

Chapter 23

Essene Eschatology

NOTE.—Read the War of the Sons of Light with the Sons of Darkness.

Essene eschatology, its doctrine of last things, was definitely apocalyptic. Believing that they had been selected to "prepare the way of the Lord," the men of Qumran were sure that a great cataclysmic event was about to occur in which they would be the heroes.

Despite their interest in Daniel and perhaps other apocalypses, these people do not seem to have written any books of this nature. Probably they felt no need for such secrecy.

The Essenes are sometimes spoken of as pacifists. The group refused to soil its holiness in secular violence. There was only one war that counted. To what extent they took part in the war against Rome is unknown. They may have thought of this as the opening stage of the great Holy War they expected. They probably defended Qumran. Josephus mentions a John the Essene appointed a general in northwest Judea.

Plans for the Holy War are best described in the Cave 1 scroll called "The War of the Sons of Light with the Sons of Darkness." This is sometimes referred to simply as "The War Scroll." The bottom portion—about a third—of each column of writing is missing. The latter columns are also damaged elsewhere and the end is missing. What we have is thirteen feet long. We probably have but half the original manuscript. Some fragments of other copies of this writing have been found in other caves. This is probably one of the last Qumran scrolls written. No mention is made of the Righteous Teacher or the Wicked Priest.

The War Scroll begins by declaring that the Sons of Light, descendants of Levi, Judah, and Benjamin, must aggressively

attack the Sons of Darkness, the army of Belial, the bands of
the Kitteans, and others. This event will take place very soon,
for the Sons of Light are suffering greatly. The author interpreted Dan. 12:1 as indicating that this is the time.

A war between Egypt and Syria will put an end to Syrian
control and leave the Sons of Light in charge of Jerusalem and
the temple. The Sons of Light "will return from the wilderness
of the people to encamp in the wilderness of Jerusalem." After
this control has been secured, preparations must be made for a
forty-year war against the world. A different nation will be
attacked each year for six years but on the seventh or sabbatical
year no war is to be waged. The campaign will then be renewed.
After forty years the Sons of Darkness will be permanently
destroyed.

The army of the LORD will be divided into a number of bat-
talions. Each will have numerous banners and mottoes, such as
"The hidden powers of God are able to destroy wickedness."
This reflects Num. 2:2. The name of every soldier is recorded
on a banner. Banners are as much as twenty feet long.

The way the troops are to be used and the tactics of battle are
described. These seem to have been copied from the Romans.
The existence of a manual of Roman military organization appears to have been taken for granted. During the years of actual
fighting, soldiers will be drafted annually "out of all the tribes of
Israel." Camp formations described follow closely the organization plan reported in the book of Leviticus to have been given
Moses in the desert. The law of the camp recorded in Num.
5:1-4 is kept.

The line-up for battle is given. "The line troops are from
forty to fifty years of age." "The line is to consist of a thousand
men. Each front line is to be seven deep. . . . All of them are
to hold shields of polished bronze, resembling mirrors." The
equipment of each soldier is described. The weapons will be
decorated with gold, silver, and precious stones. They include
swords, spears, shields, slings, and bows. The order of hurling
spears is specified. "The seven battle lines shall be flanked in
turn on the left and on the right by cavalry." The horsemen and
their horses, and their equipment, are described in detail. An
attack force is to be composed of 13,000 men; at another place
the figure is 28,000. Elaborate descriptions of varied formations and attacks are given.

Age limits of various groups are listed. No man with blem-

ishes is to participate, "for holy angels march with their hosts."
Provision is made for service groups; "those that spoil the slain,"
"those who collect the booty," burial groups, "those who guard
the arms," "those who prepare the provisions."

Priests are to play a prominent part in the war as the instruments of God. Elaborately dressed priests will direct the
fighting by means of trumpets "until the enemy are discomfited
and turn tail." The use of trumpets has been greatly elaborated
from the tenth chapter of Numbers. A large number of prayers
and addresses to be given by priests before and during battles,
and thanksgiving hymns of victory, are included in the scroll.

Details regarding sacrifices at the temple during the sabbatical
year are given. With the Essenes in charge of the temple, there
will be twenty-six courses of priests instead of the usual twenty-
four. This was to fit the sect's 364-day calendar of fifty-two
weeks.

The war will bring much suffering, "times of tribulation for
the people redeemed of God." The Sons of Light will win three
battles and lose three; "on the seventh occasion the great hand
of God shall finally subdue the army of Belial. Streaks of lightning will flash from one end of the world to the other." In the
morning it will be found that the enemy are all slain—"for they
have fallen there by the sword of God."

ASSIGNMENT

1. For what great event were the Essenes preparing? How long
   was it to take place?
2. In what ways did the Essenes seem to be copying Roman military organization? Moses' camp?
3. What part were the priests to play in the war?

SUPPLEMENTARY READING

Burrows: *Dead Sea*—Pages 390-9
Gaster—Pages 275-306, 315-21
Sutcliffe—Pages 83-9, 204-23
Yadin—Chapter 15

Chapter 24

Tobit and Son

NOTE.—Read Tobit in the Apocrypha.

The Qumran caves have produced parts of one Hebrew and two Aramaic editions of Tobit, one of the books of the Apoccrypha. This little book, apparently, was originally written in Greek between 190 and 170 B.C. However, there are scholars who argue for a Hebrew or Aramaic origin. The last two chapters were probably added later. The book became so popular that translations were also made into Latin, Syriac, and Ethiopic. Martin Luther described it as, "A truly beautiful, wholesome, and profitable fiction, the work of a gifted poet . . . a book useful and good for us Christians to read."

Tobit, an Israelite taken captive to Nineveh in the eighth century, was extremely careful in observing the rules of the Torah. An accident in connection with his pious acts cost him his sight. During a more prosperous time he had left ten talents of silver in trust in Media. He sent his son, Tobias, to secure the silver. The father employed a guide who, it developed, was the angel Raphael in disguise. On his way to Media, Raphael told Tobias of Sarah, whose seven husbands had each been killed by a demon "before he had been with her as his wife." Raphael instructed Tobias how to drive away the demon. Tobias insisted upon marrying Sarah. After a two-weeks wedding feast, Tobias, his bride, and Raphael returned to Tobit with the ten talents and half of the estate of Sarah's parents. There were further rejoicings, admonitions, and prayers. Tobit's sight was restored and he died happy at the age of 158. The names Tobit and Tobias are derived from a Hebrew root meaning the goodness of Yahweh.

In this short story, showing the influence of earlier Oriental religious ideas and writers, we find a vivid portrayal of Jewish thought of the intertestamental period. While purely imaginary, the tale gives a picture of Jewish piety and family life of the period in which it was written. Strict observance of the Law was expected. Those who not only gave first-fruits and tithes but were generous in their use of time and money for the unfortunate were assured of God's protection and reward. Although no reference to a future life is made, careful and respectful burial of the dead is highly commended.

Other legal observances reflected in this moving bit of fiction include marrying within the family, eating only kosher food, washing before eating, and purifying after touching a corpse. The personal religion and ethics pictured in this story are superior to what we find in the Old Testament. Honesty, justice, sobriety, and purity are stressed. A negative form of the Golden Rule is given: "What you hate, do not do to any one." (4:15). The way was being prepared for the teachings of Jesus.

Prayers of gratitude were expected to be addressed to God, the great, everlasting king of heaven, the holy one. God is merciful and, like a father, will restore his people who have been led into captivity. Even eventually Gentiles of "many nations will come from afar . . . bearing gifts . . . for the King of Heaven" (13:11).

Tobit was written in the Diaspora. Some scholars have suggested Antioch, the Selucid Syrian capital, where eventually followers of Jesus of Nazareth were first called Christians (Acts 11:26). However, the cordial attitude toward non-Jews suggests that the book was written in Egypt. From the time of the building of Alexandria, Egyptian Jews were more friendly with Greeks than were those of Palestine. Two stories well-known in Egypt were familiar to the author. One is "The Tractate of Khons," which tells how an Egyptian god enabled a demon to be cast out of a princess. The second is "The Story of Ahikar." Not only is Tobit's popular nephew called Ahikar, but several expressions in the book of Tobit are similar to those found in "Ahikar." The author seems to take for granted that the reader will be familiar with the story of Ahikar. The use of the organs of a fish to cure blindness and to drive away an evil spirit resembles Egyptian medicine.

Numerous Biblical references appear in Tobit, especially parallels to terms found in the Torah and ideas found in Kings.

The author was not familiar with the geography of Mesopotamia, the setting of the story. He has Tobias and his associate come to the Tigris River on their way from Nineveh to Media farther east; Nineveh was on the eastern bank of the Tigris. His knowledge of historical events in Mesopotamia was equally blurred.

A Persian influence also appears in the story. Although the Hebrew people picked up the Zoroastrian ideas of angels and demons from the Persian religion during Babylonian captivity, the concept was not emphasized by the Jews until about 200 B.C. The Old Testament has very little about this, except in the book of Daniel, written just previous to Tobit.

The picture of the angel Raphael's assuming human form and becoming a visible guide and protector of Tobit's son Tobias sounds Persian. The Persians taught that every good man is accompanied by an angel on his walk through life. The idea of a guardian angel came to be held by at least some of the Jews. This is indicated in Acts 12:15.

Asmodeus, a demon, killed each of Sarah's seven husbands on their bridal nights. Tobias finally drove him to the extreme of southern Egypt by a smoke made by burning the heart and liver of a fish with incense. This demon is the Persian evil spirit, Aeshma Daeva, one of the six archfiends serving Angra Mainyu, or Satan.

It is strange to find a friendly dog in a Jewish writing. No such dog appears any place in the Bible. Dogs were considered scavengers and unclean. However, in the Zoroastrian religion dogs were sacred.

The emphasis of the book of Tobit was probably held by the Hasideans; it was definitely later approved by the Pharisees. It is that those who observe the "three pillars of Judaism," discussed by Jesus in Matthew 6:1-18—prayer, almsgiving, and fasting—will in the long run be amply rewarded by God. Fasting does not receive much attention, although Raphael commended it to Tobit and Tobias (12:8).

In the first chapter, Tobit brags that he not only refrained from worshiping foreign gods and eating Gentile food, sins of which his friends in the tribe of Naphtali in Galilee were guilty, but that he took three-tenths of his income to the temple at Jerusalem; much of this he gave to charity. Tobit and Tobias agreed to give half the financial profit of Tobias' journey to Azarias, who they still did not know was the angel Raphael. Raphael proclaimed to them, "Almsgiving delivers from death, and it will purge away every sin" (12:9). Tobit claimed that in his youth, "I would give my bread to the hungry and my clothing to the naked" (1:17). As he took his last breath, he exclaimed, "My children, consider what almsgiving accomplishes and how righteousness delivers" (14:11). Emphasis upon giving decent burial to the unfortunate was a part of Tobit's habit of charity. This was more kindly than it would be on our part, for to the pious Jew corpses were unclean. To touch one necessitated expensive and lengthy ceremonial purifying.

Prayer had a prominent part in the life of the characters of this story. Tobit instructed his son, "Bless the Lord God on every occasion; ask him that all your paths and plans may prosper" (4:19). Raphael instructed Tobias to pray with his bride Sarah (6:17). Prayers of Tobit (3:2-6 and 13:1-18), Sarah (3:11-15), Tobias (8:5-7), and Tobias' father-in-law Raguel (8:15-17) all indicate care and sincerity. These are doubtless typical of Jewish prayers of the period in which the book was written.

What influence did the book of Tobit have on the New Testament? At least there are some parallels between the two writings. Some have suggested that Tobit's pious burying of the bodies of victims of anti-Hebrew feeling could have influenced Joseph of Arimathea to bury the body of Jesus. The story certain Sadducees told Jesus about the woman who, in accordance with the levirate, had had seven husbands but no children (Mt. 12:18-23) bears some resemblance to Sarah and her seven husbands. In Tobit's final prayer he pictures a new Jerusalem, "her walls with precious stones, and her towers . . . with pure gold" (13:16). This rather common expectation is again expressed in the Apocalypse to John.

ASSIGNMENT

1. Summarize the story of Tobit and his son.
2. For what purpose does the book of Tobit seem to have been written?
3. What legal observances are mentioned in Tobit? What were the "three pillars of Judaism"?
4. Identify: Tobias, Sarah, Azarias, Raphael, Asmodeus.
5. What is the relation of the book to Egypt? What Zoroastrian influence is noted?
6. What values do we find in this book today?
7. What was Martin Luther's evaluation of the book?

SUPPLEMENTARY READING

Dentan—Pages 50-5
Goodspeed—Chapter II
Metzger—Chapter III
Pfeiffer, R. H.: *History*—Pages 258-64
Torrey—Pages 82-8
Zimmerman

Chapter 25

Judith and Other Tales

NOTE.—Read Judith in the Apocrypha.

Shortly after the writing of Tobit, another Jewish propaganda novel appeared. Judith, written about 150 B.C., tells its readers that those who obey the laws emphasized by the Pharisees will have God's protection in the most difficult times. These laws were legalistic and ritualistic rather than ethical. Cunning, deceit, violence, were approved as long as they furthered Jewish nationalism and religion.

The author was careless about history. He says that his story took place when Nebuchadnezzar "ruled over the Assyrians in Nineveh." Actually, Nebuchadnezzar ruled Babylonia rather than Assyria. Nineveh was destroyed seven years before Nebuchadnezzar became king. He never made war with Media. Other historical names are used to give weight to the story. The Jews "had only recently returned from the captivity . . . and the altar and the temple had been consecrated" (4:3). These events took place shortly before 400 B.C., generations after the time of Nebuchadnezzar. The Jewish state is pictured as ruled by a high priest and senate, or Sanhedrin. This was not true until centuries later.

The author was attempting to make history rather than record it. The Jews were afraid of losing to the Syrians what independence they had. The latter were determined to destroy the Jewish religion. As the book of Daniel had been written to encourage Jews to fight Syria, so Judith was written to encourage them to keep up the good fight. As Daniel and his friends won out by obeying Israelite laws of worship and diet, so Judith was concerned with these and the laws of tithing and washings.

The book of Judith also has elements in common with another Jewish story written a couple of decades later, Esther. Each book has a beautiful heroine willing to risk her life for her people. Both express strong hatred for Gentiles, resulting in cruel vengeance. The theme of each might be said to be, Love your neighbor and hate your enemy. However, Judith expresses a strong orthodox Jewish religious outlook; this is missing in the book of Esther. The name Judith means Jewess.

The first seven chapters of Judith are background for the appearance of the heroine. Nebuchadnezzar, called king of Assyria, asked help from the western nations in a war with Media. Despite the refusal of the west, he defeated the Medes. He then sent his general Holofernes to punish the west. All the nations quickly submitted except Israel. An Ammonite leader told Holofernes that the Israelites could not be defeated as long as God protected them. The Assyrians encamped before the imaginary city of Bethulia and cut off its water supply. After thirty-four days, the people of Bethulia were convinced that "God has sold us into their hands" (7:25) and insisted upon surrendering. However, Uzziah, the ruler of the city, persuaded them to wait five more days for God to come to their rescue.

When Judith, the beautiful rich young widow, heard of this, she reprimanded the rulers, saying that God has saved his people in the past, and through her would do so again. After a lengthy prayer, Judith "arrayed herself in her gayest apparel . . . and made herself very beautiful to entice the eyes of all men who might see her" (10:3-4). Taking kosher food and drink with her she went to the camp of Holofernes and told the general that the Jews were so hungry that they planned to kill and eat the animals set apart for sacrifices. "On that very day they will be handed over to you to be destroyed" (11:15). She promised to tell Holofernes when her people thus lost God's protection.

For three days Judith remained in the enemy camp, carefully obeying Jewish rules of eating, bathing, and praying. The general then invited her to a banquet where he "drank a great quantity of wine." When she was left in the tent alone with the drunken general, Judith cut off his head with his sword. She put the head into her food bag and returned to Bethulia. With great rejoicing the Israelites defeated the disorganized Assyrians. "And no one ever again spread terror among the people of Israel in the days of Judith, or for a long time after her death" (16:25).

Kindness and honesty are lacking in the book. Judith was

clever with "double talk." She told Holofernes, "God has sent me to accomplish with you things that will astonish the whole world" (11:16). However, she accurately bragged to her own people, "It was my face that tricked him to his destruction and yet he committed no act of sin with me" (13:16). Courage and devotion to a cause are depicted. The use of prayer and fasting is emphasized. Like Esther, the book became popular among the Jews. Numerous translations were made. However, unlike Esther, it was not given a place among the Holy Writings, although from an esthetic and literary viewpoint it was the better book. Perhaps Esther achieved recognition because of its relation to the feast of Purim. Oddly, Josephus does not mention Judith. Like the book of Esther, it is not referred to in the New Testament.

Another book, written about 25 B.C. when the civic state of Egyptian Jews was being jeopardized by Rome, is 3 Maccabees. The Alexandrian Jew who composed it reflects the attitude of the Hasideans with their devotion to the Law. It combines into a historical romance two events of Jewish history. One occurred in 212 B.C. when Ptolemy IV (Philopator), after the battle of Raphia, attempted to enter the temple, but was persuaded not to do so by what seemed to the Jews to be a miracle.

The second event was the persecution of the Jews in Alexandria by Ptolemy VII (Physcon) about which Josephus tells. However, the author of 3 Maccabees attributes this to Philopator as revenge for the failure to enter the temple.

The king first interfered with the religion of the Jews in Egypt and altered their political status. He ran into much trouble in taking a census of the Jews, evidently as a basis for a poll tax. Jews doubtless thought that a census was contrary to the will of God as indicated in 1 Chron. 21:1-7. A Roman census in A.D. 6 gave rise to, or possibly brought about a revival of the Zealots in Palestine. Ptolemy was unable to find sufficient writing material with which to record names. He then decided to put the Jews to death, and had them gathered in the hippodrome in Alexandria. Orders for their massacre were miraculously delayed. Finally, a horde of drunken elephants was turned on them to trample them to death, but angels appeared to the elephants. This caused them to turn around and trample the persecutors of the Jews.

Ptolemy released the Jews, gave them a feast which lasted a week, wrote a testimony to their loyalty, and gave them permission to kill "more than three hundred" Jews who had deserted their religion to save their lives. As Esther came to be read in connection with the feast of Purim and other rolls at each of the general Jewish festivals, so 3 Maccabees may have been written to be read at a festival celebrated only by the Jews in Egypt.

After the conquest of Egypt, Rome came to consider the Jews as second-class citizens. We have a record of a census of the Jews in 26 B.C. as a basis for taxation. Third Maccabees seems to have been written just before this. Its immediate purpose may have been to point out God's providence and the eventual doom of race prejudice. It repeatedly emphasizes the Jews' loyalty to established government. It teaches the importance of Jews remaining true to their religion. The author expected the Jews eventually to return from the Diaspora.

Third Maccabees appears in some copies of the Septuagint, including the Alexandrian codex, but was not put into the Vulgate.

The Alexandrian codex, as well as the one found on Mount Sinai, contains the "Fourth Book of Maccabees," also called "On the Sovereignty of Reason." Written A.D. 20–54, in Alexandria or possibly Antioch, it is a discourse or sermon discussing "whether religious reason is sovereign over the emotions" (1:1). The author, influenced by Stoic philosophy, illustrates his argument by telling in extended detail the story of the martyrdom of Eleazar found in 2 Macc. 6:18-21, and of the seven brothers reported in the seventh chapter of 2 Maccabees. Fourth Maccabees connects the two incidents and reports that the mother of the seven brothers committed suicide "that no one might touch her body" (17:1). Eleazar and the seven brothers sound like Greek philosophers. The author emphasizes that the blood of the martyrs dissolves the power of tyranny.

In his collection of Pseudepigrapha, Charles includes three "Sacred Legends"—The Letter of Aristeas, The Book of Adam and Eve, and The Martyrdom of Isaiah.

The Letter of Aristeas, or "Aristeas to Philocrates," is a story of the making of the Septuagint version of the Torah. It claims to have been written by an eyewitness during the reign of Ptolemy II (Philadelphos) and his queen Arsinoe. The latter was queen between 278 and 270 B.C. However, the letter was written considerably later, which the author carelessly admits. For example: when telling of entertaining court guests at the time of Philadelphos, the author adds, "It is an arrangement which is still maintained today" (paragraph 182). The Letter has a number of historical anachronisms. It probably was written between 150 B.C. and 100 B.C., but possibly not until the following century, by an Alexandrian Jew who pretended to be a Greek in order to increase the Jewish people's self-respect and their pride in the Septuagint.

The Letter tells of Ptolemy's emancipating Jewish slaves upon the urging of the "author," and then writing to Eleazar, the high priest in Jerusalem, asking him to send seventy-two scholars who might translate the Jewish Law very exactly into Greek. The author accompanied the letter and extensive royal gifts to the high priest. He then describes the temple, Jerusalem, and Palestine in general in lavish terms.

Eleazar's carefully selected translators were received in Alexandria with unusual cordiality. At a series of seven royal banquets, the king asked questions of each of the seventy-two translators. Their answers were highly praised by Greek philosophers who found much in common between the Jewish thinking and Greek philosophy. After seventy-two days of collaboration, the translation was read to the Jewish community. It was considered so well done that a curse was pronounced upon anyone who altered it.

When the translation was read to the king, "he marvelled exceedingly at the intellect of the lawgiver" (paragraph 312). He then raised the question as to why Greek writers had not earlier incorporated parts of the Torah in their works. It was explained that some had attempted to do so, but had met misfortune at the hands of God for showing insufficient respect or for using incorrect translations.

In his "Antiquities" Josephus gives a close paraphrase of most of "Aristeas." His objective seems to have been to commend the Jews to the pagan world.

Philo tells much the same story in abbreviated form. Instead of the translators cooperating and comparing their work each day, Philo says that each worked independently, but, being inspired by God, made identical translations. Philo also adds that each year large numbers of Jews and non-Jews have a feast on the island of Pharos (where all authors say the translation was made). At this they unite in thanking God for the Septuagint.

Some scholars feel that the Letter of Aristeas had an influence upon the author of the Gospel According to Luke. Both books seem to be addressed to fictitious individuals. A number of writing techniques and emphases are held in common. A parallel is noted between the sending of seventy-two translators by the high priest and Luke's story (10:1-20) of Jesus' sending out seventy (many early copies say seventy-two) representatives. In each case, Jews are sent out to interpret their religion.

The Books of Adam and Eve are a confused collection of writings about Adam and Eve taken as literal individuals. The first of these books, upon which the others are based, is the Apocalypse of Moses, written by a member of the Jewish Dispersion apparently in the first century of the Christian Era. The Latin Life of Adam and Eve and a Slavonic Life of Adam and Eve contain parts of earlier Greek writing, but add large sections. Various early translations into several languages add and subtract with abandon, giving various Christian interpretations and predicting the birth of Christ.

The opening sentence of the Apocalypse of Moses reads, "This is the story of Adam and Eve after they had gone out of Paradise." After mentioning the birth of Cain and Abel, Abel's murder, and the birth of Seth, the story hurries on to the deathbed scene of Adam, who has his sixty-three sons gathered about him. Seth has not known about pain and death and cannot understand it. He and Eve return to the gate of Paradise to beg God for oil from the Tree of Life with which to anoint Adam, but they are told that Adam will soon die. Adam accuses Eve of bringing sin and pain to the world and causing his death. Upon his demand, Eve tells of her sin and their being driven out of Paradise. Adam dies but, in answer to the prayer of angels, is pardoned. God visits the earth, and the body of Adam is buried near the earthly Paradise, as is also that of Abel. Eve dies and her body is buried near those of Adam and Abel.

The Latin account says that after they were expelled from Paradise, Adam suggests that as penance he stand many days up to his neck in the water of the Jordan, and Eve in the Tigris. After eighteen days, Satan appears to Eve as an angel of light and persuades her to leave the water. When Satan comes to him, Adam recognizes his old enemy. Satan explains that when Adam was created he was ordered to bow down to Adam as the image of God. His refusal to do this brought about his downfall from the heavens. Adam continues to stand in the Jordan forty days.

The Martyrdom of Isaiah, written by a Jew in the first century A.D., probably in Hebrew, has come down to us only as a part of a trilogy, the Ascension of Isaiah. The other two parts, the Vision of Isaiah, and the Testament of Hezekiah, are both early Christian writings.

As he was about to die, Hezekiah, king of Judah, called his son, Manasseh, to him for instructions. The prophet Isaiah told Hezekiah that this was futile, that Manasseh would become a follower of Beliar, and that he would have Isaiah himself sawed in two. As soon as he came to the throne, Manasseh caused his nation to sin. Isaiah fled to the mountains beyond Bethlehem, where he was discovered by a false prophet. Isaiah was accused of having said that Jerusalem would be destroyed, that he had seen God (contrary to the statement of Moses in Ex. 33:20), and that Jerusalem and the princes of Judah were like Sodom and Gomorrah. As a result, Manasseh had Isaiah cut in two with a wood saw.

ASSIGNMENT

1. What historical inaccuracies are found in the book of Judith?
2. With what do the first seven chapters deal?
3. Identify: Holofernes, Bethulia, Uzziah.
4. Tell the story of the heroine, the beautiful Judith.
5. What was the purpose of the book of Judith?
6. What ideas of the intertestamental period are reflected in this book?
7. What is the story of 3 Maccabees?
8. What is the purpose and story of 4 Maccabees?
9. What "Sacred Legends" does Charles include in the Pseudepigrapha? Tell each of the stories.
10. Identify: two Eleazars, Hezekiah, Manasseh.

SUPPLEMENTARY READING

Charles: *Apocrypha*—Vol. 1—Pages 155-73; Vol. II—Pages 83-162, 653-85
Dentan—Pages 56-61
Goodspeed—Chapter VI
Hadas: *Aristeas*
Hadas: *Third and Fourth*
Pfeiffer, R. H.: *History*—Pages 285-303
Torrey—Pages 80-2, 88-93

Chapter 26

Additions to Esther and Daniel

NOTE.—Read: Additions to Esther; The Prayer of Azariah and the Song of the Three Young Men; Susanna; Bel and the Dragon.

During the reign of John Hyrcanus, twenty or twenty-five years after the writing of Judith, another propaganda story appeared. This was the book of Esther. Peace had been made with the Syrians; Idumea south of Judah had been captured. Why not reach out and include more territory? Esther was written to glorify militant Judaism. Nationalism rather than religion was foremost in the mind of the writer. Therefore, he wrote a book in which religion does not appear. Neither God nor prayer is mentioned, in contrast to the religious element running through Tobit and Judith. Non-religious Jews would not resent the book.

The setting of the story is one of the Persian capitals, Sousa, from which Nehemiah had gone to rebuild the walls of Jerusalem. Although the Jewish girl Esther had won a beauty contest and become queen, there was a strong anti-Jewish movement, which resulted in an order that all Jews be killed. Esther risked her life in an appeal to the king. As a result, Jews were given permission to kill any who attacked them. The Jews killed many thousands of their enemies. To save themselves, numerous Persians became Jews.

The Council of Jamnia in A.D. 90 questioned whether such a non-religious book should be considered as belonging to the canon. The books of the Apocrypha were vetoed. One argument against them was that they were not in the sacred Hebrew language. This argument tended to save the book of Esther, which was in Hebrew.

Long before the Council of Jamnia, possibly as early as 100 B.C., Jews in Egypt attempted to assure the book of Esther a place in the canon by adding pious sections to it. An introduction and conclusion were written, as well as three other parts inserted in the book. Thus the Septuagint edition of Esther gives a religious tone similar to that expressed in Judith. However, the Council of Jamnia rejected these additions along with other Septuagint material not found in the Hebrew Bible. When Jerome made his Latin Vulgate translation, he added the Greek concluding section and then appended the four other sections. When chapter and verse divisions were later given to the Bible, these additions were listed as Chapters 10:4-16:24. Unless one puts these parts back where the Septuagint editors intended them to be, he finds the reading awkward and with little sense.

The most obvious factor in making the new Esther a devoutly religious document is the frequent inclusion of references to God. In the five verses 10:9-13, the term God, Lord, or the personal pronoun referring to God occur thirteen times. In his letter the king refers to the Jews as "sons of the Most High, the most mighty living God" (16:16). Long, conventional prayers are attributed to both Esther and Mordecai. Despite the plotting of Esther and her uncle to make her queen, Esther is made to protest over and over that she abhorred everything connected with her being queen—"Thy servant has had no joy since the day that I was brought here until now" (14:18). God is pictured as having changed the king's attitude from anger to kindness when Esther appeared before him uninvited (15:8).

The author of the additions to Esther was careless about details. In 11:2 he says that the plot against the king was made in the second year of his reign, whereas Esther 2:16-21 puts it in the seventh year. Other very minor discrepancies appear. In the addition, Mordecai was immediately rewarded for informing the king about the plot. In the canonical Esther, Mordecai was rewarded much later.

To date, no part of Esther has been found among the Qumran or Dead Sea scrolls. This would suggest that the Essenes did not consider Esther as canonical. Possibly the fact that some Jews took this attitude toward the book of Esther was an added reason for the friends of the book in Alexandria to secure for it more religious respectability by making various pious additions.

The book of Daniel was also expanded by those who developed the Septuagint. The book did not need to be given a religious atmosphere, although there is indication that the Essenes did not treat this book with the respect they showed other Biblical writings. The additions which appeared in the Greek translation may simply have been legends which had gathered about the name of the hero of the Old Testament apocalypse, or they may have been added because they had teaching values for the Alexandrian situation.

In many copies of the Greek Bible, the story of Susanna appears as an introduction to Daniel. It may be that this was placed first because the Daniel of this story is a young man. The Vulgate puts Susanna after the universally accepted Daniel material as Chapter 13. Susanna was probably composed in Alexandria in Greek. It contains two puns on the Greek language which could not have been in an earlier Hebrew or Aramaic edition, but, of course, could have been inserted by a translator.

Like all the Daniel material, the setting of the story is in the Babylonian captivity. Susanna, the beautiful pious young wife of a wealthy Jew, innocently aroused the lustful passions of two elderly Jews. When she refused their advances, they testified publicly that they had found her in the embraces of a young stranger. The word of the elders was accepted and Susanna was condemned to die. As she was being led to execution, the young man Daniel dramatically interrupted and secured permission to question the witnesses. He quickly proved they had both given false testimony. God was praised, "And from that day onward Daniel had a great reputation among the people" (verse 64).

The third chapter of Daniel tells the story of three of Daniel's friends who were thrown into a fiery furnace because they refused to prostrate themselves before a great golden image set up by King Nebuchadnezzar. Their Babylonian names are Shadrach, Meshach, and Abednego. The latter is also known by his Hebrew name, Azariah.

Between the twenty-third and twenty-fourth verses of this chapter, the Septuagint inserts a section called The Prayer of Azariah and the Song of the Three Young Men. In Azariah's prayer nothing is said about the heat and flame. God is praised, the sins of the Hebrew people are confessed, and national deliverance is sought. Although the King's servants threw in more fuel, "and the flames streamed out above the furnace forty-nine cubits (seven times seven), the angel of the Lord came down into the furnace . . . and drove the fiery flame out of the furnace, and made the midst of the furnace like a moist whistling wind" (24-27). Then the three young men joined in a song much like Psalms 136 and 148 with the refrain given thirty-two times, "Sing praise to him and highly exalt him for ever." Everything is called to bless the Lord; sun and moon, rain and dew, mountains and hills, whales and birds, the sons of men and Israel. Their own situation is mentioned only in the concluding verses, when they call upon themselves to praise the Lord, for he has "delivered us from the midst of the burning fiery furnace."

Two other stories, Bel and the Dragon, are added as the 14th chapter of Daniel. These are two related detective stories in which Daniel is the hero. Heathen priesthood and idols are ridiculed, somewhat as had been done by Second Isaiah (Isa. 44:9-20).

Bel was Marduk, who became the patron deity of Babylon about 2250 B.C. One of the seven wonders of the world was the temple of Bel. Elaborate offerings were brought to the temple. Herodotus says it was destroyed by Xerxes I in 479 B.C. The unknown author of the Septuagint story gives the credit to Daniel who proved to the Persian King Cyrus that the food and drink offered to the idol each day were secretly consumed by the priests and their families.

The story of the dragon was also written to make fun of the Greek idol worship found on every hand by the Jews. The setting is similar to that of the story of Bel, but we know of no record of Babylonians worshiping dragons or serpents. Although Daniel killed the dragon which he refused to worship, pressure was put on the King to have Daniel thrown to the lions. As in the better-known lion story, Daniel was not harmed, his enemies were put in his place, "and they were devoured immediately." Possibly the author had method in the order of these two stories—Daniel destroyed an inanimate idol, then a living "god."

Another writing of the Daniel cycle has been found in the Qumran Cave 4, a prayer reputed to be that of Nabonidus, father of Belshazzar. Nabonidus was still the legal ruler of Babylonia when the nation was captured by Cyrus of Persia. In the prayer, Nabonidus refers to having been given a "dread disease by the decree of the Most High God." As a consequence, he was "set apart from men" in Arabia for seven years. A Jewish diviner, probably Daniel, is said to have intervened. This may be a more primitive form of the tale given in the canonical Daniel in which Nebuchadnezzar was driven from men for seven years; during this time he learned that the "Most High rules the Kingdom of men."

ASSIGNMENT

1. What is the story of Esther? Why were "The Additions to the Book of Esther" made? Of what are the "additions" chiefly composed? How must the "additions" be read in order to be understood?

2. Recount the story of Susanna. Why is it called one of the best short stories in world literature? What purpose seems to lie behind the story?

3. Who was Azariah? Who were the Three Young Men? What does the canonical book of Daniel tell about them? What is the theme of the prayer? Of the song?

4. Tell the detective stories of Bel and the Dragon. For what purpose were they written? What is the probable reason for their inclusion in the Apocrypha?

5. What light do the Qumran discoveries throw on the Essene attitude toward the books of Daniel and Esther?

6. What is the Prayer of Nabonidus?

SUPPLEMENTARY READING

Dentan—Pages 36-43, 47-9
Goodspeed—Chapters IV, VIII-X
Metzger—Chapters V, X-XII
Pfeiffer, R. H.: *History*—Pages 304-12, 433-56
Torrey—Pages 54-9

Chapter 27

Supplement to Other Old Testament Books

NOTE.—Read: Baruch; The Letter of Jeremiah; The Prayer of Manasseh; 1 Esdras.

The author of the Apocryphal book, Baruch, associated it with the prophecy of Jeremiah, but much less closely than the Daniel stories or the additions to Esther are related to the canonical books. The only book that resembles sermons of Old Testament prophets, it is purported to have been written by Jeremiah's secretary, Baruch, during the Babylonian captivity. Many church fathers considered it a part of the prophecy of Jeremiah. It is really two distinct writings.

The first (1:1-3:8), written in prose, is a confession of sins to be read publicly in "the house of the Lord." With this confession is a prayer for God's mercy. Certain expressions are evidently copied from Daniel. Other parts are a mosaic of phrases from Leviticus, Deuteronomy, Isaiah, and Jeremiah. However, the term Lord for God is frequently used. By the intertestamental period, this term had, in general, been dropped as too sacred. Evidently, this section is an early writing.

The second section of Baruch uses a later terminology for God. It could have been written any time between 100 B.C. and A.D. 100, probably about 75 B.C. The first part of this section is a commendation of wisdom, somewhat similar to that found in the book of Proverbs. In answer to the question as to why the Israelites were suffering captivity, the author says, "You have forsaken the fountains of wisdom" (3:12). Again he says, "All who hold her fast will live" (4:1). This is followed by a lament over the downfall of Jerusalem, somewhat like that found in the companion writing, the Lamentations of Jeremiah. However, there is comfort and encouragement: "He who brought these calamities upon you will bring you everlasting joy with your salvation" (4:29); "Arise, O Jerusalem . . . and see your children . . . for they went forth from you on foot . . . but God will bring them back to you, carried in glory" (5:5-6). The pretense that the book was written by Baruch during Babylonian captivity was to encourage Jewish readers without offending government officials at the time the book was written. According to the book of Jeremiah, Baruch was not taken to Babylonia, but to Egypt. Was the author not acquainted with Jeremiah, or did he expect his readers not to be?

The King James and later translations of the Apocrypha have printed, as the sixth chapter of Baruch, the Letter of Jeremiah. The Revised Standard Version gives this a separate book name, but retains the chapter and verse numbers. The twenty-ninth chapter of Jeremiah is a letter sent to the people of Judah who had been taken to Babylonia as captives. This "Letter" in the Apocrypha pretends to be much the same thing, but in reality it is a sermon written to attack idol worship in the Greek world of the intertestamental period. Jeremiah had made a similar attack (10:1-16): "They stand like scarecrows in a garden of cucumbers, and cannot speak" (10:5). Second Isaiah had done much the same (Isa. 44:9-20).

Like Bel and the Dragon, this writing makes fun of idol worship, stating eleven times, "This shows that they are no gods." These "gods" of wood or metal cannot keep cats or birds or bats from resting on them, or worms from eating them and their robes. They cannot keep themselves from being plundered by robbers or robbed even by priests. They cannot punish those who break vows made to them or restore sight to the blind. "Better therefore is a just man who has no idols, for he will be far from reproach" (verse 73).

The Prayer of Manasseh, not found in the canonical books of the Vulgate, has been put several different places in the Bible. It is most often included in a collection of hymns for public worship, placed as an appendix to the Psalms. Oddly, it seems never to have been placed where one might expect it to be, in connection with 2 Chron. 33:12, where it is reported that when, contrary to the better-known story in 2 Kings, the evil, idolatrous King Manasseh "was in distress, he entreated the favor of the Lord his God." The author of 2 Chronicles goes on to say that Manasseh's prayer may be found in both the Chronicles of the Kings of Israel—would the prayer of a king of Judah be found here?—and the Chronicles of the Seers. These records, if they ever actually existed, had long before disappeared; but some pious Jew of the intertestamental period reconstructed the prayer in a dignified form, to which the adjective "beautiful" might be applied. He probably felt it would be useful for others who had repented and were eager to turn back to God and were willing to say, "Now I bend the knee of my heart" (verse 11); "I have sinned, and I know my transgressions" (verse 12). It was for the use of those who sincerely wished to plead, "Do not be angry with me forever or lay up evil for me" (verse 12), and honestly proclaim, "I will praise thee continually all the days of my life" (verse 15). The request in verse 13, "do not condemn me to the depths of the earth," indicates that the "Prayer" was written after the idea of Hell had been accepted. This is definitely after the time of Manasseh.

When the Apocrypha are printed as a separate collection the book that appears first is 1 Esdras. Much of it is a retelling of material found in 2 Chron, 35 and 36, the book of Ezra, and part of Nehemiah 7 and 8. It has references from material of the reign of Josiah, King of Judah about 621 B.C., to Ezra's reading of the Torah upon the completion of Nehemiah's wall 444 B.C. The author differs considerably from the canonical accounts and does not seem to be bothered by internal inconsistencies. Artaxerxes is referred to as ruling between Cyrus and Darius—he was a later ruler. The account tells of three groups of Jews returning to Jerusalem at different times. Each is said to have taken back the vessels which Nebuchadnezzar had plundered from Solomon's temple.

The book is a "torso"; that is there evidently was other material at each end. It begins by telling about Josiah's extensive celebration of the Passover, without telling who Josiah was or why he sacrificed so many thousand animals. The book ends abruptly in the middle of a sentence. Probably the original manuscript or a later copy had both ends destroyed. First Esdras may not have been a rewriting of canonical material; the two accounts may be different versions of an earlier record.

The chief contribution of 1 Esdras is the Tale of the Three Guardsmen (chapters 3 and 4). In it each of these, young men of the bodyguard of the Persian King Darius, proclaims what he thinks is the strongest. The first argues for the strength of wine.

The second maintains that the king is strongest. We have the name of only the third guard Zerubbabel. He says that above these, women are stronger—" 'Many men have lost their minds because of women and have become slaves because of them.' " " 'But truth is great, and stronger than all things.' " "He ceased speaking: then all the people shouted, and said, 'Great is truth, and strongest of all!' "

This appears to be a Greek tale adapted to explain why Zerubbabel was sent to Jerusalem to build a new temple. It was to sing his praises.

First Esdras evidently was written by an Alexandrian Jew about 150 B.C. The Greek is smoother and more idiomatic than the Septuagint translation of Ezra and Nehemiah. In the Latin Bible, Ezra and Nehemiah are called 1 and 2 Esdras, and our Esdras 3 Esdras. The book we have been discussing is also at times called "Greek Ezra."

ASSIGNMENT

1. Identify the original Baruch. What is the historical inaccuracy in the book of Baruch? Distinguish between the two parts of the book.

2. What is the Letter of Jeremiah? How does the Revised Standard Version differ from earlier versions in the treatment of this book? What is the purpose of the book?

3. With what does the Prayer of Manasseh deal? What indicates that it was written after the time of Manasseh?

4. First Esdras is the retelling of what canonical material? What is the major contribution of the book?

SUPPLEMENTARY READING

Dentan—Pages 43-7, 90-2
Goodspeed—Chapters V, VII, XIV, XV
Metzger—Chapters VIII, IX, XII
Pfeiffer, R. H.: *History*—Pages 233-57, 409-32, 457-60
Torrey—Pages 43-54, 59-69

Chapter 28

Wisdom Literature

NOTE.—Read parts of Ecclesiasticus and the Wisdom of Solomon.

Wisdom literature, a type of writing common to Hebrew and other Middle East people, is represented in the canonical Old Testament by Job, Ecclesiastes, and Proverbs, and in the Apocrypha by Ecclesiasticus and the Wisdom of Solomon. Other sentences and verses here and there in the Old Testament (such as Hosea 8:7; Amos 6:12; Ezek. 18:2; and certain Psalms) belong to this category, as do some of the writings of the Pseudepigrapha and also certain Egyptian and Babylonian works.

The authors of this type of literature are generally classed as wise men, differing from other religious leaders, priests, prophets, and apocalyptists. The priest was concerned with keeping people in the right groove religiously, seeing that the ritual was properly performed. The prophet was interested in reform, progress, a better nation. The apocalyptist had the future of the individual as well as religion in mind. The wise man, or sage, made the pursuit of wisdom the chief aim of life. Proverbs composed by those who sought to be known as wise men and by others who indicated an interest in such pursuit were collected from time to time. Since King Solomon included among his achievements a reputation for wisdom—"I have given you a wise and discerning mind (1 Kings 3:12)—it was natural that extensive wisdom material was attributed to him, such as Proverbs, Ecclesiastes, and the Wisdom of Solomon.

The wise men never proclaimed, "Thus says the LORD"; they avoided pious terms. However, they were seriously religious men. Their emphases were not upon formal religion and nationalism, as was dominant among pre-exilic Hebrews. They were concerned with ethics, morality, righteousness, an abundant life. To them, these were the desires of God. Wisdom transcended nationalism. We find evidences that the Israelites were familiar with the wisdom of Babylon, Egypt, Syria, Edom, and Arabia. The book of Job reflects Edomite thinking; it may have been first composed by an Edomite. Egyptian wisdom influenced parts of the book of Proverbs.

The wisdom literature is the nearest the Hebrews came to philosophy until the Alexandrian school attempted to amalgamate Hebrew theology and Greek philosophy. The various writers would not have agreed among themselves as to just what wisdom is. Some thought of it as skill, proficiency, or craftiness. It was the ability to distinguish what is useful from what is harmful. It was not pure knowledge, although they were closely related. Prov. 15:33 proclaims that "The fear of the LORD is the instruction of wisdom," while 1:7 says that "The fear of the LORD is the beginning of knowledge; but fools despise wisdom and instruction." Wisdom is often personified, referred to as "she." At times it appears to be a part of God, even helping in the creation of the earth. A fairly close parallel can be drawn between the use of the term "Wisdom" and the later use of the term "Word," or Logos.

One of the wisdom books of the Apocrypha, Ecclesiasticus, attempts to explain the true nature of wisdom. It is the only book in the Apocrypha that gives the name of its author. In fact, it might be said to have two authors. The original is a Hebrew book written about 180 B.C. by Jesus, the son of Sirach. Jesus is Greek for the Hebrew name Joshua. This Jesus evidently was a scribe who had carefully studied the Hebrew scriptures, especially Proverbs and the Torah. He seems to have conducted an academy in Jerusalem, lecturing on ethical and religious subjects. He had had a wide experience—"I have seen many things in my travels" (34:11). He probably had his own example in mind when he said that one who studies the law of the Most High "will serve among great men and appear before rulers" (39:4).

About fifty years later, the grandson of Jesus, having migrated to Egypt, became convinced that Jews and Greeks there could profit from his grandfather's wisdom. Therefore, he translated the book into Greek. This was later divided into fifty-one chapters. In his prologue he acknowledges the difficulty of accurately translating thought from one language to another: "Despite our diligent labor in translating, we may seem to have rendered some phrases imperfectly." He goes on to say that the Law, the Prophets, and the Writings suffered also in translation. We may feel that it was unfortunate that the Jews in Palestine did not make more of the original book, for, if they had, the council of Jamnia would certainly have included it in the canon.

The Greek translation, as well as subsequent translations into other languages, is quite properly called The Wisdom of Jesus the Son of Sirach (or Sira). It is more commonly called Ecclesiasticus, but how it got this name is unknown. Perhaps it is because it was used by the early church more than any other book of the Apocrypha. *Ecclesia* is the Greek word meaning "called out" and generally translated "church."

The major part of the book is quite similar to Proverbs. Some of the pithy sayings of Proverbs are expanded into pleasant essays. It deals in a haphazard manner with many phases of everyday life: the delights of a banquet and how one should behave at table; the miser and the spendthrift; right and wrong use of speech and the value of silence; health and physicians; wealth and poverty; hypocrites and parasites; self-esteem; stubbornness and humility. The author does not hesitate to discuss men's relationship to God, divine mercy and justice, God's reward of the righteous and punishment of the wicked.

Delight in the works of the Lord is expressed (42:15-43:33); gratitude for the mercy and kindness of God is overflowing (51:1-12). In a prayer of appreciation (36:1-17), it is acknowledged that "there is no God but thee, O LORD," and the petition is expressed: "Have mercy, O LORD, upon the people called by thy name; upon Israel, whom thou hast likened to a first-born son."

We wonder what kind of family life Ben Sirach had when we read: "I would rather dwell with a lion and a dragon than dwell with an evil wife" (25:16); "Do not be ensnared by a woman's beauty, and do not desire a woman for her possessions" (25: 21); "Drooping hands and weak knees are caused by the wife who does not make her husband happy" (25:23); "A daughter keeps her father secretly wakeful, and worry over her robs him of sleep" (42:9).

The author wrote in behalf of physicians who, he believed, had the support of God: "Honor the physician with the honor due him" (38:1); "The Lord created medicines from the earth, and a sensible man will not despise them" (38:4). His section, "Let us now praise famous men" (chapters 44-50), doubtless influenced the writer of the eleventh chapter of Hebrews. In it Hebrew history is recapitulated.

Despite his conviction of the value of leisure for thought and his own experience with travel and culture, Ben Sirach felt that the greatest values were simple: "Better is the life of a poor man under the shelter of his roof than sumptuous food in another man's house" (29:22); "Better off is a poor man who is well and strong in constitution that a rich man who is afflicted in body" (30:14); those who labor with their hands "keep stable the fabric of the world" (38:34). As in Tobit, written about the same time, giving alms is highly commended: "Almsgiving atones for sin" (3:30).

Somewhat later, possibly as early as 100 B.C., but more probably about A.D. 40, another Jew who had a knowledge of philosophy, writing in Greek, produced what he called the Wisdom of Solomon. This is often considered the "Pearl of the Apocrypha." It is more Greek in form and thought than any other book of the intertestamental period. Possibly we have two authors, for the material of the first nine chapters (or perhaps through 11:4) is of a quality much superior to the remainder of the book. In respect for its pseudepigraphic character, we may refer to the book as Wisdom and to its author as Pseudo-Solomon. In it wisdom is identified with the spirit of God. "She knows and understands all things, and she will guide me wisely in my actions" (9:11). "She is a breath of the power of God, and a pure emanation of the glory of the Almighty" (7:25).

Some Alexandrian Jews were deserting the religion of their ancestors. Recognizing the ruler as a god was being required: "At the command of monarchs, graven images were worshiped. When men could not honor monarchs in their presence, since they lived at a distance, they . . . made a visible image of the king" (14:16-17).

Righteous Jews were also being plotted against by the unfaithful. "Let us lie in wait for the righteous man" (2:12). "Let us condemn him to a shameful death" (2:20). Pious Jews must be strengthened and cheered. "The souls of the righteous are in the hand of God" (3:1). "Having been disciplined a little, they will receive great good" (3:5). The lot of the righteous is far superior to that of the ungodly. Those failing to find wisdom and faith in God must be warned. The purpose of the book was to help Jews remain loyal to their faith, and perhaps commend it to Gentiles as a reasonable belief.

Jewish faith and wisdom bring the most satisfactory life, now and after death. The concept of the future life is more advanced than that of any earlier Hebrew writing. The Wisdom of Solomon has more references to immortality than has the entire Old Testament. Pseudo-Solomon seems to be refuting the argument of Ecclesiastes (which also pretends to be the work of Solomon) that death is the end of everything. He goes beyond any canonical Old Testament writer in assuming that the soul belongs to a higher order of being than does the body:

> A perishable body weighs down the soul,
> and this earthly tent burdens the
> thoughtful mind (9:15).

Wisdom "teaches self-control and prudence, justice and courage" (8:7), the four virtues emphasized by Plato. Writing as though he were King Solomon, the author expands the prayer of Solomon given in 2 Kings 3:7-9 into a lengthy prayer for wisdom, which makes up the entire ninth chapter.

The remainder of the book, starting with the tenth chapter, proclaims that "Wisdom protected the first-formed father of the world" (10:1) and saved the Israelites down through history. "Wisdom prospered their works" (11:1). "Through the very things by which their enemies were punished, they themselves received benefit" (11:5). In his enthusiasm, Pseudo-Solomon exaggerated details of the flight from Egypt under Moses. "Snow and ice withstood fire without melting" (16:22). "Land animals were transformed into water creatures" (19:19).

Old Testament theology was modified by Greek philosophy: "A perishable body weighs down the soul" (9:15). Souls exist before bodies: "A good soul fell to my lot; or rather, being good, I entered an undefiled body" (8:19-20). "God created man for incorruption . . . but through the devil's envy, death entered the world" (2:23-24).

Baruch and the Letter of Jeremiah are considered by some to be Wisdom Literature. Writings of the Pseudepigrapha which include bits of Wisdom Literature are The Psalms of Solomon, The Testaments of the Twelve Patriarchs, and The Letter of Aristeas.

ASSIGNMENT

1. What is meant by Wisdom Literature? What Old Testament books are considered Wisdom Literature?

2. Why is Solomon's name associated with Wisdom Literature?

3. How did the "wise men" differ from priests? from prophets? from apocalyptists?

4. What does the word Ecclesiasticus mean? By what other names is the book known? To what Old Testament book is it most similar? What do we know about the author of the book? What is the book's chief concern? What does the author feel are life's chief values?

5. With what is the "Wisdom of Solomon" chiefly concerned? What are its theological concepts? Why was it written?

6. What additional Wisdom Literature is found in the Pseudepigrapha? With what does each deal?

SUPPLEMENTARY READING

Dentan: Chapter VI
Goodspeed—Chapters III and XIII
Metzger—Chapters VI and VII
Pfeiffer, R. H.: *History*—Pages 313-408
Reider
Sloan: *Old Testament*—Chapter 40
Snaith—Chapter XV
Torrey—Pages 93-103

Chapter 29

Christian Use
of the Apocrypha

It was the Christians rather than the Jews who preserved the Apocrypha and other intertestamental literature. Only the Hebrew scriptures, considered as twenty-four books, were to be used by Jewish people; all other writings were considered dangerous. A Midrash on Ecclesiastes comments, "Whoever brings together in his house more than twenty-four books brings confusion." An early rabbi wrote that among those who have no part in the world to come is "he who reads the outside books."

A number of elements in the New Testament not found in the Old are familiar to readers of intertestamental literature. In the Apocrypha, we meet Pharisees and Sadducees; we come to know scribes and rabbis. In intertestamental writings, we become acquainted with angels and demons. In Tobit, the angel Raphael accompanies Tobias on his journey. In 3 Maccabees, angels drive back drunken elephants. In the Essene War Scroll, men with blemished bodies are not to participate in the Holy War "for holy angels march with their hosts." In 2 Maccabees, heavenly hosts are seen in the air. In Tobit, a demon is driven to southern Egypt.

The Old Testament scarcely mentions personal immortality. This is taken for granted in the New Testament. This transition is seen in intertestamental literature, where the resurrection of the body is mentioned several times. In 2 Maccabees 7, the seven brothers and their mother stand up against horrible suffering, convinced of a happy future life. Such expectation seems common.

Although the Messianic hope appears in the sermons of various Hebrew prophets, it is much more explicit in the intertestamental period. The Essenes went so far as to expect two Messiahs. It is in this time that apocalypticism developed and the idea that people were living near the end of the present world was not uncommon.

Much of the social, political, and religious setting of the New Testament and theological ideas found there are better understood as we see their development in the intertestamental writings. Emphasis upon observing the Torah is found much more in these later writings than in what we call the Old Testament. Merit is understood to be acquired by works, such as alms, fasting, praying. The numerous wisdom passages give some understanding of the Logos concept of the Gospel according to John and 1 John.

A number of expressions of Jesus have parallels in non-Biblical Hebrew writings, but whether he borrowed from them or they both used common terms is uncertain. The eleventh chapter of Ecclesiasticus tells of the death of a rich man, which sounds much like Jesus' parable of the Rich Fool (Lu. 12:11-21). Jesus' parable of the Unjust Judge (Lu. 18:2-8) suggests that he might have been reading Ecclesiasticus 35:12-15. Jesus' admonition to come to him for rest, "for my yoke is easy," has a close parallel in Ecclesiasticus 51. Jesus' reference to old and new wine (Lu. 5:9) bears resemblance to a verse in Ecclesiasticus (9:10). Several further reflections of Ecclesiasticus are found in the teachings of Jesus.

When Jesus taught to bring the poor and lame to a feast, some people must have recalled Tobit's order to his son to bring to the Pentecost feast "whatever poor man of our brethren you may find" (2:2). Did the Sadducees who told Jesus about a woman who had had seven husbands have in mind the experience of Sarah before she met Tobias?

In his letter to the Romans, especially in the first and ninth chapters, Paul uses numerous expressions found in The Wisdom of Solomon; one scholar reports forty parallels. In Eph. 6:11 and 2 Cor. 5:1-9, echoes of this same book of the Apocrypha are heard.

In the eleventh chapter of Hebrews, the list of heroes of faith sounds much like the section of Ecclesiasticus beginning, "Let us now praise famous men" (44:1). The reference at the end of this chapter in Hebrews to those who "were tortured, refusing to accept release, that they might rise again to a better life" was considered as early as the fifth century to refer to the story of the Maccabean martyrs of 2 Macc. 7. As The Wisdom of Solomon personifies wisdom, so both Paul and the writer of

Hebrews feel that Jesus is wisdom personified.

Numerous parallels between the book of James and Ecclesiasticus are found. James 4:5 mentions that "the scripture says" and then gives a statement found nowhere in the Old Testament, the Apocrypha, or earlier Christian writings. However, a statement in the Manual of Discipline (4:9-11) expresses somewhat the same thought.

The only direct quotation from intertestamental writing found in the New Testament is Jude 14-15, which quotes 1 Enoch 1:9. In his sixth verse, Jude refers to a story in Enoch about the punishment of disobedient angels. Jude also refers to a story in the Assumption of Moses about a dispute between the devil and the archangel Michael as to the disposal of the body of Moses (verse 9).

The Revelation of John and 1 Peter call Rome Babylon, as does Baruch, the Letter of Jeremiah, and 2 Esdras. Tobit's description of the New Jerusalem (13:16-17) appears again in Rev. 21:18-21.

Not everything in the intertestamental writing is a step toward Christianity. Note the cunning and deception of Judith, and the gloating vengeance of Judas given in the last chapter of Second Maccabees.

Since the books of the Apocrypha were included in the Old Testament used by all Christians until the sixteenth century, we are not at all surprised to find them quoted as scripture by numerous Christian writers, although some of the earliest commentators, beginning with Jerome, note that they are secondary works. First Clement, a non-canonical book that some people wanted to include in the New Testament, refers to "the blessed Judith" and recounts her experience with Holofernes. The earliest list of New Testament books we have, compiled about A.D. 200, includes the Wisdom of Solomon.

Since the Essene writings had been lost until recently, they were not used by the early church. Little use was made of the Pseudepigrapha, but we do find some references to this material. Items from the Apocrypha appear in unexpected places. The Book of Common Prayer of 1549 considers Tobias and Sarah as the ideal pair instead of Abraham and Sarah, who are generally used.

Dante's Divine Comedy includes references to six of the Apocrypha. Shakespeare named his daughters Judith and Susanna. Some eighty passages in his plays make allusion to eleven books of the Apocrypha. Chaucer, Milton, and other writers make frequent use of the books.

Handel wrote an oratorio on Judas Maccabeus; another on Susanna. Many hymns by Charles Wesley and others have allusions to details of the Apocrypha. Paintings in the catacombs, as well as later ones, often picture scenes from Judith, Tobit, Susanna, and Maccabees. The great painter Raphael was named for Tobias' guide.

Martin Luther questioned the use of the Apocrypha, not because they were absent from the Hebrew Bible from which he made his German translation, but because certain Roman Catholic teachings which he opposed were based upon references in the Apocrypha. Support for prayers and masses for the dead was found in 2 Macc. 12:43-45. Argument for obtaining merit for good works was found in Tobit 12:9; Ecclesiasticus 3:30; 2 Esdras 8:33, "The righteous, who have many works laid up with thee, shall receive their reward in consequence of their own deeds."

Even before Luther's Bible was compiled, the Dutch Bible published in 1526 printed the Apocrypha separately. Probably every Protestant Bible after that did the same, until finally the Apocrypha came to be omitted from most printings. Each of these Bibles had an introduction to an explanation of the Apocrypha, considering them of less value than the books found in the Hebrew scriptures.

Because of the Protestant attitude toward the Apocrypha, the Roman Catholic Council of Trent in 1546 pronounced an anathema upon any who would not receive all the Latin Vulgate Bible as sacred and canonical. However, in listing the books of the Bible, the Council ommitted the Prayer of Manasseh and 1 and 2 Esdras. In an official edition of the Vulgate published in 1592, these three are printed as an appendix after the New Testament. In some printings of the Roman Catholic English translation, the Rheims-Douay Version, these are printed as an appendix to the Old Testament; in others, they are omitted. Some prominent Roman Catholics have challenged the canonicity of the Apocrypha. The Church of England, the American Protestant Episcopal Church, and the Eastern Orthodox churches make some use of the Apocrypha, but in general give them a lower rating than the other books of the Bible. Today, Protestants are no longer afraid to read the Apocrypha and are finding them useful for an understanding of early Christianity.

ASSIGNMENT

1. What elements seem to be taken for granted in the New Testament, but are scarcely, if at all, found in the Old Testament?
2. What sayings of Jesus suggest the influence of interestamental literature?
3. What other parallels are found between the New Testament and the Apocrypha? What direct quotation from interestamental writing is found in the New Testament?
4. What Roman Catholic teachings are based on the Apocrypha?
5. Give the history of the inclusion in and expulsion from the Bible of the Apocrypha.

SUPPLEMENTARY READING

Goodspeed—Chapters XVII and XVIII
Metzger—Chapters XVI-XVIII
Russell—Pages 88-9

Chapter 30

The Testaments
of the Twelve Patriarchs

Until recently scholars have believed that The Testaments of the Twelve Patriarchs was written in the latter part of the second century B.C., and that late Jewish and early Christian material was inserted at a later time. This was supported by the fact that an Armenian version translated from an earlier Greek edition omits most of these last ideas.

Portions of an Aramaic Testament of Levi were found in the Cairo genizah along with the Zadokite Document in 1896. Qumran Caves 1 and 4 have revealed fragments of a similar Aramaic Testament of Levi. A monastery on Mt. Athos in Greece has a tenth century Greek Testaments of the Twelve Patriarchs. In it are two long passages not found in any other Greek copy. One of these is in the Cairo manuscript; both are in the Qumran fragments.

A Hebrew Testament of Naphtali has been found in Cave 4. It is longer than the copies we already knew. These discoveries are challenging the formerly held idea that The Testaments is a second century B.C. work with later additions. No Testaments of the Twelve Patriarchs, as such, has been found at Qumran. It has been suggested that an Essene who became a Christian knew the Levi and Naphtali testaments. Using them as a foundation, he wrote testaments for all twelve patriarchs. Of course, the non-Christian Essene idea of two Messiahs comes to mind. However, the writer could have felt that a single Messiah was descended from both Levi and Judah. It has been believed that The Testaments influenced New Testament writers and even Jesus himself. This is now open to question. Numerous parallels in vocabulary suggest relationship between the Essenes and

The Testaments: the word for Satan, Belial or Beliar, never used in the Old Testament, appears some thirty times in the The Testaments and approximately the same number of times in the Dead Sea scrolls, but oddly only once in the New Testament. Many terms and concepts have exact parallels in the Manual of Discipline.

Something of a pattern for The Testaments is set by Gen. 49 and Deut. 33. In the former, Jacob, about to die, calls his twelve sons to him and predicts the future of each. In the latter, Moses blesses each of the twelve tribes, telling how it will prosper. We have somewhat similar farewell addresses by Joshua (Joshua 23 and 24) and by David (1 Kg. 2). In The Testaments, each of the sons of Jacob, as he is about to die at the age of from 110 (Joseph) to 137 (Levi), gathers his own sons (and grandsons) about him and gives them admonition. Prediction of their future plays a minor part. Each tells his own story, the significant events of his life, and draws from it warning or advice. What little is told about each of the sons in Genesis is incorporated, but much of the material comes from otherwise unknown legendary sources.

It is the moral instructions given that make the book popular. Each of Jacob's sons, except Gad, finally becomes an apocalyptist, telling very briefly what will take place in the last days. Each testament concludes with the statement that the patriarch died, and his sons buried him in Hebron "with his fathers."

Expanding the reference to his sin given in Gen. 35:22 and 49:4, Reuben warns his sons against unchastity. Simeon, Dan, and Gad tell of having had bad attitudes toward Joseph and warn against hatred, rivalry, and enmity. Levi says that he was overly violent with Shechem (Gen. 34). Judah tells of adventures not recorded in Genesis and warns against wine, women, and greed. Asher and Benjamin plead for truthfulness; Joseph, for chastity.

Naphtali says that God "created every man after His own image" (2:5). However, like the Qumran Essenes, the author believed that "Two ways hath God given to the sons of men, and two inclinations, and two kinds of action" (Asher 1:3), good and bad. Men may be drawn to the evil inclination by women who "in their heart plot against men" (Reuben 5:3), as they allured angels "who were before the flood" (5:6). Men may also be led to evil action by the seven evil spirits whose prince is Beliar.

In time "Beliar shall be bound" (Levi 18:12) and "cast into the fire forever and they who have died in grief shall arise in joy" (Jud. 25:3-4).

Patience, prayer, humility, almsgiving, repentance, fear of the Lord, are urged. Going far beyond the Old Testament, the author advocates: "Love ye one another from the heart; and if a man sin against thee, cast forth the poison of hate and speak peaceably to him, and in thy soul hold not guile; and if he confess and repent, forgive him" (Gad 6:3). "If any man seeketh to do evil unto you, do well unto him, and pray for him" (Jos. 18:2). "Do not set down in accounts . . . evil against his brother" (Zeb. 8:5). "Love the Lord and your neighbor" (Dan 5:3). A similar teaching is expressed twice in Issachar.

Another admonition given is "Do not be drunk with wine; for wine turneth the mind away from the truth, and inspires the passion of lust" (Jud. 14:1). Note the similarity to the speech of the first bodyguard in 1 Esd. 3:17-24.

The book of Jubilees sees no hope for the Gentiles: God planned their destruction; a Jew who married a Gentile should be put to death (30:7-17). But The Testaments proclaim salvation for the Gentiles: "The twelve tribes shall be gathered together there, and all the Gentiles, until the Most High shall send forth His salvation in the visitation of an only-begotten prophet" (Ben. 9:2).

The author of The Testaments reflects an older Jewish idea that the Messiah would be a descendant of Levi. He not only has Levi say this (18:14), but also Judah (24:1-3), Dan (5:10-11), and Joseph (19:5-9). He is also sure that the Messiah is of the tribe of Judah, "great David's greater son." Judah is reported to have told his sons:

> Then shall the sceptre of my kingdom
>   shine forth;
> And from your root shall arise a stem;
> And from it shall grow a rod of righteousness
>   to the Gentiles,
> To judge and to save all that call upon
>   the Lord (24:5-6).

ASSIGNMENT

1. What form does The Testaments of the Twelve Patriarchs take?

2. What is the message of the book? What warnings are given? In what ways does the book go beyond the Old Testament?

3. What is said about evil spirits? What is Satan called?

4. What is the author's attitude toward the Gentiles?

5. What appears to be the Messianic expectation?

6. What change in understanding The Testaments has been suggested by the Qumran discoveries?

SUPPLEMENTARY READING

Burrows: *More Light*—Pages 179-80
Charles: *Apocrypha*—Vol. II, Pages 282-367
Pfeiffer, R. H.: *History*—Pages 64-6

Chapter 31

Retelling
Early Biblical History

Among the Essenes the most popular book of the Pseudepigrapha was Jubilees. It is mentioned in the Zadokite Document. Fragments of ten manuscripts of the book have been found in Caves 1, 2, and 4—all in Hebrew.

Jubilees is a Midrashic targum, telling the narrative we have in Genesis and the first fourteen chapters of Exodus with occasional additions. It was sometimes known as Little Genesis (although a bit longer than Genesis). It was also known as the Apochrypha of Moses, the Testament of Moses, the Book of Adam's Daughter, and the Life of Adam. It makes much of the number seven and divides all time into forty-nine-year Jubilee periods, beginning with the creation of the world. It considers that Judaism has existed since that time. In 36:21 we read, "And Leah his [Jacob's] wife died in the fourth year of the second week of the forty-fifth jubilee." This gives us 44 x 49 or 2156, plus 7 (one week of years) plus 4, or the year 2167.

The year of Jubilee had been established by the Hebrews as the year following seven cycles of seven years, or every fiftieth year. In this year Hebrew slaves were given their freedom, and property which one Hebrew had sold to another was returned to its original owner. "In it you shall neither sow, nor reap of what grows of itself, nor gather grapes" (Lev. 25:8-12). By intertestamental times this had become merely a method of measuring time, and the Jubilee period had been reduced from fifty to forty-nine years.

The author of the book of Jubilees was dissatisfied with the Jewish calendar. This was a calendar of twelve lunar months which made 354 days 8 hours, and 48 minutes. Seven of every nineteen years had a thirteenth month to fit into a cycle of nineteen solar years. The Jubilees writer proposed an annual calendar of fifty-two weeks divided into four seasons. The author felt that the Israelite calendar prevented the Hebrews from keeping the annual festivals at the proper time. They were thus disobeying the command of God (49:14). There is much to suggest that the Qumran Essenes adopted the Jubilees calendar.

Jubilees purports to be a revelation made to Moses on Mount Sinai by "the angel of the presence," who makes various references to heavenly tablets on which commandments are written. The supremacy the law had achieved in Judaism by the time the book was written is the major emphasis. It is a rewriting of history from the viewpoint of the Pharisees, much as the books of Chronicles were a rewriting of Samuel and Kings from a priestly viewpoint. Jubilees was an effort to counteract the Hellenizing of Judaism. The Pharisee who wrote it was probably a priest. He exalted Levi, supposed ancestor of the priests, over Judah, ancestor of the Jewish kings. Strict views on circumcision, and fasts are held. Gentiles are denounced.

Moses is directed to write the history of the world, beginning with twenty-two distinct acts of creation on the first six days. The first day included the creation of various kinds of angels. Emphasis is laid upon the Sabbath: "These shall keep the Sabbath day, and I will sanctify them unto Myself as My people, and will bless them" (2:19).

To emphasize the uniqueness of Judaism, the author says that Pentecost was observed in heaven from the creation to Noah (6:18), after which Noah and his descendants were to celebrate it, although for two periods previous to Moses it was forgotten. Detailed rules are given which do not appear in the Torah and sometimes differ from those in the Talmud. It is more advanced in thought than the Torah. Unpleasant deeds attributed to Yahweh in the Torah are attributed to Satan, as the order to Abraham to sacrifice Isaac (Gen. 22:1-2) and the attempt to kill Moses when he was returning to Egypt at the command of God (Ex. 4:24). Details in the Torah uncomplimentary to the patriarchs are omitted.

At the age of fourteen Abraham became a hero. Mastema, or Satan, sent ravens to eat seed as it was planted. Seventy times in one day Abraham drove them away. "His name became great in all the land of the Chaldees" (11:21).

New versions of stories in Genesis and Exodus were for the purpose of propaganda. The law is something as old as mankind. There is little hope for the Gentiles who do not keep the law. Advanced ideas of angels and demons are expressed. However, the picture of judgment is still that of an eye for an eye, a tooth for a tooth. As in the Dead Sea scrolls, Sabbath observance and the avoidance of idolatry are emphasized. A Greek influence is found in the teaching of the immortality of the soul rather than a physical resurrection.

Jubilees seems to have been written in Palestine shortly before 100 B.C., while John Hyrcanus was high priest. This was in Hebrew. Nearly all the Dead Sea scrolls are in that language. It was later translated into Greek, but, except for a few fragments, no Greek copy exists. Part of it has been found in a Latin translation; all of it is in Ethiopic, the older literary language of Abyssinia. Both the Latin and the Ethiopic were translated from the Greek. Bits of Jubilees also appear in numerous quotations. The author makes generous use of Genesis and also parts of the Book of Noah and the Book of Enoch.

One of the scrolls found in Cave 1 was in very bad condition. It was questioned whether it could be unrolled. A section that was successfully detached contained references to Lamech and his wife. A Greek list of apocalyptical writings included an otherwise unknown Apocalypse of Lamech. Naturally it was suggested that this scroll was the lost Lamech book, so it became known as the Lamech scroll. However, it was eventually unrolled and parts of it deciphered. It was found to be an Aramaic paraphrase or targum of Genesis, somewhat similar to Jubilees. Therefore, it is generally now called the Genesis Apocryphon.

The first column that could be read describes Lamech's fear that his extraordinary child Noah was not his but had been fathered by one of the angels (watchers) who had been having relations with human women. Lamech's wife vehemently denied this.

Occasional words and sentences of later columns have been recognized, but the next column that can be read with any satisfaction is the nineteenth. It purports to be Abram's own account of his reaching Hebron and then, because of famine, going to Egypt. Due to a dream, he decided to claim that his wife was his sister. Five years later, he had a conversation with "three men of the nobles of Egypt," but most of the words in this conversation cannot be deciphered or are missing.

However, the next column describes in detail the great beauty of Sarai. When the king heard this "he sent in haste to have her brought . . . and took her to himself to be his wife." He sought to kill Abram. Sarai saved Abram by saying that he was her brother. That night Abram wept and begged God, "Let him not have power this night to defile my wife." That night the pharaoh and "every man of his house" experienced "crushing afflictions" that lasted for two years. "All the physicians and enchanters . . . were unable to heal him."

The king asked Abram to pray for him, but Lot said, "My uncle Abram cannot pray for the king while Sarai, his wife, is with him." The king released her to her husband, who prayed for the king, and he recovered. "So I, Abram, went with very much goods, and also with silver and gold, and I went up from Egypt, and Lot my nephew with me. Lot, too, got much wealth and he took to himself a wife of . . ." The record breaks off just as we get interested in Lot's wife.

Columns 21 and 22 tell briefly of Lot's separating from Abram and building a house in Sodom. Abram was promised all the land of Palestine and so many descendants that "no son of man will be able to number them." Abram then examined the land. The place names given are very similar to those in the Book bf Jubilees. Abram went as far east as the Euphrates. "I traveled along the Euphrates until I reached the Red Sea." Did the author not know that the Euphrates does not flow into the Red Sea, or did he consider the Persian Gulf a part of the Red Sea?

The story of Abram's rescuing Lot from the kings of the east and his being blessed by Melchizedek, king of Salem, is recounted in words very similar to Gen. 14. God then reminded Abram that in the ten years since he left Haran his holdings had doubled. Abram recognized this but complained that he had no heir other than Eleazar. God replied, "This man shall not be your heir, but one who shall issue . . ." The sentence is not finished but needle-holes on the edge of the column indicate that there was originally more.

Cave 4 produced other paraphrases of parts of Genesis and Exodus, and also of 1 and 2 Samuel. A Targum of Job was found in Cave 11.

ASSIGNMENT

1. Explain the Jewish calendar. What changes did the author of Jubilees propose? Where does this new calendar seem to have been used?

2. What is the primary material in Jubilees? What is its major emphasis? As what points does it differ from material in the Bible?

3. In what way does the discovery of Satan change reports given in the Torah?

4. What is the Genesis Apocryphon? At what points do we find it differing from the canonical Genesis?

SUPPLEMENTARY READING

Burrows: *Dead Sea*—Pages 221, 239-41
Burrows: *More Light*—Pages 7-8, 178-9, 248, 309, 344, 374-6, 387-93
Charles: *Apocrypha*—Vol. II—Pages 1-82
Pfeiffer, R. H.: *History*—Pages 68-70
Torrey—Pages 126-9
Yadin—Chapter 16

Chapter 32

The Diaspora

Palestine has been considered the homeland of the Jews since the formation of Judah about 922 B.C. However, since the destruction of Jerusalem in 586 B.C., more Jews have lived outside Palestine than in. Earlier the Assyrians had captured numerous towns and villages of Judah and had taken captives to Assyria, but most of these intermarried and disappeared. Otherwise there was very little migration from Judah until Nebuchadnezzar captured Jerusalem in 597 B.C. He is reported to have deported ten thousand Jews to Babylonia. Eleven years later he destroyed Jerusalem and took many thousands more home with him.

When, approximately fifty years later, Jews were given permission to return to Palestine, many of them had put down roots in Mesopotamia and stayed. They had followed Jeremiah's advice to "build homes and live in them, plant gardens and eat their produce" (Jer. 29:5). Ezekiel had helped them develop the synagogue as a satisfactory substitute for the temple. They found the religious tolerance of the Persians pleasant. Therefore, they could "sing the LORD's song in a foreign land" (Ps. 137:4).

Although there were later migrations of Jews from Mesopotamia to Palestine, Egypt, and Asia (Turkey), large numbers remained. After the establishment of the modern nation of Israel in 1948, pressure was put upon Jews in Iraq and Iran, present-day Mesopotamia, to move to the new state. Probably the majority refused. Of those who did go to Israel some soon returned.

Those fleeing to Egypt after the murder of the governor in 581 B.C. not only took Jeremiah and Baruch along but found numerous Jews already there. The much bigger later migration to participate in the development of Alexandria is well-known. We have already noted Jewish temples erected at Elephantine

Island and in the Delta. These were generally considered unorthodox.

While some Jews were forcibly taken to other countries, not only by Assyria and Babylonia but by later conquerors, and some fled for safety, most Jewish migration was voluntary. The Jews had high health standards and large families. Therefore, they rapidly increased in numbers. They forced some people, especially the Idumeans, to become Jews. Others voluntarily joined the Jewish fellowship. The Jewish homeland is mountainous, rocky, and has never been very fertile. Considerable migration was in search of fertile farmlands. Commercial and business inducements beckoned Jews away from Palestine. Military and political opportunities opened up. Many Jews chafed under conservative religious restrictions at home and found freedom and exhilaration in foreign cities.

The territory that had originally been Judah soon became too crowded. Shortly after their return from Babylonian exile, Jews began moving north of the original border of their nation. There was little room for them in Samaria and they met opposition there. They soon found a better welcome in Galilee, where some of the native people became Jews. However, they did not stop there but moved on north into Syria. After the death of Alexander, the new Selucid Syrian government established numerous cities in the territory we now call Turkey. Jewish colonies were invited to settle there. After the Selucids gained control of Judea, they often forced Jews to become residents of these outpost cities. When Antiochus Epiphanes persecuted Jews in their homeland, many joined their cousins in these distant cities, where there was little organized opposition.

This migration did not stop in Turkey. A wanderlust and the appeal of new opportunity drew many to Macedonia and Greece. Others went on to Rome and throughout the Mediterrean world. A Jewish colony worked mines in southern Spain. The author of the book of Jonah had Jonah attempt to go there.

These Jews living abroad came to be thought of collectively as the "Scattered" or the "Dispersion." Today they are often referred to by the Greek name, Diaspora.

By the time of Jesus there were probably four and a half million Jews in the Roman world, about seven per cent of the total population. Of these, a million were in Egypt, and about the same number in the Tigris-Euphrates valley, more than a million in Syria, ten thousand in Rome. There were evidently less than three-quarters of a million in Palestine. The Jews of the Diaspora quickly adapted to the conditions and occupations of the lands in which they found themselves. Strabo, the Greek geographer writing near the end of the intertestamental period, said: "Jews are to be found in every city, and in the whole world it was not easy to find a place where they had not penetrated and which was not dominated by them."

Although there were heretics among them, most Jews kept some semblance of loyalty to their religion. Probably in any town where there were ten male Jews twelve years of age or more, a synagogue was established. The Jews insisted upon observing the Sabbath, an institution unknown to their neighbors. They tended to live in a section of the city by themselves, and would not eat with non-Jews. There were also certain foods they would not eat. They refrained from many of the amusements others enjoyed, and would not participate in the state religion. They observed ceremonies which to others seemed queer. Perhaps the most obnoxious of these was circumcision. They were intolerant of other religions and noisily raised a fuss when one of their own number proclaimed an idea which seemed to be unorthodox.

While their skills and abilities, their industry and honesty, caused them to be respected, in other ways they were despised. They insisted upon ceremonial washings and prayers in public. They felt that they were the chosen people of God and thus much superior to their neighbors.

Very early in the Diaspora, the Sibylline Oracles declared of the Jews: "Every sea and every land is full of thee, and every one hateth thee because of thy ways." But business and government found the Jews useful. Special privileges not given other religious groups were given to them. While others were compelled to recognize the Roman emperor as a god, at some times and some places the Jews were exempted from this requirement; their monotheistic prejudice was respected. They were exempted from some taxes, and Rome went so far as to collect from them for the support of their temple in Jerusalem. Jewish soldiers were even sometimes excused from military duty on the Sabbath. Some Jewish men were exempted from the military draft.

Although Jews sought respect for their religion, little attempt was made to win converts. However, there were those who were convinced that the second Isaiah was referring to them when he quoted Yahweh as saying:

> I will give you as a light to the nations,
> that my salvation may reach to the
> end of the earth (Isa. 49:6).

Many intelligent, thoughtful Greeks and Romans found something appealing in the Jewish religion. They were dissatisfied with their own religions of many gods, some of which were pictured as immoral, fighting one another and stealing one another's wives. Surely there must be some first cause, some supreme power! The Greek Zeus and the Latin Jupiter had been thought of as superior gods but very little different from other deities. The concept of the Logos has in it some idea of a summation of deities, the hint of a super-god, but this was all quite indefinite. There was no concept of personal relation with the god. The Jews taught that Yahweh was the only God, the creator and sustainer of the universe, a god who was real, near, and concerned with human beings, one who had fellowship with men. He did no wrong and insisted that at that point men should strive to be like him.

This all appealed to some thinking non-Jews, but there were two things they did not like in the Jewish religion. One was the chosen people idea, the claim that they were better than Greeks or Romans. To agree to this was obnoxious to cultured Greeks and to militarily mighty Romans. Then there was the practice of circumcision. This was repulsive to people who were not Jews, at least not Semites. It seemed contrary to nature and the divine plan for men's bodies.

Rather large numbers of Gentiles attended synagogues, made financial contributions to their support, and observed many of the Jewish customs and laws. Some adopted the Sabbath day of rest and were severely criticized by their fellows as being lazy. The Gospel of Luke reports that a Roman army officer built a synagogue at Capernaum on the shore of Lake Galilee (Lu. 7:5). Some of these Gentiles swallowed their pride, were circumcised, and became Jews. These were known as converts. However, a much larger number would not go that far. They remained friendly to the Jewish religion and ideas and came to be thought of as God-fearers.

These converts and God-fearers were fertile ground for the

seed of Christianity. The Christian religion had monotheism
plus an even greater emphasis upon ethics, morality. But it had
neither of the unpleasant items of Judaism, the superior attitude
and circumcision. The early Christians were chiefly Jews. As
they went about the Roman world with their message, they were
welcomed at synagogues and given all opportunity to speak.
Generally they were soon put out of the synagogue, but they
had won converts among the new Jews and those friendly to
Judaism. They also made converts among Jews who saw in the
Christian gospel a reformed, less narrow, Judaism, a religion
more suitable for the Diaspora. It was doubtless these factors,
as well as Roman roads, the clearing of pirates from the Mediterranean, and the use of a common language, Greek, that caused
the Christian apostle Paul to say, "When the time had fully
come, God sent forth his Son" (Gal. 4:4).

Most of the Jews who became Christians were, or had been
members of the Diaspora. In general, Jews living in Palestine
came to think of their cousins abroad as not quite faithful to the
Jewish traditions. Many of them spoke Greek more fluently
than Aramaic. Some of them adopted Greek names and wore
foreign clothing. They were not ashamed to be seen associating
with non-Jews. They began to take a brotherly attitude toward
Greeks. Palestinian Jews felt that they had become tainted with
Greek, or Hellenistic, thought. They began to call the non-
Palestine Jews Hellenists. Even those who returned to live in
Palestine were considered Hellenists in contrast to the conservative Jews who had been in Palestine for a long time. The latter
came to be called the Hebraic Jews, or Hebrews. This term
suggested something old, conservative.

We are familiar with the extensive literature produced in
Alexandria—Jonah, the Septuagint, much of the Apocrypha
and Pseudepigrapha, Philo. But the Alexandrian Jews were not
the only members of the Diaspora to commit religious ideas to
writing. Possibly some of the Apocrypha and doubtless some
of the Pseudepigrapha were written in Babylonia. The primary
Babylonian contribution was the major part of the Talmud.
Rabbis throughout the Diaspora contributed their interpretations of the Hebrew scriptures. Through the ages Jews have
continued to make outstanding contributions in philosophy,
medicine, science, government, music, and every branch of
learning and culture.

Why were the Jews of the Diaspora not absorbed by the nations in which they lived? What has held them together? Possibly the very thing that made them disliked, their conviction that they have been chosen by God, that they are his people. This has knit them into a brotherhood that has withstood all persecution.

Did the Jews of the Diaspora expect to return to their homeland? They did not quickly forget it. As long as the temple stood, many Jews felt that they should worship there from time to time, or at least once in their lifetime. After the destruction of the temple in A.D. 70, there was less to attract them to Palestine. After the second anti-Roman rebellion of 132–135, for a period of time no Jew was allowed within sight of Jerusalem. It was much safer to stay away from Palestine. While probably most individuals of the Diaspora did not plan to make new homes in Palestine, the idea has had its proponents all through the ages. The modern Zionist movement and the nation of Israel now established in the western part of Palestine are the result of this never-dying hope.

In time, early Christians came to feel that they were the real Israelites, that Pharisees and Sadducees had led their people astray, that Christians were more true to the religion of the Hebrew prophets than were the non-Christians. When we find the New Testament letter of James being addressed "to the twelve tribes in the dispersion" (1:1) or 1 Peter "to the exiles of the dispersion" (1:1), it is the Christians who are meant.

ASSIGNMENT

1. What caused many Jews to leave Palestine? Where did they go in addition to Egypt? How were they accepted? What became of their religion outside Palestine?

2. What religious literature was produced by Jews of the Diaspora?

3. What elements in the Jewish religion appealed to non-Jews? What were disliked? Distinguish between "converts" and "God-fearers." What did Judaism contribute to Greek and Roman thought? What factors made the Jews of the Diaspora unpopular?

4. What held the Jews of the Diaspora together? Distinguish between "Hellenists" and "Hebrews."

5. What was the significance of the Jewish Diaspora, or Dispersion, to Christianity?

6. What contributions through the centuries have Jews of the Diaspora made to government, philosophy, medicine, science?

Compile a list of leading Jews in these fields.

7. Discuss Zionism.

SUPPLEMENTARY READING

Mathews—Chapter VIII
Pfeiffer, R. H.: *History*—Pages 93-196
Toombs—Pages 37-40
The Interpreter's Dictionary of the Bible—Article on Dispersion

Chapter 33

Oriental Mystery Religions

The worship of Yahweh met competition as soon as the Israelites entered Canaan. The worship of Baal offered a liveliness and sensuality that appealed to some Hebrews, who preferred it to the sober and strict religion reputedly organized by Moses. The Israelites did not completely conquer Canaan; in certain ways the Canaanites conquered Israel. Several factors which had been thought to be original with the worship of Yahweh have now been found to have had an earlier existence in Baal worship. The religion taught by Moses was itself a combination of factors from the religion of his Israelite ancestors, from that of Egypt, and from the Midianites.

Syncretism also took place during the Babylonian captivity. The prophet Ezekiel found the Babylonian worship of Tammuz, with its heavy emphasis upon sex, appealing to many of the exiles. One of Ezekiel's tasks was to counteract this. Jeremiah also found Tammuz worship among the Jews in Egypt.

A more positive and helpful influence upon those in Babylonian captivity was that of a religion penetrating Babylonia from the people farther east, the Persians. This, Zoroastrianism, was an advanced religion which offered solutions to certain problems bothering the worshipers of Yahweh. They had wondered why their God did cruel things, killing Er and Onan (Gen. 38:7 and 10), and Uzzah, the farmer's son who touched the Ark of the Covenant (2 Sam. 6:7).

The Zoroastrians taught that in addition to Ahura Mazda, the god of light and good, there was Angru Mainyu, or Satan, the power of evil and darkness. This made sense to the Jewish exiles, who also adopted from the Zoroastrians ideas of angels of good and angels of evil, or demons. The concept of an eventual struggle between forces of light and darkness, emphasized by the Essenes, came from the Zoroastrians, as did elements in the picture of a future life.

The Jews who returned from Babylonian exile brought these Zoroastrian ideas with them. Doubtless the Zoroastrians continued further to influence the Jews who remained in Mesopotamia. About the beginning of the Christian era, a group of these Jews migrated from the banks of the Tigris and Euphrates to the central part of Asia Minor, or Turkey. In Paul's letter to the Colossians we learn that those with certain Zoroastrian ideas were attempting to control the Christian group in Colossae. They taught that there are angelic beings or "elemental spirits" of varying ranks which should be worshiped with feasts, fasts, vigils, and various ceremonies. Certain things were taboo, not to be touched. This group seemed to be trying to make an inferior place for Christ among their "elemental spirits."

Greek religions emphasized beauty and joy. The gods were fairy deities, never very highly respected. They might be superior to men in power, but definitely not in character. The Jews exalted God, but the Greeks exalted man. Religion among the Greeks was largely philosophical, appealing to reason and intellect. There was no message for people when they were troubled.

Neither comfort nor spiritual guidance was to be found in the religion of Rome. Roman religion became wholly political, an emperor cult, practical and unimaginative. The Pharaohs of Egypt and later the Ptolemies were considered at least sons of the gods, to be given divine reverence. Rome went beyond that. Both Greeks and Romans had developed a hero-worship in which certain distinguished men were considered as quasi-divine after death. At first acknowledged as a semi-god, Julius Caesar later had his statue erected and inscribed "to the invincible god." This started an epidemic of divinity-seeking among the Romans. Augustus claimed to have been born of a virgin. Finally, Domitian had people put to death for refusing to pay homage to him as a god. The Revelation to John in the New Testament reflects this situation.

Men were hungry for something more satisfying than the Roman religions. They added elements from the more esthetic Greek religions, but remained unsatisfied. In places still definitely Greek, the Greek gods, or more often goddesses, became increasingly popular. The Christian apostle Paul found his chief opposition in Ephesus among the worshipers of Artemis, often given the Latin name Diana. One of the seven wonders of the world was her temple there. Although originally Artemis was the goddess of chastity, Eastern influence had made her representative of the productive forces of nature. Her worship included various lewd practices. At Corinth, Paul found a great temple to Aphrodite, the goddess of beauty and love. The same excesses led to this temple having more than a thousand prostitutes.

Some people found help in Judaism, but more turned desperately to the Oriental mystery religions. To the masses there was nothing intimate about emperor-gods. Some found personal satisfaction in soothsayers and Eastern astrologers. The educated were skeptical about the value of the official religion.

As Rome extended her conquests eastward, her soldiers came into contact with Eastern religions. Sex emphasis and the worship of the Great Mother pleased these soldiers. As great numbers of free men as well as slaves from the East came to Rome they brought their religious practices with them. Their mysticism and emotionalism appealed to the religion-hungry Romans. Rome had gained the whole world and lost her own soul.

A sense of sin grew among the Roman people. Emperor worship provided no means of cleansing or expiation, no salvation. The ordinary person could not go to the emperor with his problems. The Oriental religions, on the other hand, offered comfort.

Roman emperors attempted to counteract the swing toward Oriental religions. Augustus put strict limitations upon the cult of Serapis and Isis. In A.D. 19 Tiberius expelled Orientals, including Jews, from Rome and set up a bloody persecution of others who had become devotees of Isis. However, Caligula recognized that the impossible was being attempted and favored Orientalism. In 304 Mithra was declared Protector of the Empire.

The term mystery religion implies secrecy. Therefore, many details remain unknown. Even the members had no clear-cut ideas, so each person found what he sought. In each religion there was an initiation that the new member was convinced brought him much blessedness. This gave a sense of belonging. He knew secrets most people did not know. There were those who cared for him. This made the burden of life more tolerable. Some of the cults had more or less regular congregational worship. Some had a common burial ground. In some of these religions those who wished could find licentious expression; the superstitious could find magic. On the other hand, the educated man could find symbols of truth dear to his heart; the ascetic could find freedom of spirit; the mystic, communion with deity. There was no political restraint, but rather, opportunity for self-expression of every kind.

All the mystery religions had very ancient, primitive beginnings in noting the recurrent death and birth in nature, winter and spring, sunset and sunrise. Human life does much the same, and, therefore, so must divine life. The gods died and were brought back to life. By initiation and rebirth the individual could do likewise.

Mystical, symbolic, sacramental acts were a part of this initiation in which the candidate was taught the myths and allegories. His sinful past could be washed away by water or blood. Sacrifices were a part of many rituals. The individual secured something of the god through a sacred meal. As the god returned to life, so could the person who had been brought into fellowship with the eternal life of his god. In most mystery religions virtue was not necessary to obtain a desirable resurrected life.

Stories about the gods lost their crass sensuality and immorality by being allegorized. These stories were re-enacted in sacramental dramas from time to time. By prayer and liturgy, the individual came to have a knowledge hidden from others. This is Gnosticism, which became a troublesome factor in the early church. Knowledge was obtained by magic, although reason and preaching eventually played a part. Asceticism, keeping the body under, was found in every mystery religion. Fasting was in all these religions; but bodily mutilation, absolute continence, and pilgrimages were also quite common. No price was thought too high to expiate sins and placate the deity. Suffering united members to one another and to their savior-god. The mystics made a strong appeal to feeling, but moral loyalties and spiritual perceptions were vague.

Athens, which was much more interested in religion than was Rome, developed mystery religions of its own. The most popular was the Eleusinian mysteries, developed from an agrarian cult which sought to secure fertility of the soil. The fasts, sacrifices, and washings connected with it eventually became a means of insuring the immortality of the initiate.

In Egypt, the worship of Osiris, a mythical King of Egypt, and his sister, Isis, was the chief mystery religion. Elaborate ceremonies represented the death of Osiris and his restoration by Isis. This was to give immortality to the worshiper. In the third century B.C., the Greek Serapis took the place of Osiris.

From Phrygia, in western Asia Minor, the worship of Attis and Cybele came to Rome. The chief celebration began the fifteenth of each March (the Ides). A pine tree was cut down to symbolize the death of Attis. It was treated like a corpse. The next day his resurrection was celebrated. Sexual excesses seem to have been the major part of this celebration.

The Babylonian Ishtar and Tammuz religion had its parallel in Phoenicia in Adonis and Aphrodite. Again, the god died and was resurrected, to the great joy of the goddess of love, whose happiness must be realized in sexual activity.

Although fertility and sex played such prominent parts in the mystery religions, other factors were found. This was especially true of Mithraism, a very ancient religion which developed numerous modifications. Mithra was an Iranian tribal god. In Zoroastrianism, he was a manifestation of Ahura Mazda. In the Chaldean form, he was a sun-god. In the intertestamental period, he was considered by some the supreme god. Mithraism gradually came to Asia Minor and became the chief rival to early Christianity, to which it had certain likenesses. Like Zoroastrianism, it was dualistic. It had washings, sacrifices, sacred meals, all of which were expected to bring the believer into fellowship with the god. Mithra was considered the creator and preserver of the world. The religion had a flood story, and the conviction that after the world was saved from evil the god had gone to heaven, from which he would return to give his followers immortality. There would be a final judgment, resurrection, and destruction of the present world order. Women were not accepted into this religion. Possibly this is one reason that, despite its growth in the Roman world and its fairly high morals, it gradually gave way to Christianity.

ASSIGNMENT

1. What religions influenced the Hebrews previous to Zoroastrianism?

2. Review the influence of Zoroastrianism on the Jewish religion.

3. What direct influence did Zoroastrianism have on people of Colossae in New Testament times?

4. Discuss the mystery religions. Why did they appeal to

Romans? What elements did the various mystery religions have in common? What was the chief mystery religion of Athens? Of Egypt? Of Phrygia? Of Babylonia?

5. What is Gnosticism? Asceticism?

6. Discuss Mithraism.

SUPPLEMENTARY READING

Angus: *Environment*
Angus: *Mystery*
Cumont: *Mysteries*
Cumont: *Oriental*
Dana—Chapter XI
Sloan: *Old Testament*—Chapter 35
Sloan: *New Testament*—Chapter 35

Chapter 34

The Jews' Own Religion

The Jews of the intertestamental period considered themselves chosen by the only wise and supreme God. With them he had made a covenant not offered to any other people. They believed that God had made covenants with Noah and Abraham, but chiefly with the Israelites as a whole through Moses. Although today we can readily recognize items that were contributed by Egyptian, Midianite, Canaanite, and Persian religions, this is but a recent realization. The Jew of the intertestamental period was convinced that his entire religion had been handed down to his people by God at Mount Sinai. Previous to the Babylonian captivity, the Hebrews looked down upon people of other religions as quite inferior, people with whom they should have no dealings. These people, they claimed, did not know the real God but worshiped deities who perhaps existed but were of much lesser quality and power.

Most Hebrews who had been taken from Israel to Mesopotamia intermarried and gave up their worship of Yahweh. Doubtless some captives from Judah did the same. Those who remained true to Yahweh saw certain values in the Zoroastrian religion which they adapted to their own use. This act must have made them somewhat tolerant toward people of other religions. However, during this time, monotheism was first proclaimed. Second Isaiah vehemently insisted that there is but one God.

Those who returned to Judah felt it necessary to oppose any who were not pure Jews. They refused to allow the Samaritans, who themselves worshiped Yahweh, to take part in the building of their new temple. Ezra attempted to prohibit marriage with non-Jews, ordering that all Gentile wives be divorced. Those who returned from the Captivity were convinced that they were superior to the people who had remained in Palestine, and they condemned the latter to inferior positions. The returned Jews claimed to be the ideal Israel, the servant of the LORD. On the other hand, in the Diaspora, especially in Alexandria, Jews became more friendly with those of other religions. They believed that the separatist policy was not the will of God. These non-Jews must be told about Yahweh. Although Isaiah, Jeremiah, and Second Isaiah had urged sharing their knowledge of Yahweh, the first organized demand that this be done was made by the author of Jonah, followed by the compilation of the Septuagint. Certain writings of the Apocrypha and the Pseudepigrapha contributed to this aim. In the Testaments of the Twelve Patriarchs we read of a stem which will arise out of Jacob, from which "shall grow a rod of righteousness to the Gentiles, to judge and save all that call upon the Lord" (Test. Jud. 24:5-6). Philo pointed out that Abraham, the ancestor of the Jews, was a Chaldean, and that Moses commanded the Israelites to love their Gentile converts as themselves.

There were also Jews in Palestine opposed to separatism. The authors of Ruth and Isaiah 55-66 held liberal views: "Foreigners who join themselves to the LORD, to minister to him . . . I will bring to my holy mountain" (Isa. 56:6-7).

This in no way lessened the Jewish belief that their religion was better than any other, that it had been revealed to them by God. They had suffered through their exile experience. This was a testing by God in preparation for a glorious future. Had not Second Isaiah directed, "Speak tenderly to Jerusalem, and cry to her that her warfare is ended" (40:2)? He had quoted God as saying, "I give Egypt as your ransom, Ethiopia and Seba in exchange for you" (43:3). He had promised, "You will spread abroad to the right and to the left, and your descendants will possess the nations and will people the desolate cities" (54:3).

This expectation was being fulfilled. Second Isaiah was right when he advised, "Fear not, for you will not be ashamed" (54:4). They did not forget that the prophet Zechariah was reported to have quoted God as saying, "I will brandish your sons, O Zion, over your sons, O Greece" (9:13). This was evidently written after the time of Zechariah, but was in the scriptures the Jews were using.

The Jews felt that they were succeeding because they were endeavoring to keep the law of God and, therefore, he would make them great. Not only was the law synonymous with morality and religion, it was a satisfaction. It was not man-made law, but law established by God himself, who loved his people and wanted them to have the best possible. Therefore, the Jew kept the law, not because he ought to, but because he wanted to. He was sincere in proclaiming, "Oh, how I love thy law. It is my meditation all the day" (Ps. 119:97); "I shall walk at liberty, for I have sought thy precepts" (Ps. 119:45).

The Jews had always had a certain fear of God. Back at Mount Sinai the Israelites told Moses, "Let not God speak to us, lest we die" (Ex. 20:19). Their name for God, Yahweh, meant the ever-being, the eternal. However, eventually they became afraid to speak that name lest they not do it reverently enough and God punish them. In time, they replaced the name with the common word for god, elohim, which came to be a proper noun. By intertestamental times, even this word had come to be too sacred to be commonly used. Some have interpreted this as developing a distance from God, but this does not seem to be so when we note the term that tended to take the place of Elohim—Father. Although the idea of angels grew, there was no need of an intermediary between man and God. One could come directly to God in prayer, as a son might to his father. God was near.

To fail to do his Father's will, to disobey the law, was sin. God was considered firm, but just. He expected his sons to be equally just. The first question to be asked in the Last Judgment was whether the individual had been just to his neighbor. The emphasis for both God and man was justice rather than love.

God was considered moral, pure. This picture was much superior to that held by Greeks, Romans, or followers of the mystery religions. As there were no sex stories connected with Yahweh, so his worshipers must be above scandal. Despite early Canaanite influence on the Hebrew religion, the mystery and enjoyment of sex were never confused with the mystery and joy of relations with God. Family life was much more wholesome than that of their neighbors. Young people were all expected to marry. Celibacy and asceticism were both rare.

At Mount Sinai, the Jews believed, God was able to foresee and provide for any contingency his people might face. In his law he made provision for all such. This conviction forced the Jews to ingenious interpretations of the Bible. In time, this led to allegorizing much of the scripture by Philo and other Alexandrian interpreters. The Essenes constantly saw themselves foretold in the Hebrew scriptures. In a similar way, late Old Testament writers had inserted details that were fragments of the imagination developed to fit current conditions.

The Jewish people never blamed their defeats upon God. They had been unfaithful and God had used their enemies to punish them, to reform them. He had brought them out of Egypt and enabled them to return from Babylonian exile. He had made it possible for them to defeat the Selucid Syrians. He would help them drive out the Romans. He would raise up great David's greater son, the Messiah, who would sit on David's throne, reunite all the Hebrew people, and rule over a nation as large and great as David's—probably much larger and doubtless much greater. This led to the rebellion of A.D. 66–70 and again to Bar Cocheba's revolt of 132–135. Hope had had to be deferred, but it would not die.

ASSIGNMENT

1. What did the Jewish people feel was distinct about themselves and their religion?
2. What was their attitude toward other people previous to the Babylonian captivity? How did this change during the intertestamental period? What Old Testament writings incorporate this change?
3. What was the Jewish attitude toward the law? God? sin? justice? the future?

SUPPLEMENTARY READING

Enslin—Chapters VI and VII
Moore
Parkes
Snaith—Chapters VIII and IX
Toombs—Chapter 5

Chapter 35

The Mechanics of Judaism

The Jerusalem temple was the center of Jewish worship. It had housed the Ark of the Covenant made under the direction of Moses. After David had made Jerusalem his political capital, he moved the ark there and placed it in an elaborate tent. He planned to build a splendid stone structure for it, but was dissuaded by the prophet Nathan. Just before his death, David instructed his son and successor Solomon to carry out the plans. He explained that he had not done it because "the word of the LORD came to me saying, 'You have shed much blood and have waged great wars; you shall not build a house to my name'" (1 Chron. 22:8).

Solomon's temple was a structure of hewn white limestone, covered on the interior with cedar. The floor was overlaid with cypress. It was about ninety feet long and thirty feet wide. The front room, the Holy Place, was sixty feet long and forty-five feet high. The rear room, the Holy of Holies or Most Holy Place, was a thirty-foot cube; its floor probably was higher than that of the larger room. In the unlighted smaller room stood the ark protected by two cherubim, evidently figures of winged bulls or lions with human faces. The outer room had ten candlesticks, a table or tables for the holy bread, and a small altar of incense. The temple faced east. Around both sides and the back were three stories of small rooms, totaling about half the height of the main temple. A porch or vestibule ran across the front of the building.

In line with the idea that all good things had been directed by Yahweh at Mount Sinai, the tradition developed that the temple was patterned after a tabernacle constructed by Moses in the wilderness. This tent-like structure was said to be forty-five feet long and fifteen wide, furnished much as was the temple. It is quite possible that the tabernacle never got beyond the drawing-board stage. No definite record of its being taken into Canaan or Palestine is given. On the other hand, much is made of the ark. Ruins of earlier Canaanite and Phoenician temples indicate that they were quite similar to the Jerusalem temple. The Hebrews, with no architecture of their own, had borrowed from others.

Solomon's temple was robbed of its elaborate gold decorations and equipment a number of times. It was finally completely destroyed by the Babylonian Nebuchadnezzar in 586 B.C.

What became of the ark? It may have been taken to Babylonia as a trophy in 586, or possibly when Nebuchadnezzar first conquered Jerusalem eleven years earlier. It may have been burned when the temple was destroyed. In the third place, it may have been hidden by the Jews. Second Macc. 2:5-7 says that Jeremiah hid it and other temple equipment in a cave on Mount Sinai, which he so sealed that no one could find it "until God gathers his people together again and shows his mercy." Second Bar. 6:5-10 reports that just before Jerusalem was destroyed, Baruch saw an angel descend and take the ark and numerous other pieces of temple equipment. He ordered the earth to "guard them unto the last times, so that when thou art ordered, 'thou mayest restore them.' . . . And the earth opened its mouth and swallowed them up."

When the Jews started coming back from Babylonian captivity in 538 B.C., they cleaned off the temple site and erected an altar. Soon they rebuilt the foundations of the temple, but other interests interfered with the construction of a new edifice. Zerubbabel returned from captivity determined to build the temple, but made little progress until the prophets Haggai and Zechariah came to his support in 520. The building was completed in 516 and came to be known as Zerubbabel's temple. It was probably identical in dimensions to Solomon's temple, but much inferior in materials and decorations. There seems to have been but one seven-branched candlestick. The Holy of Holies was empty—it had no replica of the ark.

Additions to the temple were made at later times. We read in Ecclus. 50:1-2 that "Simon the high priest, son of Onias . . . repaired the house and fortified the temple. He laid the foundations for the high double walls. . . . In his days a cistern for water was quarried out." The verses that follow give a detailed description of the service of sacrifice. This was about 300 B.C.

This temple was plundered from time to time. Antiochus IV,

Epiphanes, did much damage in 168. First Macc. 4:38 reports that Judas and his friends "saw the sanctuary desolate, the altar profaned, and the gates burned. In the courts they saw bushes sprung up as in a thicket. . . . They saw also the chambers of the priests in ruins."

In his extensive construction program, Herod the Great offered to build a new temple for the Jews. By this time Zerrubbabel's temple had the prestige of years. Jews did not want it destroyed, but were happy to have it renovated. This was begun in 20 B.C. A new enlarged porch or vestibule, a new floor, a new roof, additional columns and courts, as well as more magnificent decorations resulted in what came to be recognized as a new temple, Herod's, larger and possibly more elaborate than Solomon's. This was not considered completed until A.D. 64, long after Herod's death. It was destroyed six years later. Reform Jews today call their synagogues temples. Jews of the Diaspora did not get to visit the temple often, but Rome attempted to collect from them a tax for its support.

Special sacrifices were made on festive occasions. There were also daily sacrifices. Some were made in the name of the people and paid for by offerings and taxes. Others were made in the names of individuals who brought or paid for their own animals.

While the chief elements of the temple services were sacrifices (not only animal but cereal offerings and drink offerings), music was also a part of worship. While the burnt offering was being consumed, priests blew trumpets and clashed cymbals. After the drink offering was poured out, a psalm was sung, a different one for each day of the week.

The Chronicles account makes much of temple music, evidently developed after the second temple was built. Choirs were composed of Levites. The congregation joined in refrains and hallelujahs. So important did temple music seem to the compiler of Chronicles about 250 B.C. that he credited its organization to David.

In the intertestamental period, various musical instruments were used at the temple, including, in addition to trumpets and cymbals, psaltries, harps, other stringed instruments, timbrels, and pipes. In Herod's time there was added an organ which had thirteen pipes and two bellows. Temple choirs were composed of men and boys.

Three great festivals and two or more minor ones were celebrated annually. The greatest of these was the Passover, observed in late March or early April. It celebrated death passing over the homes of Israelites as they were about to start their exodus from Egypt. To this had been annexed the Feast of Unleavened Bread in honor of the beginning of early harvest. This resulted in an eight-day celebration.

The feast of Pentecost (fifty days), or Weeks, also called Harvest or First Fruits, seven weeks after Passover, brought great crowds to Jerusalem, especially from the Diaspora. At the Passover season the Mediterranean was too rough for smooth travel; seven weeks later it was almost ideal.

The Feast of Tabernacles, or Booths, was the great harvest celebration in September or October. It began on the night of the harvest full moon. Families lived on their housetops. There was an all-night festival, when the court of the women at the temple was lit by great candelabras. Young priests whirled lighted torches in acrobatic dances. Temple choirs and musicians provided music all through the night.

The Feast of Lights, or Hanukkah, commemorated the rededication of the temple in 165 B.C. after the "abomination of desolation." It provided torchlight processions and illuminations each December. Also developed during the intertestamental period was Purim, celebrated in February or March in recognition of the deliverance of the Jews from Haman, as told in Esther.

Temple activities were conducted by priests. There were so many—five or six thousand—that individual priests served only a few hours during the year. Since their duties at the temple required their presence in Jerusalm only four or five weeks a year, most priests had their homes outside the city. Many of them lived in Jericho.

In intertestamental times the leader of the priests, known as the high priest, was a man of great authority. The later Hasmonean high priests called themselves kings. The Selucid Syrians, and later the Romans, took to themselves the right to appoint high priests, naming men they found most cooperative, sometimes the man who offered to pay the most for this remunerative position. With it came great profits from sacrifices, taxes, and gifts.

The origin of the position of high priest is quite indefinite. Moses is reported to have appointed his brother Aaron and Aaron's sons as priests. Ezra 7:5 refers to Aaron as chief priest.

In telling of the establishment of the cities of refuge, both Num. 35 and Jos. 20 refer to high priests, but these accounts were not brought into their present form until during, or shortly after, Babylonian captivity. Eli was the leading priest of his time and was succeeded by Samuel, but neither the title of high priest nor that of chief priest is applied to either of them.

Although Samuel reprimanded Saul the King for functioning as a priest, making sacrifices (1 Sam. 13:13), we find both David and Solomon supervising the activities of priests as though they were the chief priests. David had two leading priests, Abiathar a descendant of Eli, and Zadok. Ezra reported that Zadok was a descendant of Aaron. Eventually, the Pharisees and Essenes insisted that high priests should be descendants of Zadok.

In the stories of temple reform of Joash, and later of Josiah, high priests are mentioned. Haggai and Zechariah refer to high priests, as does Nehemiah. Apparently, the title came into definite existence after the Babylonian captivity. The high priest a bit later became the most important man among the Jews. He was "anointed," supposedly selected by God. His influence went beyond the temple, beyond religion, to all phases of Jewish life.

Herod the Great's father controlled the Jews by controlling the high priest. Herod himself used the position to his own advantage, as did his descendants and the procurators until the destruction of the temple. During this period at least twenty-eight men were high priests. Under the Romans only Sadducees held this position. It was no longer hereditary, but was shared by a number of families. These formed an inner circle who came to be known as the chief priests. The high priest served as head of the governing body of Judea, the Sanhedrin.

The Sanhedrin, or great council, came into existence some time between 300 and 250 B.C. The writers of Chronicles, living at about that time, suggest that a judicial council, presided over by a chief priest, was appointed by Jehoshaphat, who ruled Judah about 850 B.C. (2 Chron. 19:8-11). The idea of the Sanhedrin could have been based upon the story of Moses, appointing seventy elders who were given "some of the spirit that was upon him" (Num. 11:16, 24-25). When we meet the Sanhedrin it has legislative and executive power as well as judicial. Local communities had small Sanhedrins of five to twenty-three members, but the national group had seventy members plus the presiding high priest. Rome changed its attitude toward the Sanhedrin from time to time. In general, it took away certain powers, including that of putting people to death, but allowed it to continue to govern in many matters. During the division of Herod's kingdom, the Sanhedrin had authority over only the territory of Archelaus and the first group of procurators, except in matters definitely religious. The Sanhedrin had its own building in the southern part of the temple area. This was an impressive stone structure. After the destruction of the temple in A.D. 70, the Sanhedrin, which had been chiefly related to the priests, was replaced by the council, which for some time met at Jamnia but dealt only with religious questions.

Fortunately for the Jews, the destruction of the temple did not leave them without religious centers. Ezekiel in Babylonian captivity seems to have led in the establishment of synagogues, local organizations of Jews who met at regular times to pray together and read and discuss their scriptures. Oddly, the word synagogue does not appear in the Old Testament or the Apocrypha, although synagogues are doubtless referred to in Ps. 74:8—"They burned all the meeting places of God in the land." Reflecting the Jewish feeling that all good things were established at God's command by Moses, both Josephus and Philo report that synagogues had their origin in the time of Moses. Eventually, synagogues developed into social and educational centers. The rulers of each synagogue became the local sanhedrin. Synagogues filled so many needs of the Jews that, when they returned from captivity and built a new temple, they kept their synagogues.

The regular Sabbath synagogue service was begun by a psalm or prayer of thanksgiving, the repetition of the shema (Deut. 6:4-9; 11:13-21; Num. 15:37-41), prayers chanted by a cantor, an assigned reading in Hebrew from the Torah, translation of this into the common language of the people (Aramaic or Greek)—this was the origin of the Targums—, a selected reading from the Prophets, its translation, and an address or discussion based on the reading. If a priest was present, he was asked to pronounce a benediction; otherwise, a closing prayer was offered.

Synagogues originally met in homes, but by the intertestamental period, many synagogue buildings had been erected. In the towns these were the most important structures. Every town had a synagogue. The cities had several. In Jerusalem, Hellenists returning from Egypt had their own synagogues, as did other groups of foreign Jews. Some served as hostels for visiting Jews. Sometimes separate trades had their own synagogues.

Titus said that, when he conquered Jerusalem, there were 394 synagogues there. At this time there were probably a thousand synagogues throughout the Diaspora. We have evidence of at least eleven in the city of Rome. Long before A.D. 70, the temple was not much more than a symbol; the synagogue had become the real center of the Jewish religion.

The synagogue developed the use of the Torah, caused the Jews to become the people of a book. Chanting or singing fostered the development and use of the collection we call The Psalms. It was the synagogue leaders, mostly Pharisees, who maintained religion after the destruction of the temple. They developed a school for the study of the Torah at Jamnia. It was this group that in A.D. 90 "sealed" the scriptures, limited to Torah, Prophets, and Holy Writings.

The emphasis upon the Torah encouraged young men to make a special study of the scriptures. The chief training school was in Jerusalem. These specialists in the Bible came to be called rabbis or teachers, "great ones." Rabbis commonly led the discussions or preached the sermons in synagogue services and taught in the synagogue schools. Rabbis were definitely not priests.

During the intertestamental period, we meet not only rabbis, but also scribes. Scribes, recorders, secretaries, were mentioned even before the time of Solomon. Scribes came into prominence after the Babylonian captivity. Ezra and Nehemiah make frequent reference to scribes. Ezra himself is considered the father of the scribes from a religious standpoint. He was also a priest. The prophet had practically disappeared. The Torah had been canonized. Therefore, copies of it were needed and its interpretation desired. To produce both of these became the task of the scribes. While earlier scribes were associated with the priests, the division between temple and synagogue, between priests and rabbis, developed more scribes associated with rabbis and their interests in the scriptures. There came to be little if any difference between scribes and rabbis. Probably many men were called by both titles.

ASSIGNMENT

1. Review the history of the temple. What had preceded the temple? Give the circumstances, date, and builder of each of the three temples. What became of each?

2. What later attempts were made to build Jewish temples? How is the term temple used in current Judaism?

3. Discuss the practice of sacrifices; the use of music at the temple.

4. What were the chief temple feasts?

5. What is the origin of the synagogue? In what major ways did it differ from the temple? Why was it continued after Babylonian captivity? Under Roman control, how did the attitudes of Pharisees and Sadducees toward temple and synagogue differ? What caused these differences to develop? to be maintained? Outline the regular Sabbath service of the synagogue. What contributions did the synagogue make to Jewish life and religion?

6. Distinguish between priests, rabbis, and scribes. What is known about the development of the position of high priest? What was meant by "chief priests"?

7. Tell the history of the Sanhedrin.

8. What relation did Jews of the Diaspora have to the temple? to synagogues?

SUPPLEMENTARY READING

Enslin—Chapter VIII
Moore—Part I, Chapters V and VI
Parkes—Chapter 1
Pfeiffer, Charles—Pages 58-64
Pfeiffer, R. H.: *Religion*—Pages 205-13
Schauss
Snaith—Chapter XVII
The Interpreter's Dictionary of the Bible—Articles: Festivals, Synagogue, Tabernacle, Temple

Chapter 36

The Changing Concept
of God

It was difficult for Jews to recognize that their concept of God grew. They had no systematized theology. They were sure that God had told all that needed to be known to Moses on Mount Sinai. What each writer did was to express factors of this truth in his own words. As we look back now, we see an evolution in these expressions. However, during the intertestamental period, the Jews could not see this growth. They could not get an over-all picture as we are privileged to do. One concept, however, is found in all Jewish pictures of God—deity, more than a principle, is always personal. God is portrayed as exalted, but not remote.

During Babylonian captivity, the Jews came to the definite belief that there is but one God: "I am the LORD, and there is no other; besides me there is no God" (Isa. 45:5). The question of the character of God still needed to be faced. It is in the intertestamental period that we see steps leading to Jesus' picture of deity. Second Isaiah had quoted God as saying, "I am the LORD your God, the Holy One of Israel" (42:3), but that was not enough. What was the relation between this holy God and sinful man?

Socrates had talked about a Divine Purpose which had to do with the guidance of man. Aristotle had talked about a Prime Mover, or First Cause. Various Greeks discussed the Logos, a summary of knowledge. Late Jewish writers had discussed Wisdom. Perhaps the Greeks and the Jews were not so far apart! Philo proposed bringing them together. Possibly the Jews had thought of God as too definitely a big man. Attempts were made to move away from this. One of the Targums translated Gen.

3:8 as, "And they heard the voice of the Word of the Lord God walking in the garden." Intertestamental writers described God as a spirit existing in all places: "How vast the territory he possesses! It is great and has no bounds" (Bar. 3:24-25). "The Spirit of the Lord has filled the world, and that which holds all things together knows what is said" (Wisd. 1:7). In the Letter of Aristeas we read, "There is only one God, and his power is manifest throughout all things, every place being full of his dominion" (132).

On the other hand, in adopting Greek theological thinking, care must be taken to avoid accepting the Greek symbols of deity found in statues or idols. "Though we speak much we cannot reach the end, and the sum of our words is 'He is the all.' . . . For he is greater than all his works" (Ecclus. 43:27-28). His concern is universal. In the Additions to Esther, Mordecai prays, "The universe is in thy power (13:9). Pseudo-Solomon declares, "The whole world before thee is like a speck that tips the scales" (Wisd. 11:22).

The universality of God was recognized: "The compassion of man is for his neighbor, but the compassion of the Lord is for all living beings" (Ecclus. 18:13). This tended to challenge the concept of the Jews being God's pets, his chosen people. We wonder if it was the Palestinian Ben Sirach, or his Alexandrian grandson who prayed, "Cause the fear of thee to fall upon all the nations . . . and let them know thee, as we have known that there is no God but thee, O Lord" (Ecclus. 26:2-5). This was Jewish witness in a polytheistic environment. The compiler of the Prayer of Azariah has his hero conclude, "Let them know that thou art the Lord, the only God, glorious over the whole world" (verse 22). "He is king over the heavens, and judges kings and kingdoms" (Ps. of Sol. 2:34). In the Testaments of the Twelve Patriarchs it is stated that God will use Israel and its Law to save all Gentiles.

Second Isaiah pictures God as maintaining:

> I am the LORD, who made all things,
> who stretched out the heavens alone,
> who spread out the earth—Who was with me?
> (44:24).

Similarly, the intertestamental writers frequently emphasized that Yahweh is the creator of the universe. Ezra is reported to have addressed God, "O sovereign Lord, didst thou not speak at the beginning when thou didst form the earth—and that without help?" (2 Esdras 3:4). The song of the Three Young Men (verses 29-68), the prayer of Jonathan in 2 Macc. 1:24-29, of Mordecai in Add. to Esther 13:10-12, of Judith in Jud. 9:12, as well as various expressions in the wisdom literature, emphasize that God created all things and is to be praised for his goodness. The absolute sovereignty of God was basic for the Essenes.

Creation was by the word of God, apparently instantaneous, without the toil by which men make things. "Thy word accomplished the work" (2 Esdras 6:38). "By the words of the Lord his works are done" (Ecclus. 42:15).

Despite unpleasant events in their own experience, the Jews of the intertestamental period were sure that God had a hand in all history. In 1 Macc. 4:30-33, Judas expresses the conviction that God has given David victories and will do the same for him. In summarizing her success, Judith proclaims that "God is the Lord who crushes wars; for he delivered me out of the hands of my pursuers" (Jud. 16:3). Ezra similarly praises God in 2 Esdras 3:9-11. The Habakkuk Commentary proclaims, "The mysteries of God are marvelous" (7:8). The apocalyptic writings suggest that at times God does not interfere in the affairs of men, but he has done great things in the past and will do even greater things in the immediate future. The present unhappy situation is God's punishment for sin.

Especially in the Qumran writings, God is pictured as determining whether each individual will be righteous or evil. "Thou hast created the righteous and the wicked" (Thanksgiving Hymns 4:38).

That God is both eternal and holy is proclaimed numerous times. He is the all-knowing: "The Most High knows all that be known . . . No thought escapes him" (Ecclus. 32:18-20); "Thou knowest all things" (Add. to Esther 13:12).

In contrast to the Greek pictures of their gods, the Jews emphasized the righteousness of Yahweh. God is good. No longer do we find him doing cruel things as he is portrayed in the early Old Testament. Tobit prays, "Righteous art thou, O Lord; all thy deeds and all thy ways are mercy and truth, and thou dost render true and righteous judgment for ever" (3:2). Azariah says much the same thing in his prayer (Pr. of Az. 1:3-4). So do Esther (Add. to Esther 14:7), Pseudo-Solomon (Wisd. 12:15), Baruch (2:6), and Ezra (2 Esdras 8:36).

Justice, not love, is the form righteousness generally takes. Tobit feels that God will afflict Jerusalem "for the deeds of your sons, but again he will show mercy for the sons of the righteous" (13:9). Second Maccabees says of Antiochus Epiphanes, "The all-seeing Lord, the God of Israel, struck him an incurable and unseen blow" (9:5). Pseudo-Solomon believes that "Men could fall at a single breath when pursued by justice and scattered by the breath of thy power. But thou hast arranged all things by measure and number and weight" (Wisd. 11:20).

However, God is pictured as long-suffering. "The Lord is patient with them and pours out his mercy upon them" (Ecclus. 18:11). Baruch is reported to have addressed Jerusalem, "You were handed over to your enemies because you angered God," but continues, "Take courage, O Jerusalem, for he who named you will comfort you" (Bar. 4:6 and 30). The Prayer of Manasseh reads, "Thou art the Lord Most High, of great compassion, long-suffering and very merciful" (verse 7). The same concept of God is given in 2 Esdras 7:132.

The apocalyptic picture of God's heavenly court with its many attendants was a means of depicting God's majesty and greatness. The king was the lawmaker. Judith portrays strict obedience to the Law as the approach to God.

With a growing concept of noble qualities of God, there developed a new respect for God. As in the Old Testament the name given to God, Yahweh, came to be considered too holy to pronounce, so during intertestamental times the word God itself, Elohim, came to be less and less used. The author of 1 Maccabees went to the extreme of never using the words Lord, or God (although the King James translators remedied this shortcoming by inserting the word God at six different places). Synonyms, such as King, Most High, Holy One, the Almighty, Father, the Name, Heaven, or He, are used through the intertestamental writings. Nearly a hundred titles or names are found. Sometimes the greatness of God is indicated by piling title upon title: "Lord, Lord, king of the heavens and ruler of all creation, holy among the holy, monarch, all-powerful ruler" (3 Macc. 2:2).

God is not often thought of as speaking directly, as was frequently reported in the Old Testament. In 2 Esdras, God speaks directly at times and at other times through angels. An angel directs Habakkuk to Daniel (Bel 34-39). Daniel tells Susanna's judges that "the angel of God has received the sentence of God" (verse 55), and "the angel of God is waiting with his sword" (verse 59). In 1 Macc. 7:41, an angel kills 185,000 Assyrians. In 2 Maccabees, angels and other non-human manifestations are quite active. We are familiar with stories in the beginning of the New Testament reporting messages delivered by angels to Zechariah (Lu. 1:11-20), Joseph (Mt. 1:20-21), Mary (Lu. 1: 26-38), and the shepherds (Lu. 2:9-14).

A number of times in intertestamental writing God is spoken of as revealing himself through Wisdom.

On the other hand, common people might offer prayer to God. This was unusual in the Old Testament. Here again is progress. The priest no longer is necessary for communion with God. Despite Hannah's breaking of the taboo against ordinary people offering prayer (1 Sam. 1:21-28), we find very few laymen praying until the beginning of the intertestamental period. Nehemiah, neither priest nor prophet, prayed from time to time. The author of the book of Daniel, writing in 165 B.C., has his hero risk his life rather than give up a habit of praying toward Jerusalem three times daily (Dan. 6:6-13).

Related to this is the Prayer of Azariah. Various characters in Tobit practice prayer. Earlier in this chapter reference has been made to prayers of Baruch, Ezra, Pseudo-Solomon, and Esther (in the Additions). This is leading in the direction of the admonition given in the first New Testament book written, "Pray constantly" (1 Thess. 5:17).

Prayer in the intertestamental period is not chiefly making requests of God. It is largely praise, adoration. Prayers in intertestamental literature are commonly modeled after psalms found in the Old Testament.

ASSIGNMENT

1. What did Philo attempt to do? What contributions to an understanding of God did the Jews make to the Greek world?
2. What was the Jewish thought of God as creator? his eternity? holiness? righteousness? justice? long-suffering? majesty?
3. Discuss the change from the common use of the term Yahweh to the term Elohim. Why did this take place? Why did the term Elohim drop out of common use? What terms took its place? What did this indicate about the changing concept of God?
4. Discuss the intertestamental idea of God's manifestations.

5. Discuss the changing use of prayer (who might pray; type of prayer).

SUPPLEMENTARY READING

Charles: *Religious Development*—Chapter V
Moore—Vol. I, Part II
Toombs—Pages 69-72
Abingdon Bible Commentary—Pages 200-13

Chapter 37

The Utopia of the Future

The Jews were unceasingly optimistic. As early as the first writing prophet, Amos, 750 B.C., we find an expectation of the day of the LORD when God and his chosen people would be permanently established and all would go well. It would be a day of light. Amos and later prophets warn, "Woe to you who desire the day of the LORD . . . It is darkness, and not light" (Amos 5:18), justice and not joy. God was seeking for justice. The Hebrew people were not practicing it. It was essential that "justice roll down like waters, and righteousness like an overflowing stream" (5:24).

While the prophets were pessimistic about the immediate future, they felt that not all would be lost, that God would in time "raise up the booth of David that is fallen" (Amos 9:11). Isaiah believed a remnant would be saved, that from this remnant would rise up a man anointed of God, the Messiah, who would lead his people to great victory. This concept had probably existed since the kingdom of Israel was broken into two parts about 922 B.C. Isaiah believed that, with the coming of the Messiah, "the earth shall be full of the knowledge of the LORD as the waters cover the sea" (Isa. 11:9). Not every picture of the golden future depends upon a Messiah or even political supremacy. For some, it was a purely theocratic state.

Probably the first concept of the Messiah was of one who would reunite Israel and Judah. Later it was believed that his kingdom would be as great as David's, then larger. The popular belief was that he would overcome any enemy. In the later intertestamental period this was Rome. Some went so far as to believe that the Jews would supplant the entire Roman Empire. Post-exilic people were convinced that the utopia was coming when every Jew would sit "under his vine and under his fig tree" (Zech. 3:10). Probably similar statements were at this time interpolated in the writings of earlier prophets, as Mic. 4:4.

They felt that certainly the time of David and Solomon must have been better than the present. Of this romantic golden past it was said, "Judah and Israel dwelt in safety, from Dan even to Beersheba, every man under his vine and under his fig tree, all the days of Solomon" (1 Kg. 4:25). This contradicted the fact that such supposedly happy men were so oppressed by taxation and forced labor that they broke into rebellion. It was believed that God would soon restore such a splendid time for his own people.

The day of the LORD, which Amos had insisted would be a time of judgment, would be a day of victory for a righteous God and, therefore, for the restored and righteous Israel. The judgment would be for the heathen world. This could be a permanent Kingdom of God, but this does not imply that its individual members would not die.

The Psalms indicate a growing feeling of value and satisfaction achieved through communion with God. Certain prophets thought the time would come when it would be unnecessary to ask if one knew the LORD, for all would know him. Sin would be destroyed.

The Jews kept looking for a glorious age that never came. Every change in government raised new hopes. By intertestamental times, they came to believe that the utopia would come only by the interference of God in history. Darker and darker pictures of the day of the LORD were drawn. In the writing of the Pseudepigrapha called the Assumption of Moses, we are told of such a time when "the sun shall not give his light . . . the circuit of the stars shall be disordered" (10:3-6). The Sibylline Oracles (5:512-530) expects a war among the constellations. A definite Persian or Zoroastrian influence can be found here.

Only as the Jews came to think of there being but one God, the creator and sustainer of the universe, could such ideas be held. While their picture of God improved, their attitude about the world grew worse. The world was considered too evil to contain the Kingdom of God. In varying degrees it was felt that the present world must be destroyed. Apocalyptic writings emphasized this. The Qumran Thanksgiving Hymns expected evil to be destroyed by a river of fire. "Wickedness Thou shalt exterminate forever and Thy righteousness shall be revealed in the presence of all Thy deeds" (14:16). The War Scroll expects the Sons of Light to destroy the Sons of Darkness.

It was commonly thought that only righteous Jews living at the time of the great cataclysmic event would participate. The prophet Jeremiah had thought that God was concerned with all people. Ezekiel, his successor, tended to limit God's concern to the Hebrew people. Ezekiel seemed to be winning during the intertestamental period. The Testaments of the Twelve Patriarchs accept a few Gentiles, but these will be subordinate to Israel. In the Psalms of Solomon, chapter 17, Gentiles who are saved will become servants.

This is not entirely a selfish concept. The highest satisfactions could be attained only by sharing in the life of the community. Great suffering would accompany the bringing about of this new age or new world. No two apocalypses agree as to details. It was vivid but complicated and obscure. Some accounts have definite contradictions from chapter to chapter. Perhaps the Essenes with their expectation of a war between the Sons of Light and the Sons of Darkness had the most definite picture.

This new world is not to be non-material. Members are sometimes pictured as living a thousand years and begetting a thousand children. The yield of fruit and grain will be ten thousand fold. In Enoch 90 the old temple and its ornaments are removed, and God brings a new and much larger temple and sets it on the old temple site.

The golden age was not always described as unending. Second Esdras pictures the Anointed reigning four hundred years to correspond to the four hundred years of Egyptian bondage. After this, he and all mankind will die. Then come the resurrection and final judgment ushering in another new age. God himself is to be the judge. Elsewhere we find this period a thousand years. The Messiah is also sometimes considered the final judge. In some pictures there is a messianic age without a Messiah. It is the kingly role of God that is important. This they all have in common.

The dream of the Messiah was largely limited to the prophets, although nowhere in the Old Testament is the term actually used as we find it in the New Testament. While numerous intertestamental writers expected a new age, a new world, they made little reference to a Messiah. From the time of the prophets until that of John Hyrcanus, there was little interest in the Messiah. This probably explains why Judas Maccabeus was not proclaimed the Messiah. John Hyrcanus seems to have wanted to be called the Messiah. Therefore, there is little reference to the Messiah in the Apocrypha, more in the Pseudepigrapha. There is a very strong Messianic expectation in the Qumran literature.

The personality of the Messiah is never mentioned in the Apocrypha. Nevertheless, the author of Ecclesiasticus has in mind a messianic descendant of David when he says, among similar statements,

> He gave a remnant to Jacob
> and to David a root of his stock (47:22).

In the Pseudepigrapha, the Psalms of Solomon (17:5) expresses the same conviction, while Jub. 31:18-19 refers to the Messsiah as coming from David's tribe, Judah.

In 2 Esdras 13:3, the Messiah seems to be a heavenly being who "flew with the clouds of heaven." Another writer in the same book quotes God as saying that after four hundred years "my son the Messiah shall die" (7:29). In the vision of the eagle in the 11th and 12th chapters, he appears as a lion with a man's voice who destroys the Roman Empire. In Enoch, he is a human being from Israel, appearing as a white bull and later as a lamb with black horns (90:37-38).

Enoch 37-71 describes a divine Messiah in existence before the beginning of the world. In the last judgment he is to be the defender of the righteous. He will be able to uncover all secret things of the world.

The Psalms of Solomon describes the Messiah as a human king, "This king is the Lord Messiah" (17:36). He will become God's official representative. He will destroy the Romans and the Sadducees and restore the dispersed tribes of Israel to Palestine. Wisdom, justice, mercy, holiness, and freedom from sin are his characteristics. The Messiah of 2 Esdras is also expected to restore the lost tribes of Israel.

The Messiah "will not trust in horsemen or in chariot; nor in the bow; nor shall he multiply to himself gold and silver for war; nor shall he rely on a multitude in the days of war" (Ps. of Sol. 17:37). Another part of 2 Esdras pictures violence against the enemies of God, who seem to be the same as the enemies of the Jews. In a vision the writer saw the Messiah send "forth from his mouth, as it were, a stream of fire, and from his lips a flaming breath . . . and burned them all up" (13:10-11). A bit further on it is explained that the Messiah "will destroy them without effort by the law (which is symbolized by the fire)" (verse 38).

As the Qumran community was divided between priesthood and laity, so the Essenes generally refer to a priestly Messiah and a lay Messiah, Aaron and Israel, "the prince of the whole congregation." However, there is some hint that the descendant of Levi and the descendant of Judah may be the same person. A similar idea may be found in the Testaments of the Twelve Patriarchs. At one place the Talmud refers to "the two sons of oil—these are the two anointed ones, one anointed for battle and one anointed to be king of Israel." This is further complicated in the Manual of Discipline, where there is reference to three coming messianic persons, prophet, priest, and king. The Zadokite Document mentions a Righteous Teacher who will arise at the end of the days (6:11). This may mean that he will be the forerunner of the Messiah. If it means that the founder of the sect was expected to return as the Messiah, it is to be noted that he was not considered the Messiah in his first earthly life. On the other hand, the Thanksgiving Psalms, generally attributed to the Righteous Teacher, make something like messianic claims for the author. He refers to God's "separating by me the righteous from the wicked."

The book of Jubilees and the Dead Sea Scrolls reflect the Greek belief in the immortality of the soul, rather than the resurrection of the body. A universal judgment was expected. In the Thanksgiving Psalms we read, "Everything is engraved before thee with a pen of remembrance" (1:24). The Manual of Discipline reports that God "has ordained a period for the reign of error, and in the appointed time of punishment, he will destroy it forever" (4:18-19), but this punishment is not described.

ASSIGNMENT

1. What were the major expectations of the Jewish people? What place in world affairs did they want to hold? Why?

2. Trace the hope for the Messiah. Describe the various pictures of the Messiah in the intertestamental period.

3. What was meant by "the day of the LORD"?

4. What attitude toward the present world developed in the intertestamental period? What influence did this have on the idea of the utopia of the future?

5. What picture of the utopia of the future did the apocalyptists draw? How material? How long was it to last?

SUPPLEMENTARY READING

Charles: *Religious Development*—Chapter II
Enslin—Chapter IX
Gaster—Pages 337-40
Klausner—Part II
Moore—Vol. II, Part VII, Chapter II
Snaith—Chapter X

Chapter 38

The Resurrection

Second Esdras teaches that after the Messianic Age "the world, which is not yet awake, shall be roused, and that which is corruptible shall perish. And the earth shall give up those who are asleep in it . . . and the chambers shall give up souls which have been committed to them" (7:31-32).

The idea of the resurrection was a late Hebrew concept. The Sadducees rejected it because it is not found in the Torah. It probably was not held until the Babylonian captivity. Earlier religion probably was not concerned with the individual. It was a relationship between God and the Hebrew nations, Judah and Israel. A partial continuation of the individual after death was accepted. This state was known as Sheol, a very hazy existence in which the "shades" of people found neither suffering nor enjoyment. Without the physical body, it was felt, there could be no real personality. "There is no work or thought or knowledge or wisdom in Sheol" (Eccles. 9:10). No one will return from this "land of gloom and deep darkness" (Job 10:21). Such a one is "weary" (Job 3:17), "has no strength" (Ps. 88:4), and dwells "in the land of silence" (Ps. 94:17). He is no longer in the hand of God. Morality has nothing to do with his state in Sheol or the Pit, although there is separation by nations. The Septuagint in translating the Hebrew Sheol uses the Greek term Hades.

The idea of continuation after death played no part in early Hebrew religion. The first reference to this appears only incidentally in 1 Sam. 28 when King Saul seeks guidance from the deceased Samuel.

As the Hebrew concept of God grew, and God came to be thought of as just, a solution needed to be found for the questions: Why do some people not receive justice in this world? Why does a good God allow good people to suffer? Doubtless the Persian Zoroastrians helped the Jews develop an answer. They concluded that reward and punishment would be found in the next life. This led to concepts of heaven and hell.

The Wisdom of Solomon suggests some such division: "The souls of the righteous are in the hand of God, and no torment will ever touch them. In the eyes of the foolish they seem to have died . . . but they are at peace. . . . Their hope is full of immortality . . . because God tested them and found them worthy of himself" (3:1-5). On the other hand, regarding the wicked, "The Lord will laugh them to scorn. After this they will become dishonored corpses, and an outrage among the dead for ever . . . and they will suffer anguish" (4:18-19).

Among the Old Testament prophets an emphasis on the importance of the individual developed. Jeremiah suggested this. The book of Proverbs emphasizes it. As people began to dream of a utopia of the future, they became convinced that God would raise up the faithful dead to share in this great experience, that they might be a part of the restored, glorious Israel.

This was a physical kingdom; therefore a physical resurrection was necessary. This differed from the Greek idea of the continuation of the spirit or soul. God had created the earth and its inhabitants. He would create a new world. Therefore, mutilated bodies would be recreated. The seven brothers of 2 Macc. 7 believed this. One of them, as he was about to be dismembered, "quickly put out his tongue and courageously stretched forth his hands and said nobly, 'I got these from Heaven, and because of his laws I disdain them, and from him I hope to get them back again'" (verses 10-11). The same book tells of an elder of Jerusalem: "With his blood now completely drained from him, he tore out his entrails, took them with both hands and hurled them at the crowd, calling upon the Lord of life and spirit to give them back to him again. This was the manner of his death" (14:46).

The Old Testament has but two references to the resurrection of individuals, both in Apocalyptic passages. Isa. 26:19 (inserted in the book of Isaiah probably about 300 B.C.) reads regarding pious Israelites:

> The dead shall live, their bodies shall rise.
> O dwellers in the dust, awake and sing for joy!

This chiefly refers to Israelites who had given their lives for their religion. Surely God would provide them some further opportunity. However, some scholars are convinced that this does not refer to individuals but to spiritually inert or "dead" Judah.

Dan. 12:2 promises, "Many of those who sleep in the dust of the earth shall awake, some to everlasting life, and some to shame and everlasting contempt." Resurrection here was to be limited to the very good and the very bad, those deserving additional reward or punishment; the others would doubtless remain in Sheol. Other verses sometimes quoted refer to avoiding death rather than a return from death.

In the early intertestamental writings we find belief that righteous Israelites will rise to eternal life in God's kingdom (2 Macc., Enoch 91-92, Ps. of Sol.). The parables of Enoch 37-71 promise that righteous Israelites will enjoy life on a new earth, while the wicked will be raised to final judgment and everlasting torture.

The Aussumption of Moses provides for the resurrection of good spirits after the final judgment. They will be taken to the heavens where they can look down on the torture of the wicked in Gehenna. In 2 Bar. 30 only the righteous are to rise, but in chapters 50 and 51 both righteous and evil will rise; the good will become more beautiful and the bad more ugly.

Sheol, or Hades, had not disappeared from men's thinking by intertestamental times. Ecclesiasticus suggests that the only desirable future possible is a good reputation and stalwart sons. There will be no great satisfaction in Hades. "Give and take and beguile yourself, because in Hades one cannot look for luxury" (14:16). "How can you reject the good pleassure of the Most High? . . . There is no inquiry about it in Hades" (41:4). "Who will sing praises to the Most High in Hades as do those who are alive?" (17:27). Bar. 2:17 reads, "The dead who are in Hades, whose spirit has been taken from their bodies, will not ascribe glory or justice to the Lord." This was the natural end of those who died "full of years," but it was also used as punishment for sinners when God "leadeth down young men into Hades before their time" (Test. Reuben 4:6).

Later additions to Ecclesiasticus suggest punishment and moral distinction. Some moralization of Sheol is found in Enoch 22, where we first find three parts in Sheol; one for righteous Israelites, one for wicked Israelites who have not been sufficiently punished, and a third for other wicked people. Evidently no non-Israelites were considered righteous. For those in the first two sections there will be a bodily resurrection to the earth, where they will receive proper reward or punishment. Some intertestamental writers omit the third division of Sheol.

The concept of hell and heaven took the place of Sheol. Gehenna or the Valley of Hinnom, south of Jerusalem, contained the city dump where garbage constantly burned. The bodies of criminals and beggers were put there. The stench, worms, and fire seemed appropriate for a place for the wicked. Even throughout the Diaspora, Gehenna came to be a symbol for the hottest part of Sheol.

A special final place for the righteous developed. It was natural that, as the Jews had fled to walled cities, especially Jerusalem, for protection, their dream of a desirable future life contained similar protection. "The saints shall rest in Eden, and in the New Jerusalem shall the righteous rejoice" (Test. Dan 5:12). During intertestamental writing the term Paradise came to be used, "place of rest . . . paradise of delight" (2 Esdras 7:36). The Septuagint used this term for the Garden of Eden. Enoch (32:3) is said to have visited such a Paradise. Other earthly locations were suggested. Later intertestamental writers moved Paradise to the third heaven. We note this in 2 Enoch 8:1. One function asssigned to the Messiah was that of opening Paradise to the righteous and allowing them to eat from the tree of life. In some passages Paradise is an intermediate stopping place for the righteous; in others it is permanent.

In time, the term Heaven took the place of Paradise. This term evolved. First, it was a region above, in which the sun, moon, and stars moved. Then, it came to designate the abode of God and his angels. During the intertestamental period, it came to mean the destination of the righteous dead. The apocalyptists had numerous heavens, as many as seven. The Talmud also describes these seven.

Under the Greek influence, Jews of the Diaspora tended to think that death meant the immediate release of the soul from the evil body to eternal life. This is the picture given in 2 Bar., in Jub. 23:31: "Their bones shall rest in the earth, and their spirits shall have much joy," and in 1 Enoch 91-104. The Wisdom of Solomon at a number of places teaches such immortality: "God created man for incorruption, and made him in the image of his own eternity" (21:23); "The righteous live forever" (5:15).

Late intertestamental writers believed that, at a cataclysmic turning point of history, the dead of former generations would be brought back to life. Generally, only pious Israelites were to experience this. "Those who died in grief will rise up in joy, and those in poverty for the Lord's sake will be enriched . . . those who died for the Lord's sake will wake in life" (Test. Jud. 25:4).

In both the picture of bodily resurrection and that of spiritual immortality, we find the belief that man is made for eternal fellowship with the living God.

In the literature of this period, resurrected people are capable of experiencing pain or pleasure. Second Esdras 7:80 tells of the wicked wandering "about in torments, ever grieving and sad, in seven ways." In 7:91 the righteous "see with great joy the glory of him who receives them, for they shall have rest in seven orders." They lament because they know that men on earth are committing lawless deeds (1 Enoch 9:10).

As in the Zoroastrian and Egyptian religions, some type of final judgment, generally in the nature of a court trial, is connected with most pictures of a future life. This may be conducted by God, by the Messiah, or take place automatically. Sometimes a preliminary and then a final trial are suggested. Judgment of nations tends to be replaced by judgment of individuals. Second Esdras raises the question, "whether on the day of judgment the righteous will be able to intercede for the ungodly" (7:102). The answer is, "Every one shall bear his own righteousness or unrighteousness" (7:105). Judgment is generally pictured as final. However, the Apocalypse of Moses has the angels praying for the departed Adam (35:2). The Testament of Abraham tells of two tests, a judgment by fire, and one of balances in which a man's good deeds are weighed against the bad. Those souls whose good and bad deeds balance may be helped by the prayers of the righteous (chapter 14).

Earlier thinking declared total destruction for the wicked. By the latter part of the intertestamental period, it was felt that all people would have a future life, good or bad. It was not until the first century A.D., when Jewish thinkers were less nationalistic and conceited, that the problem of those not totally righteous or entirely wicked was given serious consideration. Some felt that in his mercy God would not condemn these to

Gehenna. Others felt that such would eventually be released from Gehenna. From this came the Roman Catholic teaching of purgatory.

The earlier concept of the resurrection was that one returns to live in the new world, a definitely physical world. Therefore, the resurrection body was physical. "God himself shall fashion again the bones and ashes of men, and shall raise up mortals once more as they were before" (Sibylline Oracles 4:181-192).

But as thinking moved away from life in the earthly utopia to a spiritual heavenly existence, a different kind of body was needed. In 2 Enoch 22:8 the angel Michael is told, "Go and take Enoch out of his earthly garments . . . and put him into the garments of my glory." A spiritual counterpart of the physical body was coexistent with it until the day of resurrection. Later in the same book it is said that after judgment the physical bodies of men will be gradually changed into spiritual bodies (50:3-4), which will need no food or anything earthly (56:2).

ASSIGNMENT

1. Why did the Sadducees reject the idea of resurrection? When did this idea come into Hebrew thinking? What had been the earlier concept?

2. What led to the idea of heaven and hell?

3. How did Jews and Greeks differ in their concept of life beyond the grave?

4. Differentiate between the terms: Sheol, Hades, Gehenna, Paradise, Heaven. What seems to be the origin of the Roman Catholic idea of purgatory?

SUPPLEMENTARY READING

Dentan—Pages 72-3
Enslin—Pages 113-4
Moore—Vol. II, Part VII, Chapter I
Russell—Chapter 7
Toombs—Pages 87-90

Chapter 39

Non-human Beings

The word angel means messenger. Human beings were in early Old Testament accounts sometimes called angels. At other places we find "the angel of Yahweh," who seems to be Yahweh himself. With the possible exception of Ex. 32:2, the one pre-exile reference that would suggest a different type of angel is in connection with the punishment for David's taking a census. When the angel of destruction "stretched forth his hand toward Jerusalem" the LORD interfered (2 Sam. 24:16).

The idea of angels as distinct beings was Zoroastrian. Zechariah, showing various Zoroastrian influences, is the first Biblical writer to mention angels as mediums of revelation from God. Earlier prophets reported that Yahweh spoke directly to them.

Various orders of angels are mentioned as cherubim, seraphim, ofannim. The apocalypse of Daniel has ranks among angels, and for the first time angels are named—Michael, the "prince" of Israel, and Gabriel. It is stated in the Palestinian Talmud that "the names of angels were brought by the Jews from Babylonia." All names have the root "el" or God. Michael means, "Who is like God"; Gabriel, "Son of God"; Raphael, "The healing of God."

The intertestamental wisdom literature makes no mention of angels. But the apocalyptic literature has numerous references to angels and other non-human beings. God was coming to be thought of as having less direct contact with men and having a resplendent group of attendants in his heavenly court. There are myriads of unidentified angels. Enoch 71 refers to "ten thousand times ten thousand angels flying about the house." The Qumran Essenes believed that, in their final great war, angels would fight beside the Sons of Light. Second Baruch 51:11 and Test. Levi 3:3 refer to a similar army of angels.

Certain superior angels, or archangels, come to have personalities as well as names. We recall Tobias' friend, the angel

Raphael. Groups of angels are called Sons of Heaven, Sons of God, Holy Ones, Watchers, Ministering Angels, Angels of the Presence, Angels of Sanctification. According to Jubilees, these last two groups of angels carefully observe the Sabbath (2:18) and circumcision (15:27).

Naturally, intertestamental writers were interested in the origin of angels. Some thought of them as pre-existent. The Book of Jubilees has them made on the first day of creation; Enoch, on the second day. They seem to have many of the physical and mental characteristics of men, but do not eat or drink, nor do they propagate their kind. They do not die but can be annihilated by God. They are highly moral but have limited knowledge.

The chief function of angels is to display the glory of God and praise him continually. They convey the prayers of men to God (Tobit 12:12) and bring messages from God to men. Messenger angels are winds; those who make up a heavenly choir are fire. Nations have special patron angels. The chief angel of all, Michael, is the patron of Israel. In 3 Maccabees, angels turned the drunken elephants on the enemies of the Jews. In 2 Maccabees, Maccabeus "sought the Lord to send a good angel to save Israel." As a result, "a horseman appeared at their head, clothed in white and brandishing weapons of gold" (11:7-8).

All righteous Israelites have individual guardian angels according to Jub. 35:17. That a similar concept was held by early Christians is indicated by Matt. 18:10 and Acts 12:15.

The book of Enoch influenced the Essenes. Fragments of ten manuscripts were found in Cave 4. Parts of similar writings, probably previous to Enoch, have also been found. The seven names of angels given in Enoch appear in part in the War Scroll, the Manual of Discipline, and the Zadokite Document. The term "holy ones" used in Daniel and Enoch appears in several of the Essene writings. The angel of light in Essene literature is also called the spirit of truth and the prince of light. Other angels are likewise called princes. The angels of the presence appear in various scrolls.

A lower type of angels is in charge of the natural phenomena, as rain, snow, frost, wind, fire, thunder, and lightning. The Dead Sea Thanksgiving Psalms refer to these as spirits who took on the form of holy angels (1:10). They do not observe the Sabbath as other angels do, for their functions go on at all times (Jub. 2:2-3). In the Slavonic version of Enoch, the stars are ruled by two hundred angels. Enoch 82:13 refers to angels of the four seasons. Enoch and the Testaments of the Twelve Patriarchs mention an angel of peace.

These nature angels may represent a compromise with Greek and Roman religions, where similar beings were considered gods. The seventy angels of the nations are probably other heathen gods transformed. They are even in danger of losing their heavenly places. Enoch tells of the fall of angels referred to in the New Testament writings (Jude 6 and 2 Pet. 2:4). The Babylonian god Nabu eventually became the angel of the inkhorn of Ezekiel and the Recording Angel of later popular Christian terminology.

Not all Jews accepted the idea of angels. The Sadducees rejected the concept of angels and evil spirits because neither concept appears in the Torah and, therefore, must be modernism injected into the Jewish religion.

The problem of evil and its seriousness was ever present in Hebrew minds. Satan and evil spirits are scarcely known in the Old Testament. But as the picture of Yahweh grew to be more ethical, an explanation of evil became necessary. The idea of evil spirits helped solve the problem, but since Yahweh was thought of as all-powerful, these spirits were in some way associated with him. "An evil spirit from the LORD came upon Saul" (1 Sam. 19:9) enticing him to try to kill David. Still, why should God do this?

Again the Zoroastrians came to the rescue of the Jewish people. Their religion taught of a power of darkness and evil as well as one of light and right. As mentioned in Chapter 2, the story of 2 Sam. 24, about God telling David to take a census and then punishing him, was rewritten after the Babylonian captivity as Satan inciting David (2 Chron. 21:1). Satan is mentioned in only two other places in the Old Testament, both post-exilic. In Zech. 3:1-2 there is a fleeting reference to Satan as the accuser of the priest Joshua. In the book of Job, Satan appears as a member of the court of Yahweh, commissioned to tempt Job. He is an adversary of God, the accuser (in Greek *diabolis*). Jubilees attributed to Satan, or Mastema, the suggestion that Abraham sacrifice his own son Isaac (17:16; 18:9 and 12) and the attempt to kill Moses as he was returning to Egypt (48:2-4), both attributed to God in Gen. 20:2 and Ex. 4:24.

In intertestamental writing, Satan heads up the power of evil. Other names are given him: Prince of Deceit, Devil (from *diabolis*), Asmondeus, Mastema, Belial (the Worthless One), and Beliar. "Through the devil's envy, death entered the world" (Wisd. 2:24). Probably this gave rise to the popular identification of the serpent with Satan in the Garden of Eden story (Gen. 3:1-7). In the Apocalypse of Moses version of the Books of Adam and Eve, Eve says, "The devil answered through the mouth of the serpent" (17:4). The Testament of the Twelve Patriarchs and Jubilees have much to say about Satan. The former pictures him as the cause of hatred (Gad 4:7), malice (Benj. 7:1), and derision (Reuben 4:7). A spirit of Beliar led Dan to conspire against Joseph (Dan. 1:7) and Potiphar's wife to try to seduce him (Jos. 7:4). Jubilees says that Mastema brought about corruption among the "Sons of Noah" (11:5) and caused sickness (10:8). One of the functions of the Messiah will be to subdue Beliar and deliver the righteous from his control.

A hierarchy of evil spirits under the direction of Satan was believed in by the Zoroastrians. These became popular in intertestamental writing. The angel Raphael taught Tobias how to drive away the evil spirit or demon who had caused the death of Sarah's seven husbands. The Testaments of the Twelve Patriarchs describes demons as evil things of human experience— envy, lust, anger, hatred, lying, adultery. The righteous man is given power to tread on these. Their task is to tempt people and to torment those who yield to their temptations. At the final judgment they will be punished and driven from the earth. The book of Jubilees (10:3-9) describes demons as children of fallen angels. Jubilees also attributed to them responsibility for idol worship. However, some suggest that God will use them as executioners at the last Judgment.

As other gods were considered to be uncertain angels, so some were demoted to demons. Several New Testament references call the chief demon Beelzebub. This was a Philistine god (2 Kg. 1:2). In the Life of Adam and Eve (17:1), Satan was rejected from glory and in anger caused Adam and Eve to be expelled from the Garden of Eden.

Between Satan and the host of common evil spirits was a hierarchy of demons. Enoch 6:7 lists the names of nineteen leading demons.

Intertestamental period writers accepted the Zoroastrian idea of evil spirits, but made their own attempts to explain their origin. First Enoch used the fallen angel idea. Satan, one of the top angels, persuaded a group of lesser angels to rebel against God. They were thrown out of heaven. Coming to earth, they taught men the arts of civilization. They became interested in human women and thus became the fathers of a race of giants (similar to the statement in Gen. 6:4). God killed the giants but their souls continued to tempt human beings. The fifth chapter of Jubilees tells of the sin of these angels. The fifth chapter of the Testament of Reuben does the same more briefly.

Numerous intertestamental writers give expression to the Zoroastrian expectation of a great conflict between God and his angels and Satan and his angels in which the latter would be completely defeated.

The Essene Manual of Discipline, while not mentioning a variety of angels, says that "God created men to rule the world and appointed for him two spirits . . . truth and perversity." "He has made men heirs to them that they might know good and evil. But when the time of Inquisition comes, He will determine the fate of every living being in accordance with which of the two spirits he has chosen to follow."

ASSIGNMENT

1. Where did the Hebrews get the idea of demons and angels? What did the word angel originally mean?

2. What names of angels are given? What does the ending "el" mean? What titles are given to groups of angels?

3. What is meant by guardian angel? What other tasks were assigned to angels?

4. What relation did angels have to gods of other religions?

5. What problem did the idea of Satan solve for the Hebrews? What other names were given to Satan? Explain demons. What was their task?

6. How did the concept of demons and angels change during the intertestamental period?

SUPPLEMENTARY READING

Gaster—Pages 340-2
Moore—Vol. I, Part II, Chapter III
Snaith—Chapter XIII
Toombs—Pages 72-7

Chapter 40

Men of the Law

The author of 1 Maccabees indicates a primary interest of his own time when he portrays the dying Mattathias saying, "My children, show zeal for the law, and give your lives for the covenant of our fathers" (2:50). This book was written in Palestine while the temple was still prominent. In the Diaspora —Babylon, Alexandria, and elsewhere—especially later in the intertestamental period, the Law came to be the most important factor in Jewish thinking and religion. Virtue was identified with observance of the Law. "Observe, therefore, my children, all the law of the Lord, for there is hope for all them who hold fast unto His ways" (Test. Jud. 26:1). Even Philo, with his Greek tendencies, carefully observed the Law and denounced Jews who did not, calling them sons of Cain. Emphasis upon the law was an attempt to suppress prophecy. Prophecy sought for progress, change. Jews of the intertestamental period feared that change meant adopting Greek or Roman concepts. The Law was considered eternal.

Probably "Law" is not the best translation of the Hebrew word "Torah." The term "law" fails to carry over into English the sense of teaching, instruction, direction, or revelation included in "Torah." In some instances the Greek word used by intertestamental writers and translated into English as "law" included more than the first five books of the Bible. It is everything that God had made known to men. At some places "wisdom" would be a proper translation.

The synogogue became the center of the study of the Law. In every synagogue the place of honor was given to the scroll or scrolls of the Torah. It was read with all reverence. It was not only translated but carefully interpreted to the audience, for it was a gift from God, revealing his mind and will. This concept of the origin of the law runs through intertestamental writings.

Ecclus. 45:5 says that God gave Moses "the commandments face to face, the law of life and knowledge." It was believed that God made the Law even before he created the world, in order to guide people into a good life. Therefore, the Jewish religion differed greatly from that of other people. It was not the worship of an arbitrary deity interested only in being glorified, and enjoying ordering people about. In *Against Apion* Josephus says that Jews know their laws better than their own names. "This is in consequence of our having learned them immediately as soon as anything, and of our having them, as it were, engraved on our souls" (2:19).

The students of the Law, the Pharisees, became the leaders after the destruction of the temple in A.D. 70. Their center at Jamnia was established for the study of the Torah. Since that time the Law has been the heart of Judaism. All the rest of the scripture was considered a commentary upon the Law. But this was not enough. The Mishna and later the Gemara were based entirely upon the Torah.

The Pharisees were determined to "put a fence around the law," to help people obey the Law. This oral law thus developed and eventually became the heart of the Talmud. It was an attempt to apply the Law to new conditions and situations not definitely mentioned in earlier writings. This "tradition of the ancients" was unwritten and continued to grow until about A.D. 200. In accord with the belief that all good things had been revealed by God to Moses on Mount Sinai, none of the oral law was admitted to have been made after the time of the great lawgiver. But some was considered to have existed even longer. Laws for all mankind had been given to Adam (Jub. 3:10-14) 30-31) and by Noah (Jub. 7:20). In Jub. 1:27-28, and elsewhere, angels of God give the laws to Moses. Doubtless parts of the oral law had been developed long before the time of the Pharisees, probably written down and later lost. Jews of the Diaspora, other than those in the region of Babylon, did not take the details of the oral law as seriously as did those in Palestine.

The Pharisees taught that, if any one found a conflict between the written and the oral law, the latter should be followed. This was not egotism upon their part but an attempt to ease some of the older regulations. They were sure that God had originated the oral Torah, that God was even kinder than one would believe if he got his picture entirely from the written Torah.

At times the oral law definitely contradicted the written Torah. Deut. 15:1-3 commands the cancelling at the beginning of every seventh year of all loans made to fellow Israelites. Naturally, moneylenders refused to make loans near the end of this period. Eventually Jewish authorities declared that a lender could reclaim the loan at any time he saw fit.

The Pharisees were correct in considering themselves liberal and progressive. They accepted and developed many concepts not held by earlier Hebrews and current Sadducees. It was they who enlarged the canon of the scriptures by adding the Prophets and later the Writings. They emphasized the declaration of one of the Psalmists, "Thy word is a lamp to my feet" (119:105).

The Torah was to the Jews what the flag has been to many people, or the king (or queen) to others. The Jew would defend the law with his life, not only its teachings, but physical copies of it. Many a Jew has died in attempting to protect the sacred Torah in a synagogue threatened by anti-Semitic violence. We find this loyalty to the law expressed in Bar. 4:1-2:

> She is the book of the commandments of God
>   and the law that endures forever.
> All who hold her fast will live,
>   and those who forsake her will die.

To neglect the law is sin: "It is no light thing to show irreverence to the divine laws" (2 Macc. 4:17). "Justly do they perish who have not loved thy law" (2 Bar 54:14). We have several instances of people giving their lives by refusing to disobey the law. First Macc. 2:32 tells how the Selucid Syrians "prepared for battle against them on the Sabbath." The Jews refused to fight on the Sabbath, "and they died, with their wives and children . . . to the number of a thousand persons" (2:38).

To the intertestamental writers the Torah is Wisdom. Ecclesiasticus says, regarding the utterances of Wisdom, "All this is the book of the covenant of the Most High God, and the law which Moses commanded as an inheritance for the congregations of Jacob" (24:24-25). The first Psalm was probably written during the intertestamental period as an introduction to our book of Psalms: "Blessed is the man" whose "delight is in the law of the LORD, and on his law he meditates day and night" (verses 1-2).

Most Jews of this time, and probably all later times, believed that the Torah would never be destroyed. "Thy law . . . does not perish but remains in its glory" (2 Esdras 9:37). "It endures forever" (Bar. 4:1). That Jesus held this is indicated in Mt. 5:18.

Various rabbis claimed that the law had been offered to all nations of the world, but only Israel accepted it. That the law was still meant for other people as well as for Jews is an advance step found in some intertestamental writings: "The imperishable light of the world was to be given to the world" (Wisd. 18:4). Regarding the law and non-Jews, 2 Esdras 7:21 says, "God has strictly commanded those who came into the world . . . what they should do to live." The Testaments of the Twelve Patriarchs says, "The light of the law was given to lighten every man." The Jew must set an example for others—"If ye be darkened through transgressions, what, then, will all the Gentiles do, living in blindness?" (Test. Levi 14:4). Those who argued for the universality of the law found scriptural backing in such statements as that of Isa. 26:2, "Open the gates, that the righteous nation which keeps faith may enter in."

As among the first writing prophets, there were some intertestamental writers unafraid to be critical of the law with its emphasis on form. Ecclesiasticus taught, "Let all your discussion be about the law of the Most High" (9:15), but "in wisdom there is the fulfillment of the law" (19:20), rather than in ritual. "The Most High is not pleased with the offerings of the ungodly; and is not propitiated for sins by a multitude of sacrifices" (34:19). "If a man fasts for his sins, and goes again and does the same things, who will listen to his prayer? And what has he gained by humbling himself?" (34:26).

It was the tendency to emphasize form rather than attitude, ritual rather than intelligence, that disgusted Jesus of Nazareth. He did not attack the law, but like the Pharisees, believed that it needed to be improved. In Mt. 5:17 we find him saying, regarding the Law and the Prophets, "I have come not to abolish them, but to fulfill [round out, complete, fill full] them." The Matthew compiler then proceeds to give six examples of improvements Jesus felt should be made. Jesus did not hesitate to go contrary to the oral Torah.

With Jesus' emphasis on using intelligence and out-going love in religion, the early Christians were perplexed as to what attitude they should take toward the law, especially toward rules and regulations. Were they above the law? Paul, brought up as a strict Pharisee, suggested: "A man is not justified by works of the law" (Gal. 2:16); "You are not under the law but under grace" (Rom. 6:14). On the other hand, Paul found definite value in the law. In Gal. 3:24-25 he says that the law is like the *pedagogos,* the custodian or servant who takes the boy to the teacher in the morning. When he has done that his task is accomplished. So, says Paul, the law brought people to Christ.

ASSIGNMENT

1. Just what is meant by the term Torah? What was considered the origin of the law? Why is Moses called the great lawgiver?

2. What is meant by the oral law? The Talmud? How and why did Sadducees and Pharisees differ in their attitude toward the law?

3. Why was the law so greatly emphasized? In what major ways did emphasis upon the law make the Jewish religion differ from other religions? What was the relation of this emphasis to the idea of theocracy?

4. What attitude toward the law was taken by Jesus? By Paul?

SUPPLEMENTARY READING

Charles: *Religious Development*—Chapter V
Moore—Vol. I, Part I, Chapters III and IV
Snaith—Chapter XIV
Toombs—Chapter 5

SUGGESTIONS FOR FURTHER READING

Angus, S., *The Environment of Early Christianity*. Scribner's, 1931.
————, *The Mystery Religions and Christianity*. Scribner's, 1928.
Black, Matthews. *The Scrolls and Christian Origins*. Scribner's, 1961.
Bruce, F. F., *Second Thoughts on the Dead Sea Scrolls*. Eerdmans, 1961.
Burrows, Millar, *The Dead Sea Scrolls*. Viking, 1955.
————, *More Light on the Dead Sea Scrolls*. Viking, 1958.
Carcopino, Jerome, *Daily Life in Ancient Rome*. Yale University Press, 1940.
Charles, R. H., *The Apocrypha and Pseudepigrapha of the Old Testament*. London, Oxford Press, 1963.
————, *Religious Development Between the Old and New Testaments*. Holt, n. d.
Church, Alfred J., *Roman Life in the Days of Cicero*. Macmillan, 1924.
Cross, Frank Moore, Jr., *The Ancient Library of Qumran and Modern Biblical Studies*. Doubleday, 1958.
Cumont, Franz. *The Mysteries of Mithra*. Dover Publications, 1956.
————, *Oriental Religions in Roman Paganism*. Dover Publications, 1956.
Dana, H. E., *New Testament World*. Broadman Press, 1937.
Daniel-Rops, Henri, *Daily Life in the Time of Jesus*. Hawthorn, 1962.
Dentan, Robert C., *The Apocrypha, Bridge of the Testaments*. Seabury Press, 1954.
Enslin, Morton Scott, *Christian Beginnings*. Harper, 1938.
Fosdick, Harry Emerson, *A Guide to Understanding the Bible*. Harper, 1938.
Fritsch, Charles T., *The Qumran Community*. Macmillan, 1956.
Gaster, Theodore H., *The Dead Sea Scriptures in English Translation*. Doubleday, 1956.
Goodspeed, E. J., *The Story of the Apocrypha*. University of Chicago Press, 1939.
Hadas, Moses, *Aristeas to Philocrates*. Harper, 1951.
————, *The Third and Fourth Books of Maccabees*. Harper, 1953.
Harris, M. H., *Hebraic Literature*. Tudor Publishing Co., 1941.
Howe, Carl G., *The Dead Sea Scrolls and the Living Church*. John Knox Press, 1958.
Howlett, Duncan, *The Essenes and Christianity*. Harper, 1957.
Johnston, H. W., *The Private Life of the Romans*. Scott, Foresman and Co., 1932.

Klausner, Joseph, *The Messianic Idea in Israel*. Macmillan, 1955.

Lamb, Harold, *Alexander of Macedon*. Doubleday, 1946.

————, *Cyrus the Great*. Doubleday, 1960.

Manson, Joseph, *The Thanksgiving Hymns*. Eerdmans, 1961.

Mathews, Shailer, *A History of New Testament Times in Palestine*. Macmillan, 1910.

Metzger, Bruce, *An Introduction to the Apocrypha*. New York: Oxford, 1957.

Moore, George Foot, *Judaism*. Harvard University Press, 1927.

Parkes, James, *The Foundations of Judaism and Christianity*. Quadrangle Books, 1960.

Perowe, Stewart, *The Later Herods*. Abingdon, 1959.

————, *The Life and Times of Herod the Great*. Abingdon, 1959.

Pfeiffer, Charles F., *Between the Testaments*. Baker Book House, 1959.

Pfeiffer, Robert H., *History of the New Testament with an Introduction to the Apocrypha*. Harper, 1949.

————, *Religion in the Old Testament*. Harper, 1961.

Reider, Joseph, *The Book of Wisdom*. Harper, 1957.

Rowley, H. H., *The Relevance of Apocalyptic*. Harper, n. d.

Russell, D. S., *Between the Testaments*. Muhlenberg Press, 1960.

Schauss, Hayyim, *The Jewish Festivals*. American Hebrew Congregations, 1938.

Schurer, Emil, *A History of the Jewish People in the Time of Jesus*. Shocken Books, 1961.

Sloan, W. W., *A Survey of the New Testament*. Philosophical Library, 1961; Littlefield, Adams, 1962.

————, *A Survey of the Old Testament*. Abingdon, 1957.

Snaith, Norman H., *The Jews from Cyrus to Herod*. Abingdon, n. d.

Stendahl, Krister, *The Scrolls and the New Testament*. Harper, 1957.

Sutcliffe, Edmond F., *The Monks of Qumran*. Newman Press, 1960.

Tedsche, Sidney, and Zeitlin, Solomon, *The First Book of Maccabees*. Harper, 1950.

————, *The Second Book of Maccabees*. Harper, 1954.

Toombs, Lawrence E., *The Threshold of Christianity*. Westminster, 1960.

Torrey, Charles Cutler, *The Apocryphal Literature*. Yale University Press, 1945.

Van der Ploeg, J., *The Excavations at Qumran*. London: Longrens, Green and Co., 1958.

Yadin, Yigall, *The Message of the Scrolls*. Simon & Schuster, 1957.

Zimmerman, Frank, *The Book of Tobit*. Harper, 1958.

Abingdon Bible Commentary. Abingdon, 1929.

The Interpreter's Bible. Abingdon, 1952-56.

The Interpreter's Dictionary of the Bible. Abingdon, 1962.

General Index

Aaron, 183-4, 198
Abednego, 136
Abraham, 1, 4, 9, 11-2, 22, 31, 79, 151, 159-60, 176, 208
Acre, 62
Additions to Esther, 33, 134-5, 138-9, 192
Adonis, 174
Aegean Sea, 11
Aelia Capitolina, 72-3
Aeshma Daeva, 124
Against Apion, 41, 212
Agrippa I, 66-9
Agrippa II, 67-72
Ahura Mazda, 13, 170, 174
'Ain Feshkha, 94, 96
Alexandra Salome, 56-7, 85, 98
Alexander the Great, 12, 15-8, 20-1, 24, 27, 34, 42, 53, 164
Alexander Janneus, 56-7, 85, 92, 114
Alexandria, 16-8, 24, 27-32, 41-2, 60, 67, 70, 123, 129-31, 135-6, 142, 144, 146, 163, 176-8, 189, 211
Alexandrine Codex, 130
Am-ha-arez, 79-83, 86
American School of Oriental Research, 92
Ammon, 45
Amos, 6, 98, 194-5
Angels, 85-6, 94, 117, 121, 124, 129, 149, 159-60, 170, 178, 181, 192, 203, 206-10, 212
Angra Mainyu, 12, 124, 170
Anabasis, 41
Anthony (*see* Mark Anthony)
Antigonus, 60, 63
Antioch, 18-9, 24, 62, 123, 130
Antiochus III, (the Great), 18, 20, 57
Antiochus IV, (Epiphanes), 18-20, 41, 43, 45, 48-9, 89, 164, 181
Antipas, 61, 64, 66-7, 69
Antipater I, 57
Antipater II, 57-60

Antiquities, 41, 131
Aphrodite, 172, 174
Apocalypse, apocalyptic, 50-4, 119, 191, 196, 199, 201, 203
Apocalypse of Baruch, 36
Apocalypse of Moses, 132
Apocalypse of Peter, 36
Apocalypse to John (see Revelation to John)
Apocalyptists, 50-2, 143, 148-9, 155
Apocrypha, 30, 32-8, 43, 54, 71, 97, 108-9, 122, 127, 134, 138-41, 143-5, 150, 153, 167, 177, 185, 197
Apollos, 32
Arabs, Arabia, 11, 45, 57, 66, 91-2, 98, 137, 144
Aramaic, 30, 122
Archelaus, 61, 64-5, 69, 91, 98, 185
Architecture, 23
Aretas III, 57-8
Aretas IV, 66
Aristeas, 28, 36, 108, 130-1, 147
Aristobulus I, 56
Aristobulus II, 57-60, 188
Aristotle, 16
Ark of the Covenant, 6, 170, 180-1
Arsinoe, 130
Art, 23
Artaxerxes, 141
Artemis, 171
Ascension of Isaiah, 133
Asher, 155
Asceticism, 173, 175, 178
Asia, Asians, Asia Minor, 17-8, 42, 163, 171, 174
Asideans, 44
Asmodeus, 124-5
Assassins, 68
Aswan Dam, 26
Assumption of Moses, 36, 151, 202
Assyria, Assyrians, 2, 10-1, 29, 127-8, 163-4, 192
Astarte, 27

INDEX OF OLD TESTAMENT REFERENCES

INDEX OF NEW TESTAMENT REFERENCES

INDEX OF APOCRYPHA REFERENCES

INDEX OF PSEUDEPIGRAPHA REFERENCES